IMAGES
of America

CHATTANOOGA'S FOREST HILLS CEMETERY

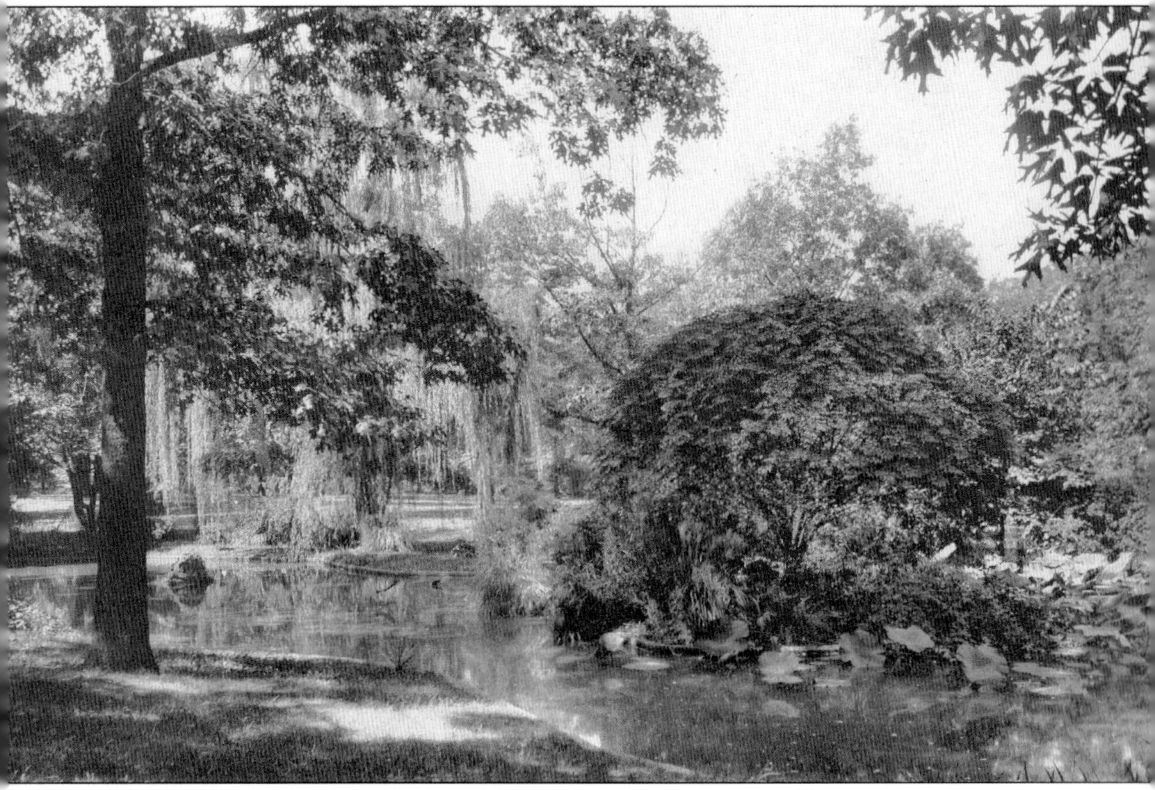

Believing the growing city of Chattanooga needed a new cemetery, 11 businessmen met in August, 1874, to form a cemetery association. Each association member contributed $3 to defray the cost of the charter. Adjacent to A. M. Johnson's new town of St. Elmo, the cemetery, originally named Oakland but renamed Forest Hills, covers 100 acres with space for 70,000 graves. Although bodies from other cemeteries and family plots were moved there, the first burials did not take place until 1880.

On the Cover: Albert Bowen (1864–1923) of Chickamauga, Georgia, was buried by the Harry Chapman Company located at Eighth and Pine Streets. Bowen's family paid $750 for his cemetery plot. His funeral cost $690. Expenses included: casket $375, vault $150, embalming $25, flowers for the door $5, use of cars $120, and use of the hearse $15. (Photograph courtesy of Forest Hills Cemetery.)

IMAGES
of America

CHATTANOOGA'S FOREST HILLS CEMETERY

Gay Morgan Moore

ARCADIA
PUBLISHING

ISBN 978-0-7385-8694-6

Published by Arcadia Publishing
Charleston, South Carolina

Printed in the United States of America

Library of Congress Control Number: 2010931188

For all general information, please contact Arcadia Publishing:
Telephone 843-853-2070
Fax 843-853-0044
E-mail sales@arcadiapublishing.com
For customer service and orders:
Toll-Free 1-888-313-2665

Visit us on the Internet at www.arcadiapublishing.com

This book is dedicated to Forest Hills Cemetery superintendent Barbara Chandler. Without her enthusiastic assistance and support this book would not have been possible.

CONTENTS

ACKNOWLEDGMENTS

It is impossible to thank all of the many people who have contributed to this book. There are, however, a number of individuals without whom it would never have been completed. My heartfelt thanks go to Forest Hills Cemetery superintendent Barbara Chandler. She not only provided the impetus for the book by creating the annual Forest Hills Cemetery Historical Stroll, but also offered her support and hours of assistance during this book's creation. I also wish to thank the Forest Hills Cemetery board of directors for their support of this project.

I am particularly grateful to the many people who shared their family histories and, often, their precious photographs. Their stories make this book what it is, a history of the people—both widely-known and not so well-known—who made Chattanooga what it is today. I enjoyed meeting and talking with each of you.

Mary Helms, head of the local history and genealogy department at the Chattanooga-Hamilton County Bicentennial Library, and her staff, Karen Brown, Suzette Rainey, and April Mitchell, were unfailingly pleasant and helpful during my hours at the library. I am grateful to James Reece, also of the library's local history staff, who patiently scanned the many images from the library's photography collection. Thanks, Jim!

I also wish to thank Carmen Davis of the Bessie Smith Cultural Center, Susan Sawyer of Erlanger Medical Center, Steve Cox of the University of Tennessee-Chattanooga Special Collections Department, Maria Matthews of Girls Preparatory School, and Jeff Webb, webmaster of the St. Elmo Web site—all of whom provided additional photographs.

Thank you also to Maggie Bullwinkel, my editor at Arcadia Publishing, for her enormous patience and support.

Last, but certainly not least, I wish to thank my husband, Sandy, who not only reads my work but also patiently endures my preoccupation and general lack of attentiveness during the process. I am deeply grateful for his support and encouragement.

The historic photographs included in this book are from the Chattanooga-Hamilton County Bicentennial Library photographic archives unless otherwise noted. The contemporary images were taken by Sandy Moore and the author.

Introduction

Chartered in 1851, Chattanooga grew rapidly during the 1840s and 1850s aided by the advent of railroads, increased river traffic, large deposits of coal and iron nearby, and a developing tourism industry on Lookout Mountain.

When the Civil War began, residents of Hamilton County were deeply divided in their loyalties. Hamilton County residents voted not to secede, while the city residents voted to secede. When Tennessee seceded from the union, most families remained in the area, while others either moved further south or north as young men were forced to choose sides. A few residents, like Confederate sympathizer Harriet Whiteside, were forcibly moved north. The widow of Lookout Mountain developer James Whiteside, she and her younger children were forced to leave their mansion and most of their possessions when they were taken by rail to Indiana.

During the war, Chattanooga was alternately occupied by Confederate and Union forces and was the site of several battles, including those on Missionary Ridge and Lookout Mountain. The Battle of Chickamauga, one of the largest and mostly costly engagements of the war, was fought over the border in Georgia. The city was shelled on numerous occasions. Union general John Wilder, who later moved to Chattanooga, reported using the steeple of the First Presbyterian Church to sight his artillery when he ordered the shelling of Chattanooga.

When peace came in 1865, Chattanooga was in ruins. The postwar population included 5,776 civilians, 3,000 Union soldiers, and 3,500 former slaves living across the river at Camp Contraband. Most citizens lived in, and ran their businesses from, tents and makeshift buildings. Determined to rebuild, they often lacked capital. Unlike much of the south, Chattanooga looked north and began inviting ambitious young men with "brains, money, and muscle," to come to the city and help rebuild. Northerners, lured south by such advertisements in northern newspapers, were joined by men who had fought in and around Chattanooga with both armies and had seen the potential of the city.

The boom was on! There was money to be made and many came to earn their share. By 1870, the population of the city had grown to 6,903. In 1880, the population numbered 12,892; it topped 29,000 in 1890. Hamilton County's population grew by more than 40,000 during the same period.

Confederate colonel Abraham Malone Johnson returned to Chattanooga after the war ready to rebuild. In 1866, he began to buy property on the east side of Lookout Mountain, adding to that inherited by his wife, Thankful Whiteside. In 1879, he subdivided the property into residential lots. He named the village St. Elmo from the title of an 1866 novel by Augusta Evans. A popular novelist, Evans spent several summers on Lookout Mountain and used the area as a backdrop for her story. The village grew rapidly into Chattanooga's first suburb as improved roads and later the first incline railway up Lookout Mountain opened.

In 1874, Johnson began meeting with a group of men, including Theodore Montague, Xenophen Wheeler, Dr. P. D. Sims, and Tomlinson Fort, among others, to establish a new cemetery. Each of the board members donated $3 to meet the cost of the charter. Located on more than 100 acres of rolling hills adjacent to St. Elmo, the cemetery, originally called Oakland, was renamed Forest Hills. Although bodies were removed from private family plots and other cemeteries, the first burial did not take place until 1880. Ironically, the first burial was British surveyor Walter Hayter, who was hired to survey the property and died suddenly at age 23.

With space for 70,000 graves, Forest Hills Cemetery is the final resting place for more than 45,000 area residents. Unique for the time, the cemetery offered burial to African American residents, though originally segregated.

Today Forest Hills Cemetery is not only an active cemetery, but also a place for the living to enjoy its changing seasonal beauty.

This book was inspired by the annual Forest Hills Cemetery Historical Stroll. The event features more than 20 characters dressed in period costume who recount the lives of some of the interesting people buried there. Each year several volunteers play their own ancestors. While it would seem that expanding the Forest Hills Cemetery story from a 20-plus character stroll into a book would exhaust the number of interesting stories to tell, the opposite is true. There are many more fascinating stories that could be included here.

The book is divided into 11 general topics. The first chapter includes those who were instrumental in building the cemetery and St. Elmo, as well as several other unusual stories. Since the business of Chattanooga is business, chapter two features some of the many people who helped develop the economic life of the area. Before the advent of electronic media, newspapers were the most important means of information and public discussion. Chapter three includes some of the men and women who wrote and published Chattanooga's newspapers. Chapter four features those who were employed as civil servants in local, state, and national government. Since women were largely excluded from business and public life, they often led the civic organizations that cared for the less fortunate and improved the quality of life in the city. Therefore, chapter five includes civic leaders and the clergy, among them a number of women. Education was important to the growth of Chattanooga, and a number of educators are featured in chapter six. Chapter seven is devoted to the medical community, while arts, entertainment, and local athletics are covered in chapter eight. Although many former members of the armed services are buried in the local national cemetery, chapter nine includes members of the military from the Civil War through the Cold War.

Note: Efforts were made to acquire either a historic photograph of the people featured in this book or a picture of their monument. However, some were buried in unmarked graves or their grave markers have deteriorated over time to the point that they can no longer be identified. In such cases, a general picture of the cemetery was substituted.

One

Forest Hills Cemetery and St. Elmo

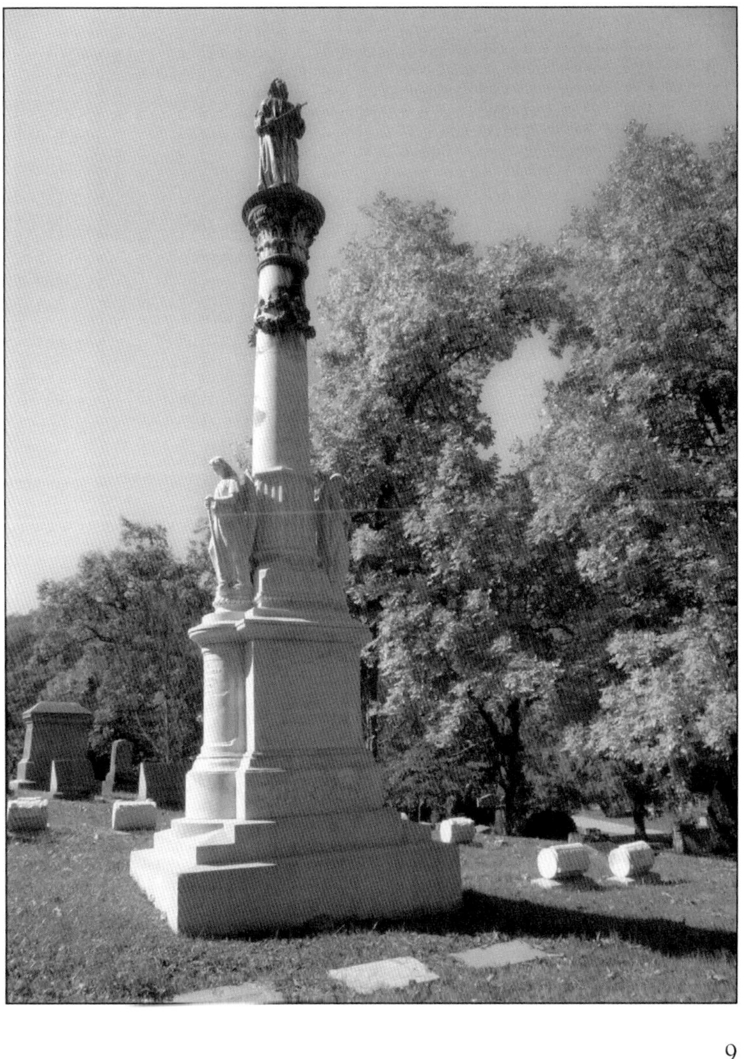

Born in Georgia, Col. Abraham Malone Johnson (1830–1903) came to Chattanooga in 1851 to work for the railroad. During the Civil War, Johnson rose to the rank of colonel in the Confederate Army. In 1886, he subdivided the farm his wife had inherited on the side of Lookout Mountain and named the community St. Elmo after the title of the novel by Augusta Evans, who spent several summers on Lookout Mountain and described the area in her book.

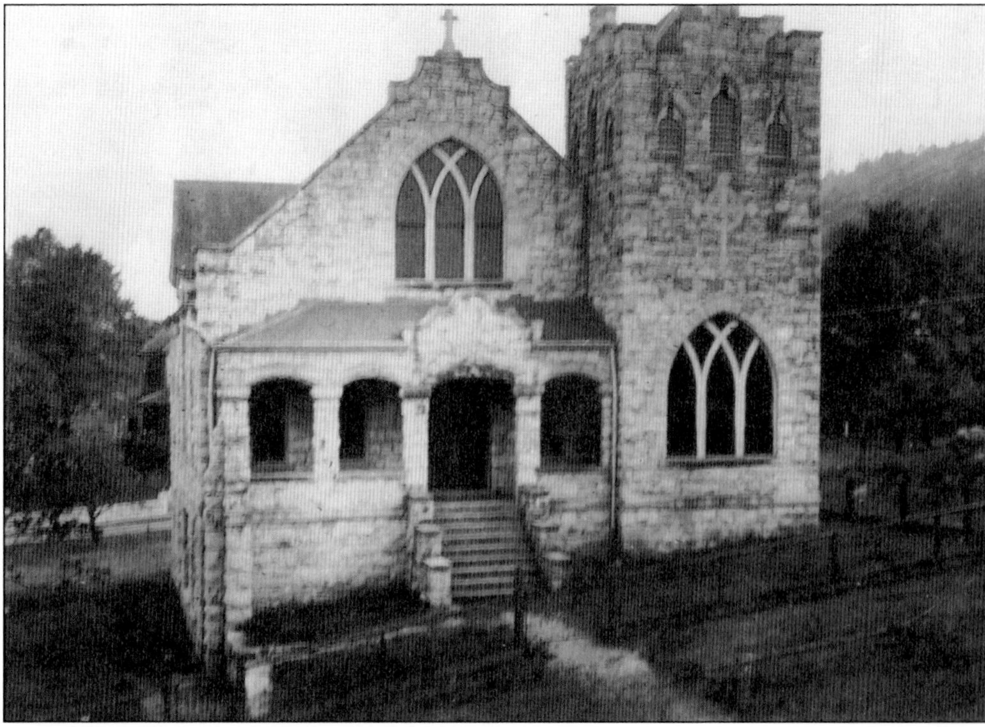

Born into wealth and engaged to another man, Thankful Whiteside Johnson (1838–1890) eloped with tinsmith and railroad postal route agent Abraham Malone Johnson in 1857. Her inheritance formed the basis for the St. Elmo development. Following her death, Johnson donated the land for the Thankful Memorial Episcopal Church in her honor. Some of the church's stained-glass windows came from the Johnsons' home. (Photograph courtesy of Jeff Webb.)

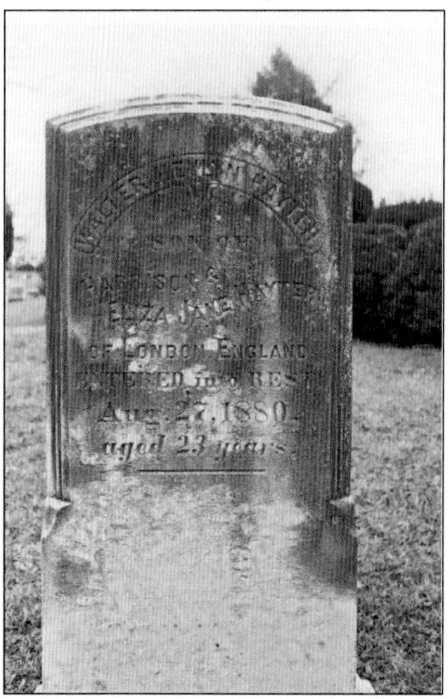

The first person buried at Forest Hills Cemetery was Walter Haylan Hayter (1857–1880). Born in London, England, the young engineer was hired by the cemetery association to survey the property. When he died unexpectedly in his hotel room, the *Chattanooga Times* lamented that "he had no one in the city to mourn him."

During its first years of operation, Forest Hills Cemetery had a gate house at the entrance. The longtime gatekeeper, Confederate veteran Henry Gothard (1844–1932) rang a bell to signal the cemetery workmen to retire as a funeral procession approached the gates. As the procession entered the grounds, Gothard stood and saluted. He also kept daily watch over the bicycles and roller skates left in his care by children on their way to Lookout Junior High School, located near the cemetery entrance.

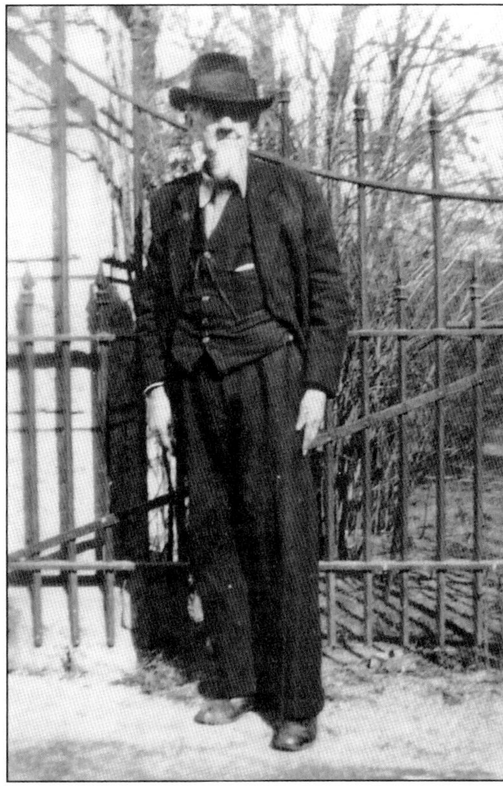

In the early years, the caretaker lived in a home on the cemetery grounds. Located at the rear of the cemetery, the home was said to have had a stable in the basement. There was also a small cemetery shelter house. Both buildings were eventually torn down and the handmade bricks from the home were used in the 1940s to build the present office at the cemetery entrance.

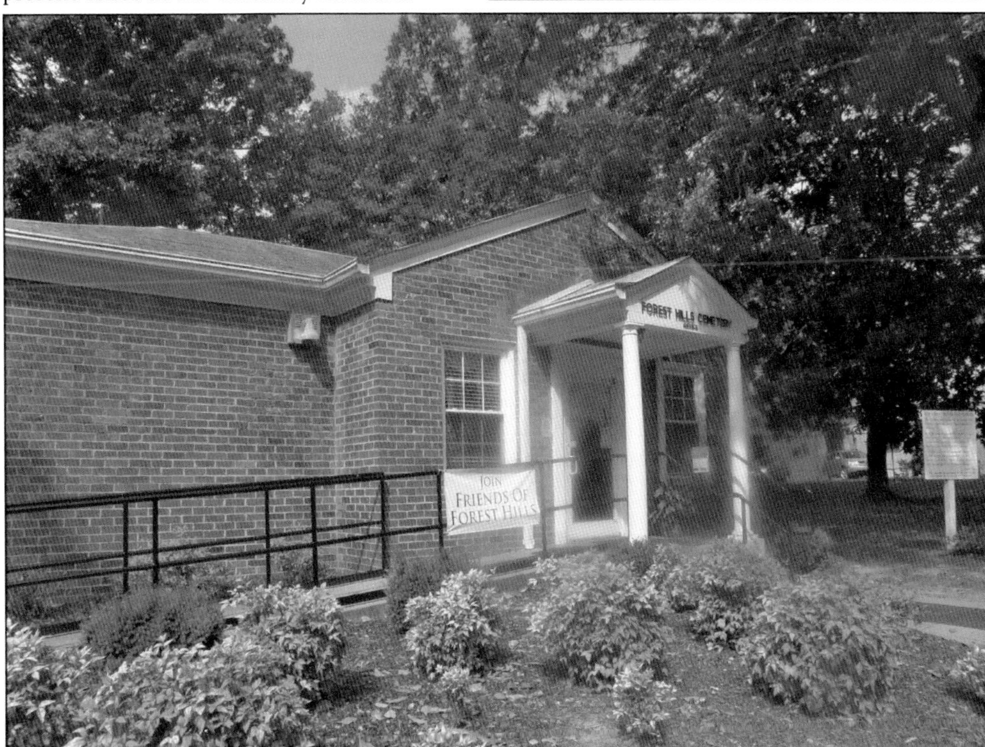

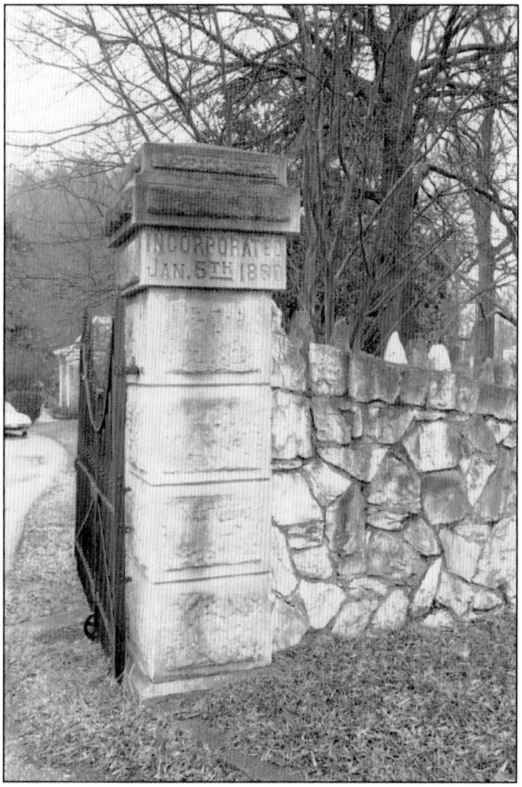

The Forest Hills Cemetery caretakers kept the ledgers noting not only the place and date of burials, but also the causes of death. Early entries listed such causes as yellow fever, brain tumor, consumption (tuberculosis), old age, or "crazy." Many small children and babies died, as well as mothers and their babies from childbirth complications. Shotgun wounds, hanging, and murder were not uncommon causes of death.

The Vine Street Orphans Home was granted a plot in the cemetery for the children who died while living there. The orphanage, now the Chambliss Home, is the oldest charity in Chattanooga. Begun in 1908 by the Women's Christian Charity, the home was located on Vine Street. As described in the *Chattanooga Times*, the two-story brick building had 10 rooms and was "supplied with all of the conveniences." Below is a photograph of the home after it was relocated to Germantown Road.

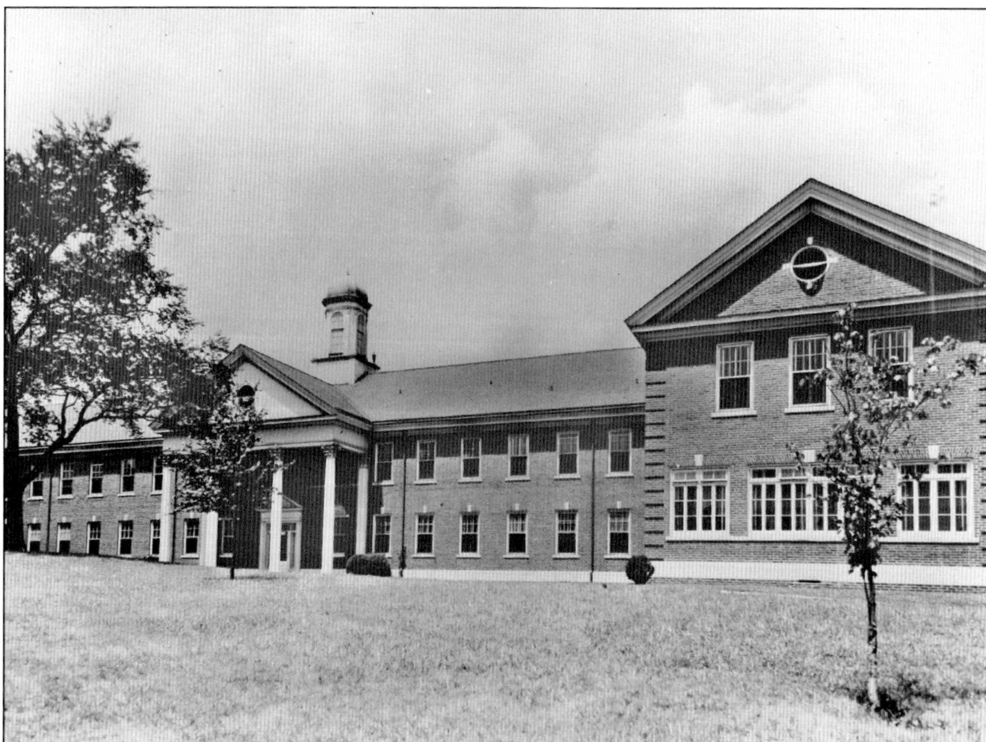

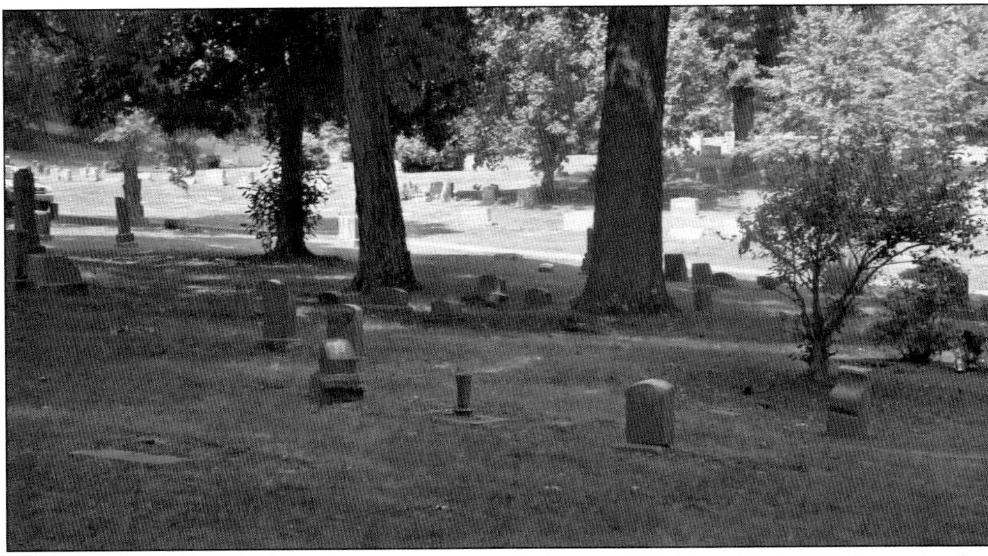

Identified in his obituary as a "prominent negro," George W. Nolan (1845–1884) was the first African American buried at Forest Hills Cemetery. He was employed as a porter on the East Tennessee, Virginia & Georgia Railroad. The cause of death was "heart disease." Unique during reconstruction in the south, Forest Hills Cemetery offered burial, although segregated, to both white and black citizens.

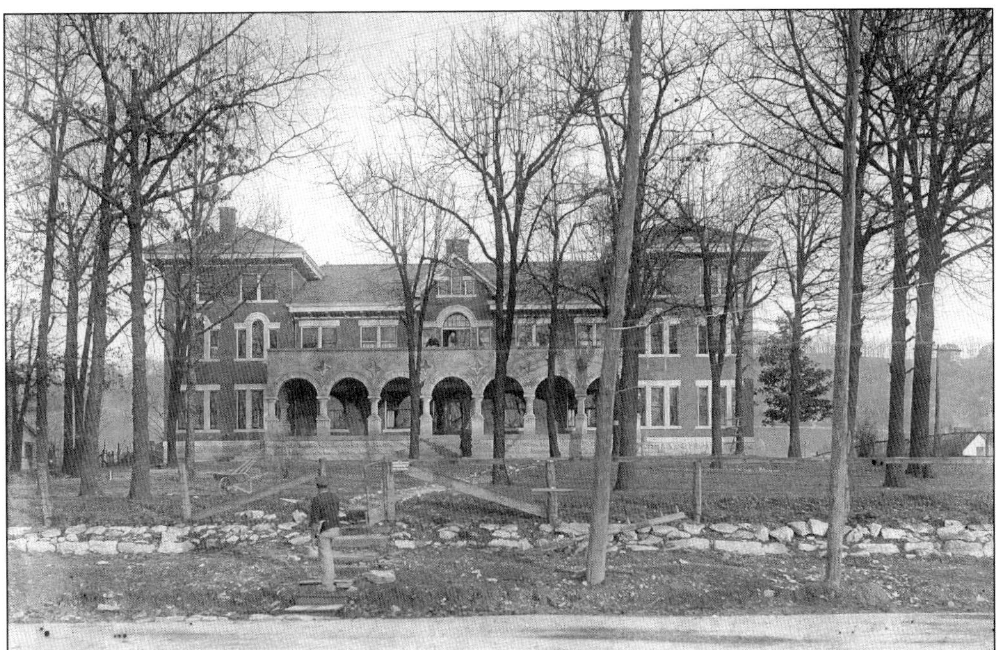

Founded by the Women's Home Mission Societies of several churches in response to the plight of some of the older women in their congregations, the Old Ladies Home was organized in 1902. Originally in a rented home, a new residence was built in 1904 on Dodds Avenue. Later the name was changed to the more appropriate Oak Manor. Women not otherwise provided for were buried in Forest Hills Cemetery.

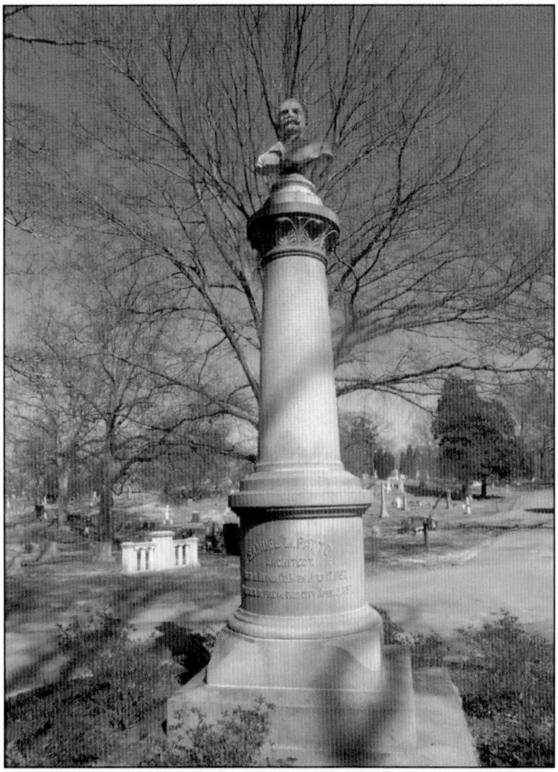

Mississippian Samuel Patton (1857–1897) came to Chattanooga in 1888. An architect, he designed the Loveman's building, Patten Hall, the Watkins home at Vine and Palmetto, Windcrest on Missionary Ridge, and the Richardson building. He was living on an upper floor of the Richardson building when it caught fire. Unfortunately, he designed it with only one exit and was unable to escape. No trace of his body was found. This monument was erected in his honor.

While Forest Hills Cemetery can accommodate more than 70,000 graves, to date only about 45,000 persons are buried there. When the cemetery opened, many bodies were moved from private family burial grounds and the Citizens Cemetery, located adjacent to the University of Tennessee campus. Many families purchased plots, the largest of which has space for 85 graves.

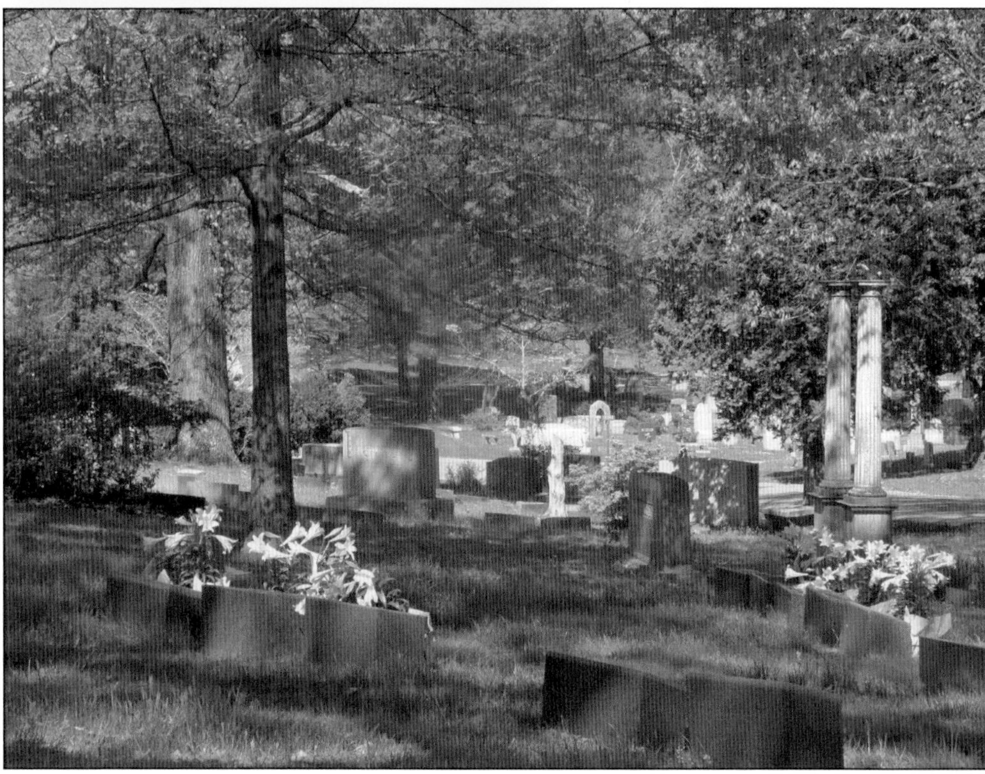

Chattanooga's Florence Crittenden Home found it necessary to have a plot in the cemetery. Providing a safe home for unmarried pregnant women to have their babies, the home was chartered in 1891 through the work of the Women's Christian Association. Originally located on Cypress Street, in 1930 a new home was opened on Thirty-third Street.

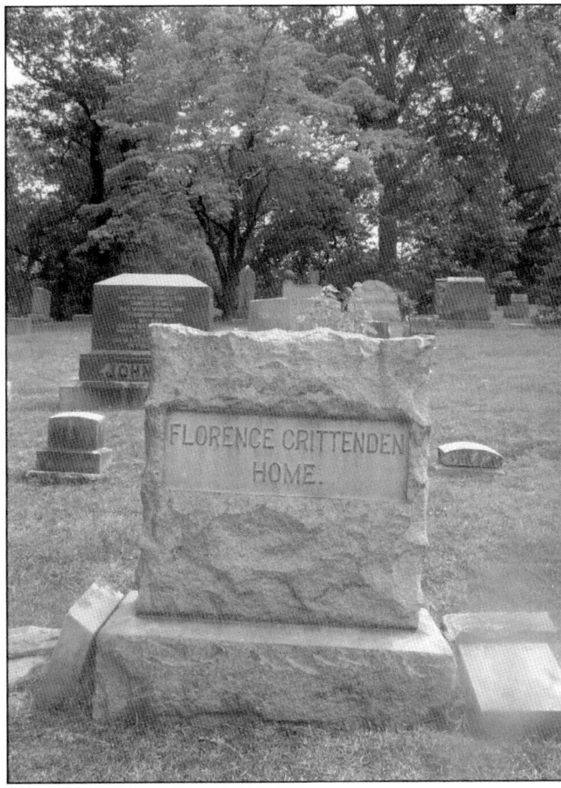

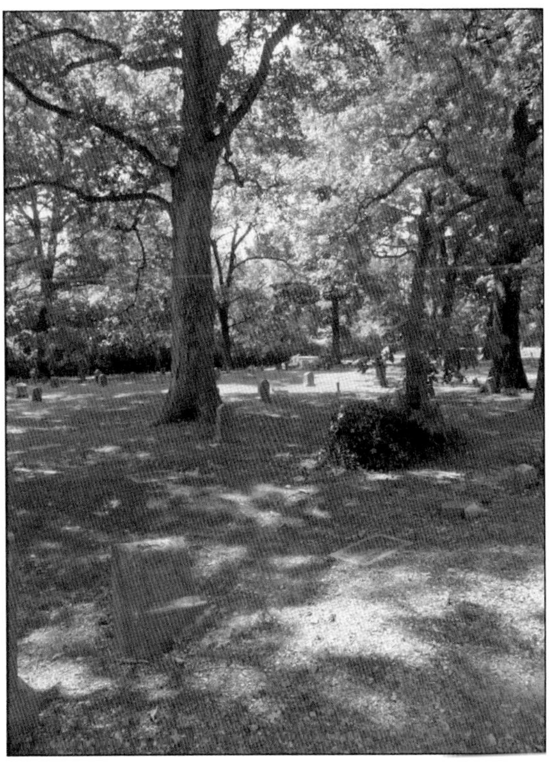

When Mariah Kibble Aiken (1828–1933) died, she was believed to be the oldest resident of Hamilton County. Born into slavery near Murfreesboro, Tennessee, she was owned by the Walter Kibble family. Although freed after the Civil War, she remained with the family and reared their daughter, Anna, with whom Mariah reestablished contact several years before her death.

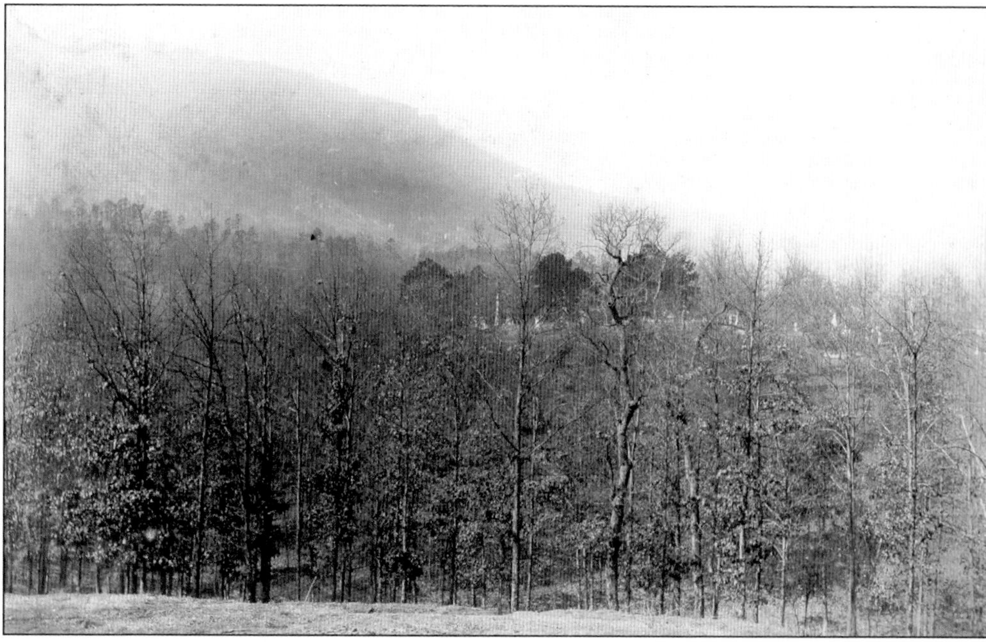

From the 1880s until 1906, Chattanooga had a small population of Chinese residents. Never numbering more than 18 men, most were single and all were engaged in the laundry business. One of these men was Wah Lu (1856–1887). The *Chattanooga Times* described an annual ceremony, referring to it as a "picnic," in which the Chinese community and invited guests brought food, wine, and incense to the cemetery and offered prayers for the well-being of the dead.

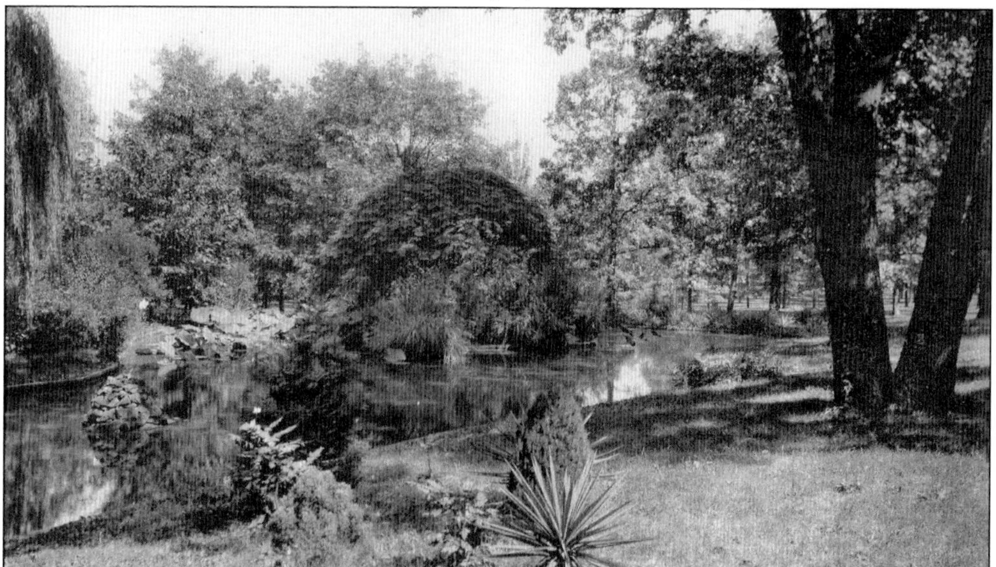

Yee Men (1857–1891) had only been in Chattanooga for three weeks when he committed suicide. The *Chattanooga Times* carried a detailed report of his traditional Chinese funeral, calling the proceedings "one of the most peculiar ever held in Chattanooga." Yee's clothing and bedding were collected from his home, and pieces of paper were scattered to announce the funeral. The decedent's clothes and other belongings were burned and coins were dropped into his grave, followed by the placing of food at the grave, lighting of joss sticks, and ritual recitation of prayers.

Chan Yu (1857–1887) was suffering from typhoid fever when he committed suicide by stabbing himself in the abdomen and throat. By 1906, all of the Chinese had disappeared from Chattanooga. A newspaper account alludes to opposition to a law, considered degrading by the Chinese, that they be photographed.

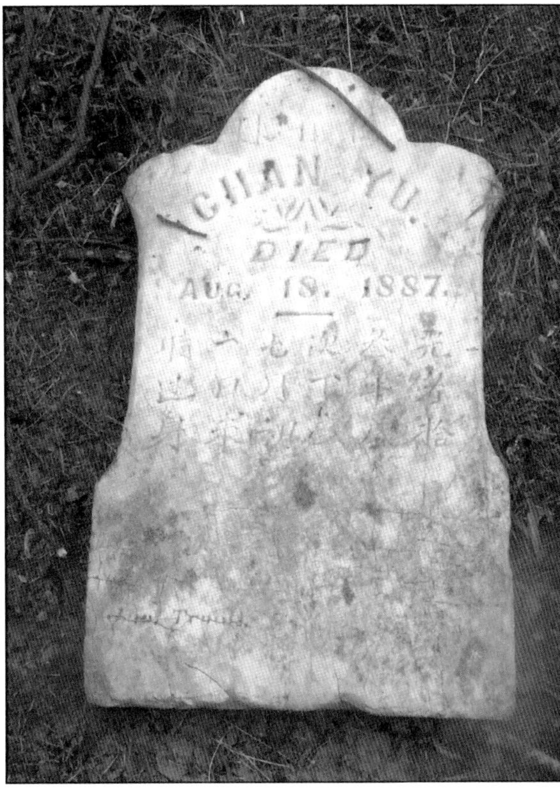

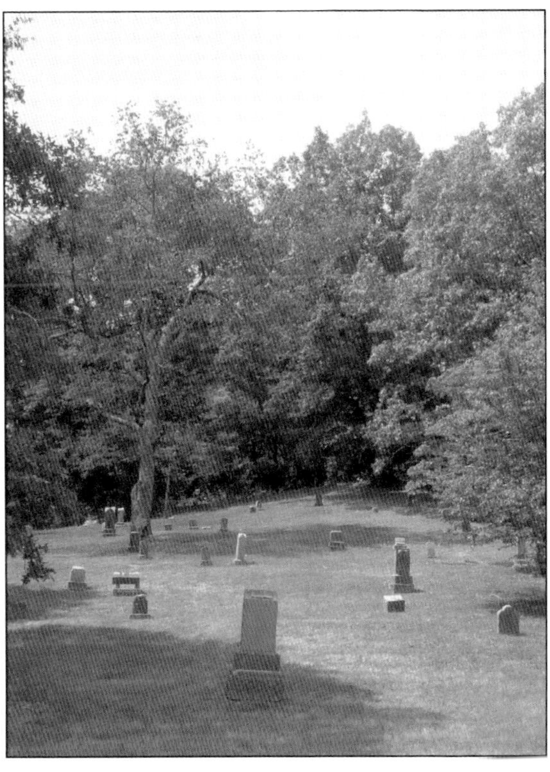

Jennie Weaver (1829–1904) came to Chattanooga in 1853, with her owners, the family of Francis Marion Walker. Her obituary emphasizes the love and esteem for her by this family and her affection toward them. It also admonishes former slave owners "to render the declining days of the survivors (slave nannies) more tolerable, if not happier and more comfortable than is possible to them under their generally hard environments."

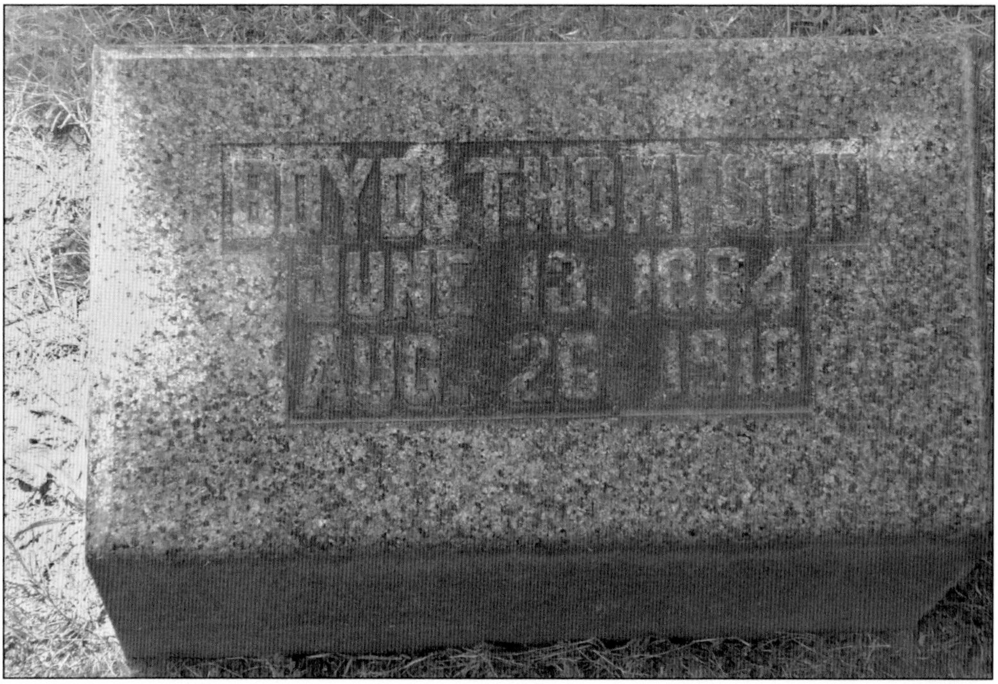

Boyd Thompson (1884–1910) was killed in a pistol duel with Will Synder on Market Street near Eighth Street in front of Gottschalk's Store on August 26, 1910. According to newspaper reports, the duel was the result of a three-year feud between the men. Synder was seriously wounded, but recovered. His killing of Thompson was ruled self-defense.

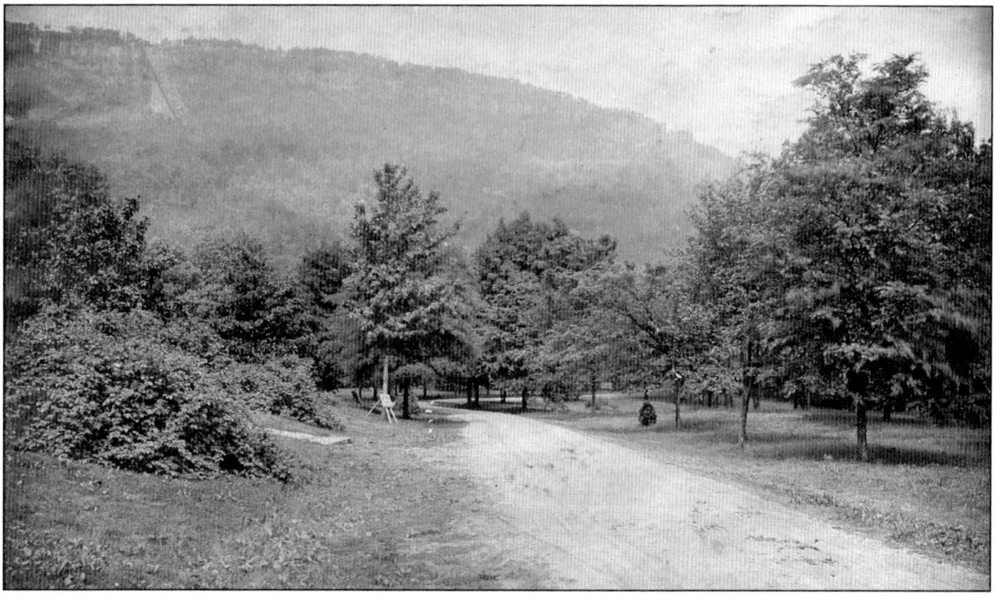

Effie Cawthorn (1864–1904) stated that she "was ordered by God to save her son, Clifford, from being a bad man and a felon" when she killed him with a hatchet. She also stated that she had intended to kill her other children and herself when she set fire to their home. Ruled temporarily insane, she was a widow who had previously attempted to take her life and was reportedly exhibiting increasingly strange behavior prior to the murder. She died several years later in a Knoxville asylum.

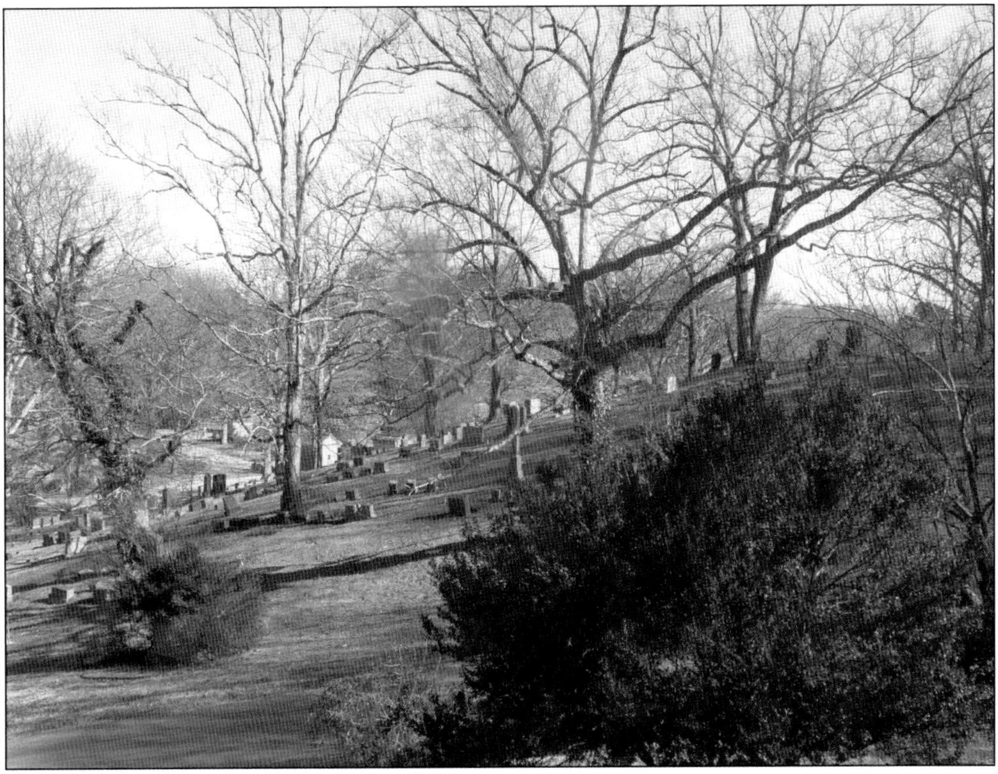

Three amputated limbs were buried in separate lots in the 1920s. The amputated foot of Joseph Bruce was interred in August 1926, while the amputated leg of C. P. G. Caves and the amputated arm of Dr. Edward Denton were buried in April 1927 and February 1928, respectively.

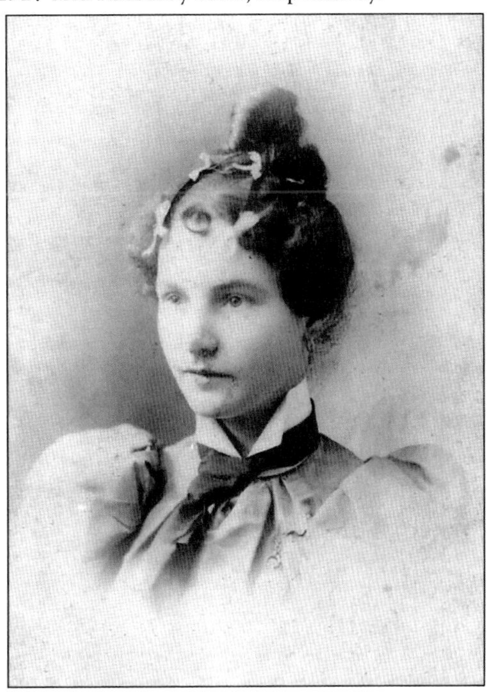

Edith Cruse Mullins was only four years old when her mother, Lillian Cruse (1874–1916), died of tuberculosis, but she still recalls seeing her mother's coffin carried by a horse-drawn hearse into Forest Hills Cemetery. After her mother's death, Edith went to live with her aunt and uncle, Abbie (1881–1967) and Ira (1867–1946) Marcy, who reared her along with their daughter Violet (1887–1951).

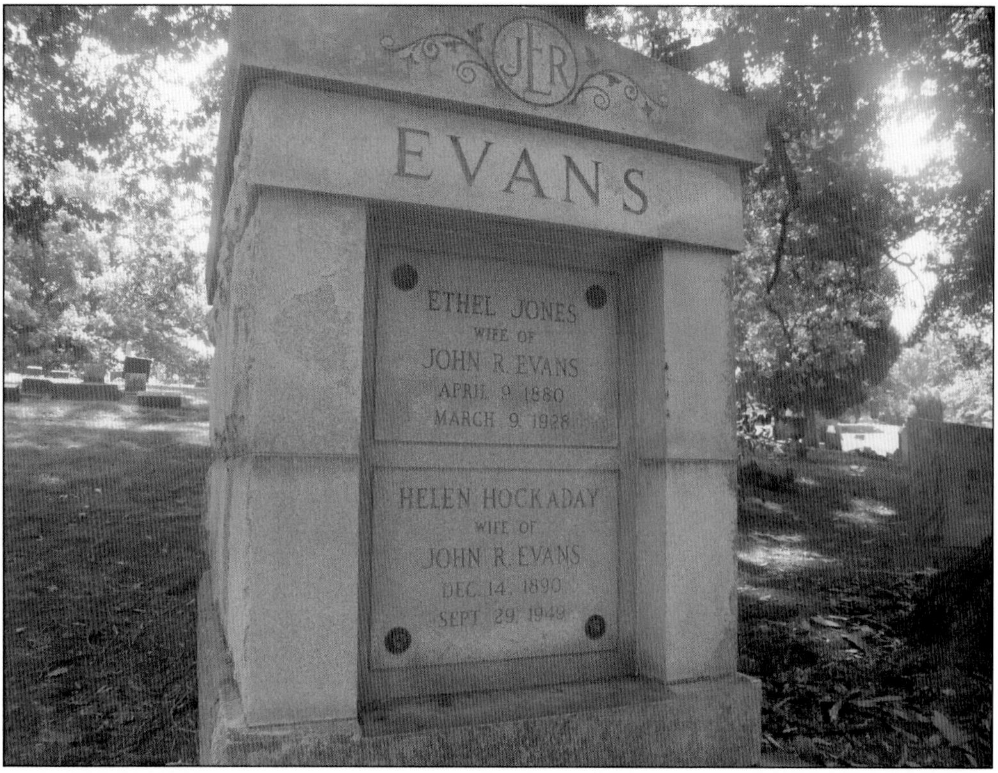

Named by the *Chattanooga Times* as the most popular newsboy in the city, John Evans (1878–1959) won a trip to the Chicago World's Fair in 1893. At 17, he opened a grocery. He opened an insurance agency in 1908 and by 1923 he was president of the Tennessee State Realtors. By the time of his death his two wives, Ethel (1880–1928) and Helen (1890–1949) already occupied the two spaces in his mausoleum. His grave is located beside the mausoleum.

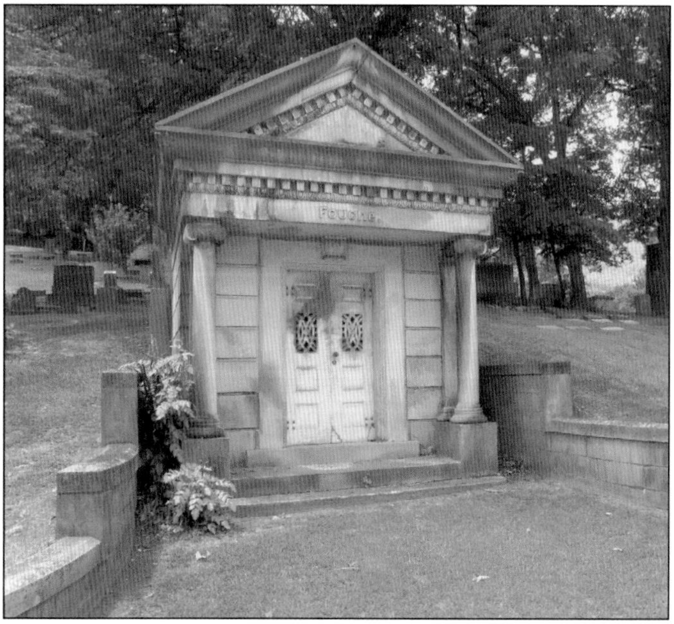

This mausoleum contains the remains of Morton (1833–1898) and Adelphia Pratt Fouche (?–1919). The couple came to Chattanooga in 1889 from Rockwood, Tennessee, where Morton was president of the First National Bank of Rockwood. In 1895, he was appointed clerk of the U.S. District Court, a position he occupied until his death. Their only surviving child, Eleanora (1849–1886) married Tennessee Supreme Court chief justice David Snodgrass (1851–1917).

Finley Alexander Seagle (1862–1934) came to Chattanooga from Wytheville, Virginia, in 1883. By 1892, he owned the Chattanooga Lumber Company. He served as a commissioner and later mayor of St. Elmo from its incorporation in 1905 until 1930. He married Mary Alice Brown in 1887. The couple reared their eight children in the new town. As a commissioner, he was instrumental in establishing the St. Elmo Elementary School and the Lookout Mountain Junior High School.

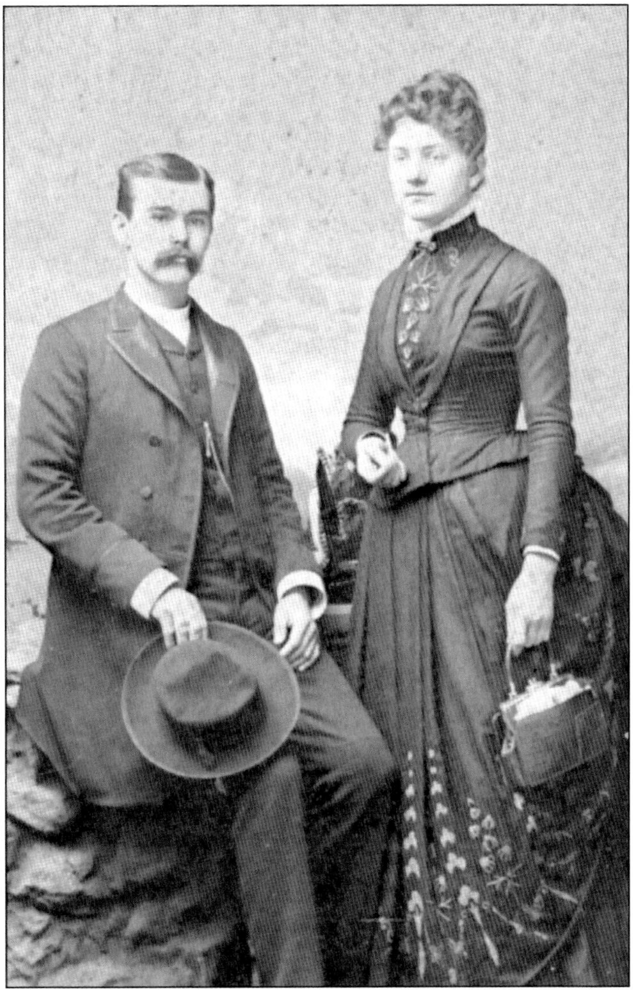

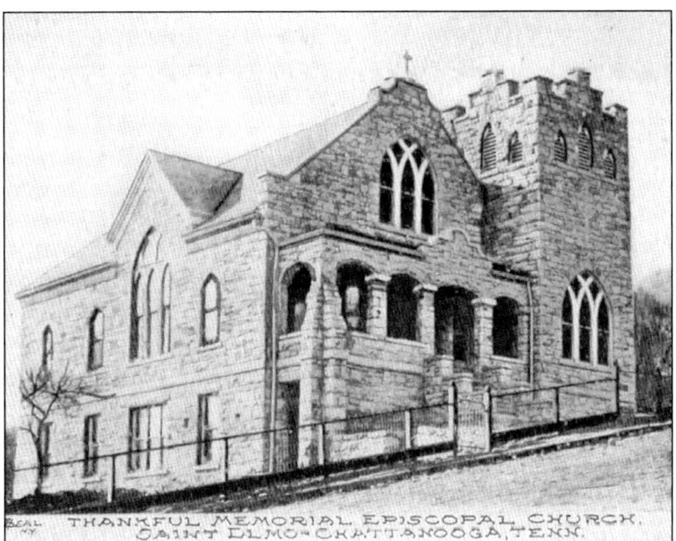

Welsh-born David Davies (1827–1917) immigrated to the United States in 1845. A peddler by trade, he worked in the iron industry throughout the Civil War. After the war, he was employed at the Roane Iron Company. He lived in St. Elmo, where he served as the senior warden of the Thankful Memorial Episcopal Church. Reportedly a hearty eater of anything and everything, he had perfect teeth and took up smoking at age 88.

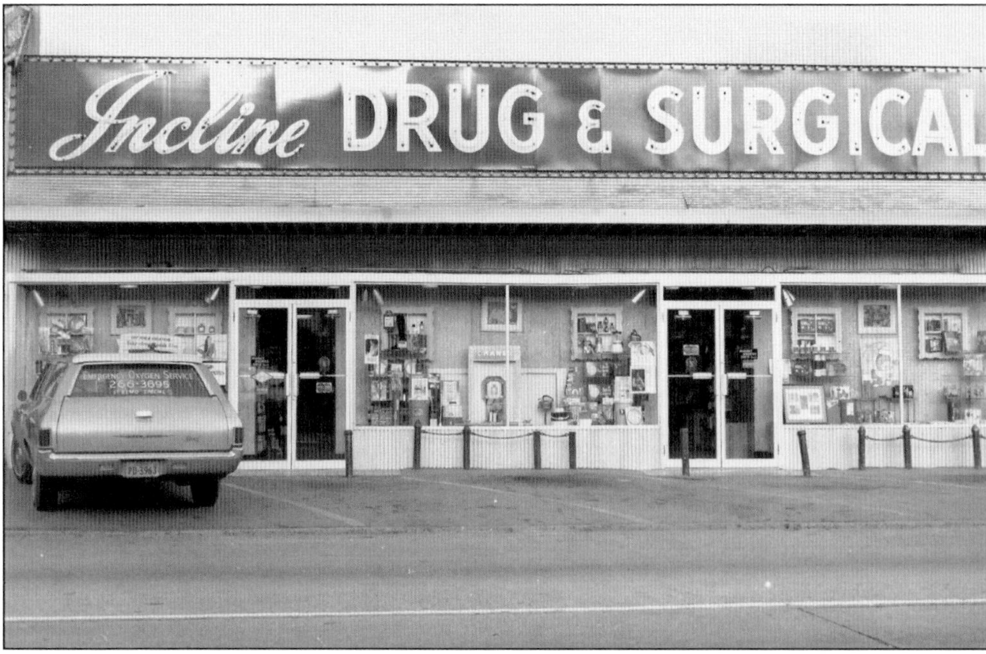

In 1939, Martin McDonough Sr. (1902–1984) opened the Incline Drug Company on St. Elmo Avenue across the street from the entrance to the Incline Railway. Beginning the business with only $490, his first prescription was for a 35¢ eye solution. The drug company grew and later included a gift shop and surgical supply company. (Photograph courtesy of Jeff Webb.)

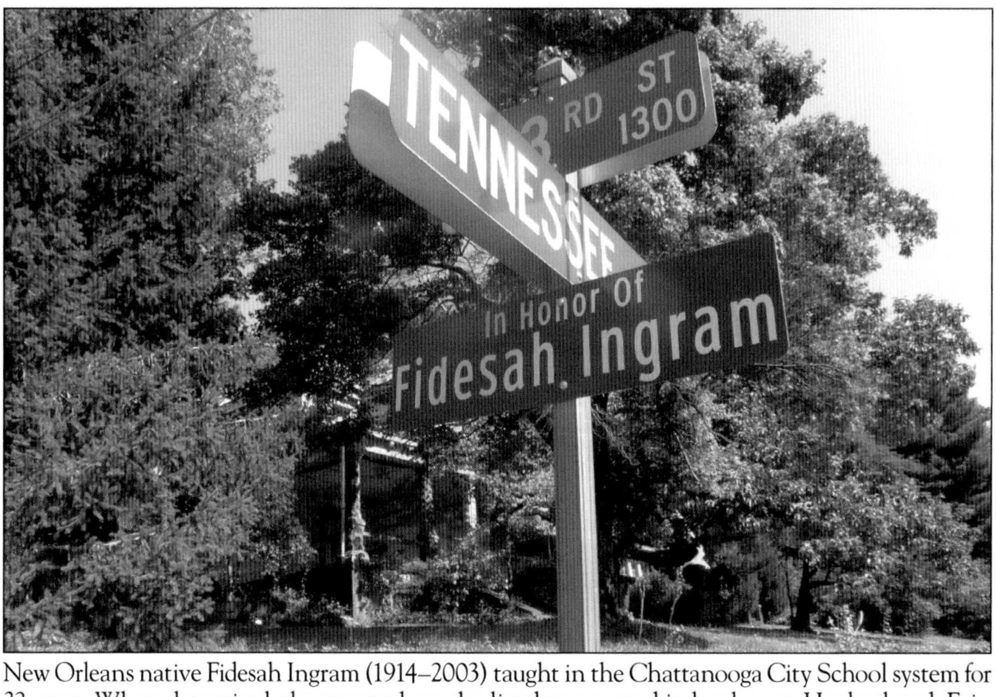

New Orleans native Fidesah Ingram (1914–2003) taught in the Chattanooga City School system for 32 years. When she retired, the street where she lived was named in her honor. Her husband, Fain (1912–1961), began his career as a teacher at the Cave Springs Georgia School for the Deaf, where he taught furniture making. They purchased this home at the corner of Tennessee Avenue in 1937.

Two

Business and Industry

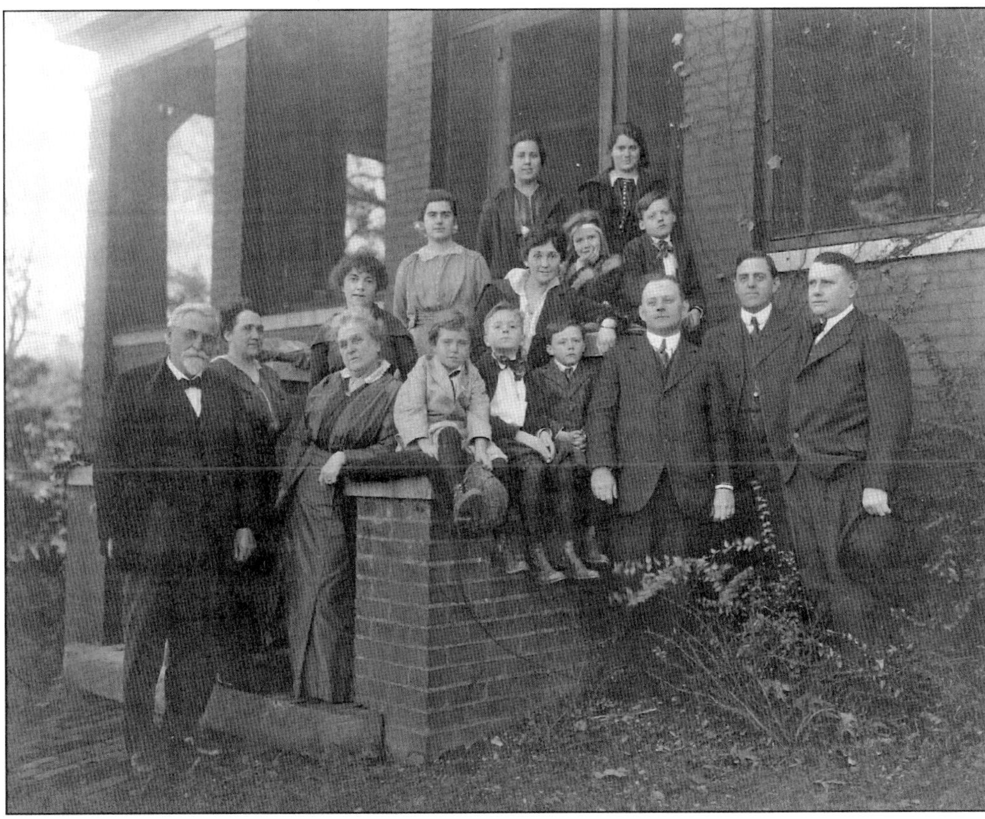

George Washington Wheland (1843–1929), pictured at the far left, enjoyed having all of his family for dinner or family picnics at his St. Elmo home. Following his service in the 118th Ohio Volunteer Infantry, he built Wheland Foundry. Specializing in making grist and cane mills and later engines and sawmills, he remained president of the company until his death. (Photograph courtesy of Margaret Cate.)

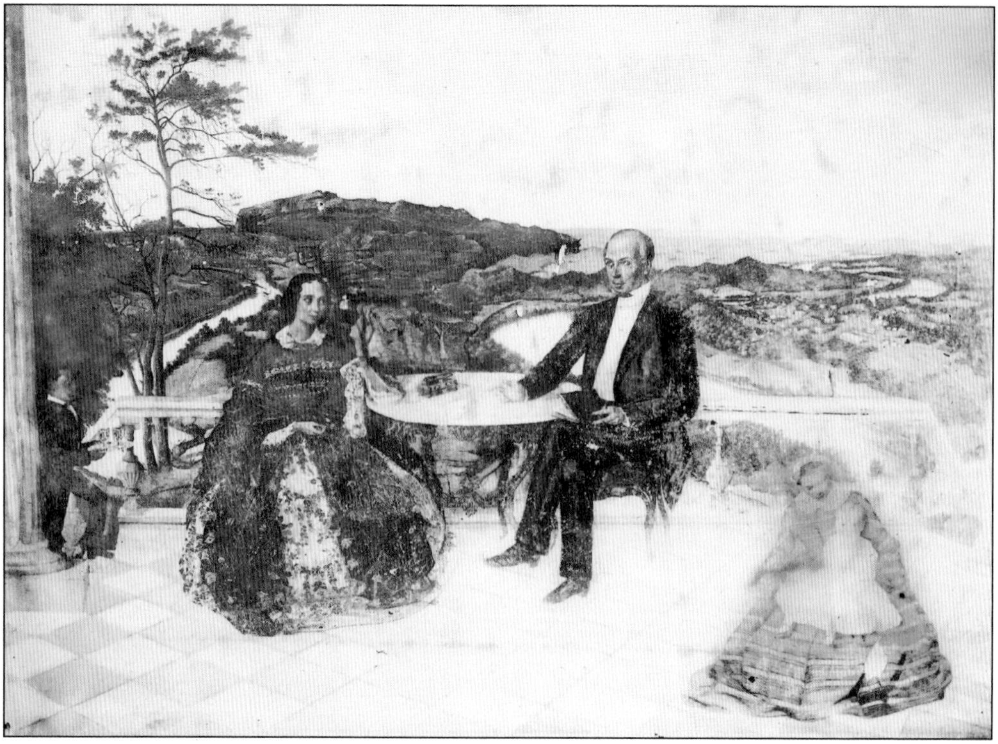

James Anderson Whiteside (1803–1861), a lawyer and early state legislator, moved to the town of Ross's Landing in 1839. Seeing the potential of the area, he was instrumental in bringing railroads to the valley. Recognizing the potential for tourism on Lookout Mountain, he purchased the Lookout Mountain Turnpike and built a hotel on the eastern brow. He gave money and encouragement to many churches and was known as the "godfather of Chattanooga churches." He married twice and was the father of 14 children.

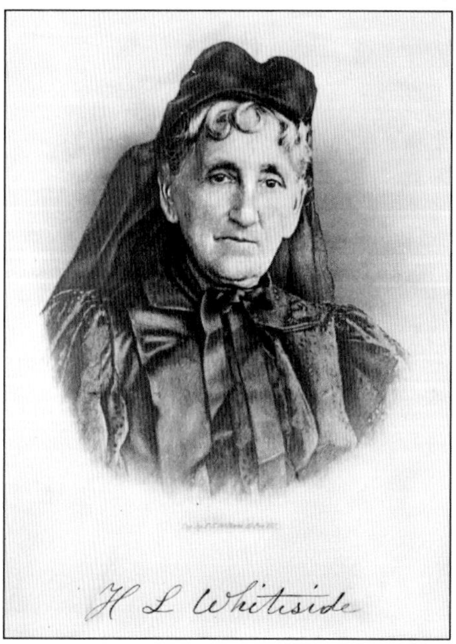

Harriet Straw (1824–1903) arrived in Chattanooga from Wytheville, Virginia, in 1843 to take a position as a tutor to the children of the newly widowed James Whiteside. Beautiful, educated, and intelligent, she married Whiteside in 1844 and bore him nine children before his death in 1861. At his death, she gained control of his sizeable estate, which included much of Lookout Mountain. Over the next 42 years, her desire to build and maintain control of her fortune led her to file lawsuits against her children, stepchildren, and many others in the community.

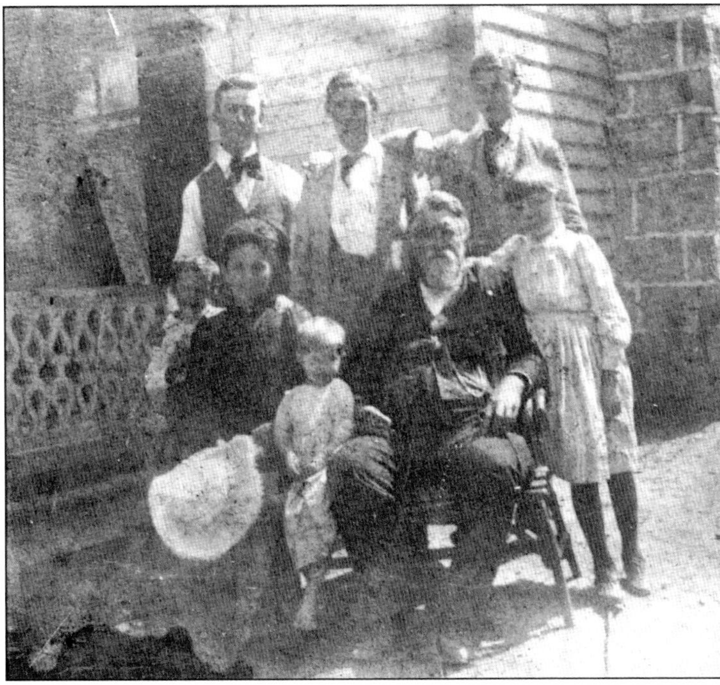

The grandson of one of the first white settlers at Ross's Landing, Francis Marion Gardenhire (1836–1905) inherited and added to his family's extensive estate, much of which occupied a 2-mile strip along the Tennessee River east of the city. Serving the Confederacy, he was imprisoned during the Civil War, but returned home and married Leona Rogers in 1868; she died in 1927. The Gardenhires reared seven children at their home on East Third Street.

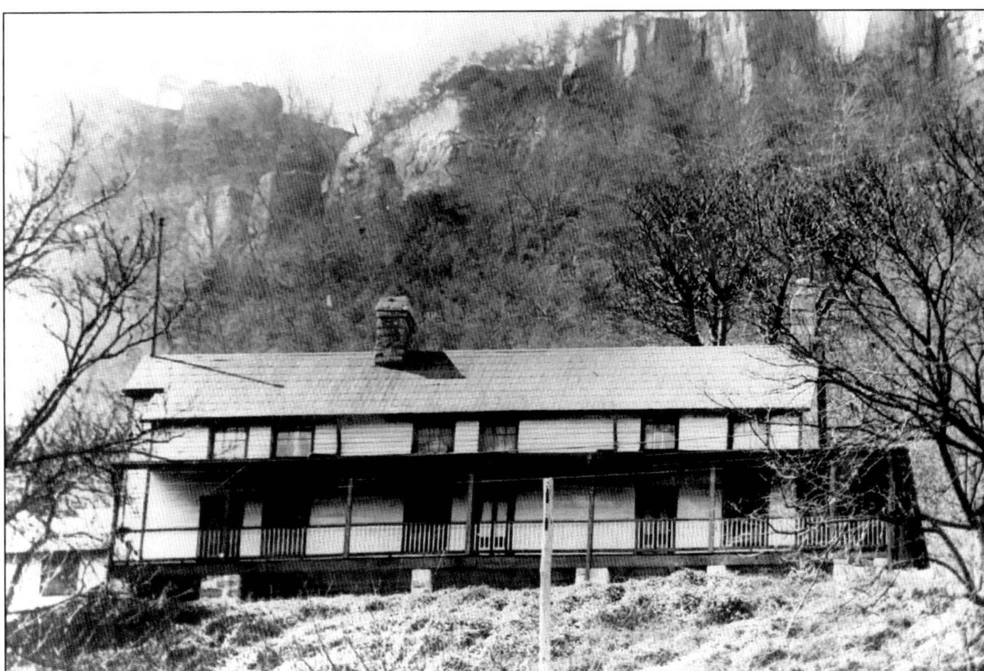

Arriving in Chattanooga in 1851, Robert Cravens (1804–1886) founded the East Tennessee Iron Company. With James Whiteside and others, he purchased 16,000 acres on Raccoon Mountain and began a coal mining business. By 1860, Cravens was wealthy and had a home on the side of Lookout Mountain. Serving as Gen. Joe Hooker's headquarters, the home was destroyed during the Battle of Lookout Mountain. Cravens returned after the war, rebuilding the home with profits from the purchase and resale of army wagons.

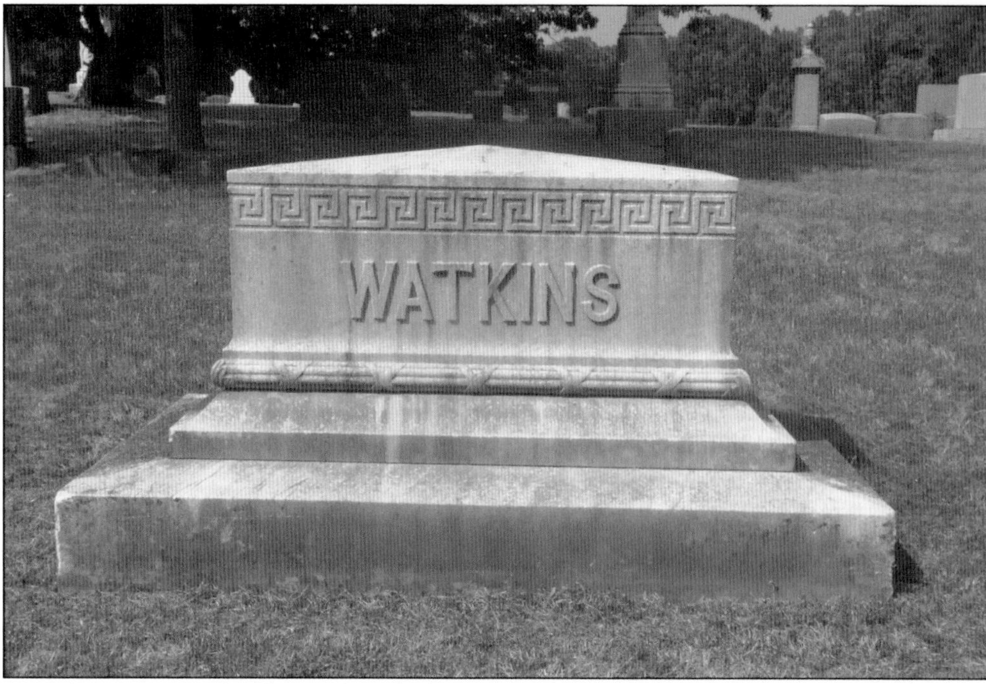

Reared in poverty and without a formal education, Richard "Dick" Watkins (1836–1894) followed his brothers to Chattanooga and opened what became the largest hardware store in the state. A captain in the Confederacy, he saw action in Chattanooga, Resaca, Vicksburg, Peachtree Creek, and Mobile. A leader in the development of the railway up Lookout Mountain and the Lookout Inn, he was later elected mayor of Lookout Mountain.

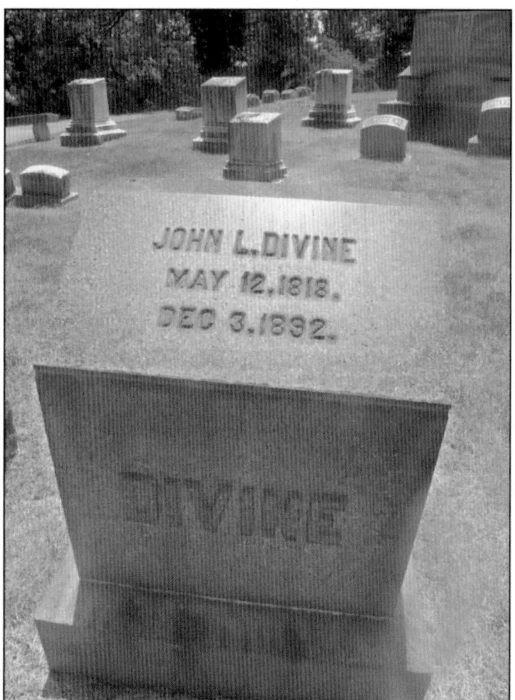

John L. Divine (1818–1892) was born in Maryville, Tennessee, a few months after his parents emigrated from Ireland. At age 20, he was on his way to Mississippi when he stopped off in Chattanooga. All of his money was stolen and he was forced to remain in the city. Over the years he made his fortune in the mercantile business, the livestock trade, real estate, and banking, and managed to marry two women from well-to-do families, Elizabeth Williams (1829–1859) and Rachel James (1841–1929).

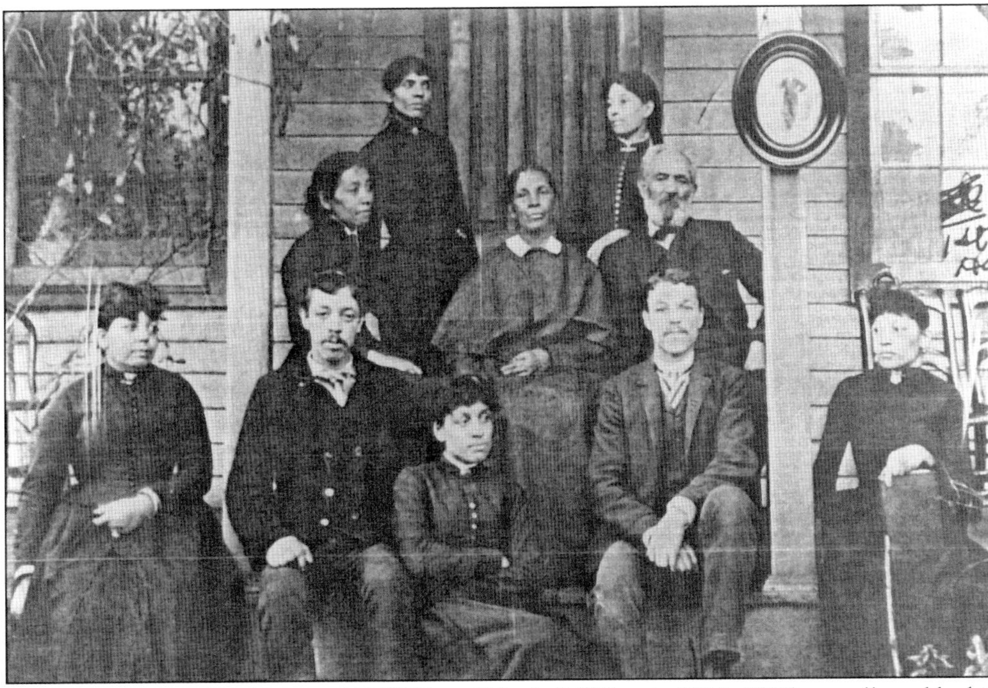

Born a slave to a Cherokee, in 1839 William "Uncle Bill" Lewis (1810–1896) was allowed by his owner—for the sum of $350 per year—to come to Chattanooga to set up a blacksmith shop. Over the next few years he was able to purchase his freedom as well as that of his wife, son, mother, aunt, two brothers, and a sister. By 1870, he owned a substantial amount of real estate. Shown here with his family, Lewis is at far right of the second row and his nephew John Lovell is second from left of the first row.

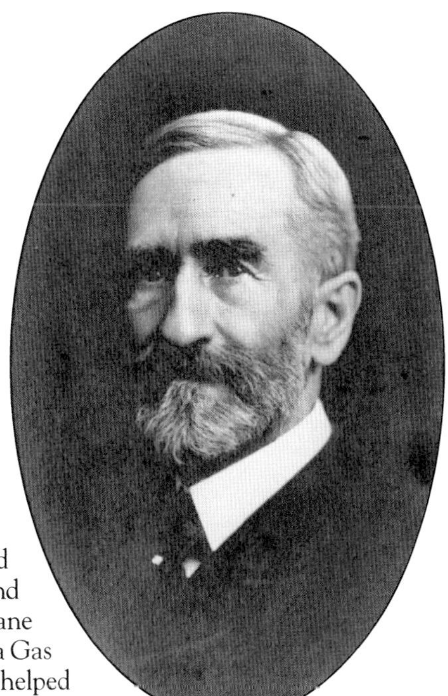

A member of the 140th Ohio Infantry, Theodore Giles Montague (1836–1910) was one of the many men who responded to a newspaper advertisement assuring former Union soldiers they were welcome in Chattanooga. The only qualifications desired were, "capital, brains, and muscle." Once in Chattanooga, Montague helped found the First National Bank. He was associated with the Roane Iron Company, Lookout Water Company, Chattanooga Gas Company, and Chattanooga Pipe and Foundry. He also helped establish Forest Hills Cemetery.

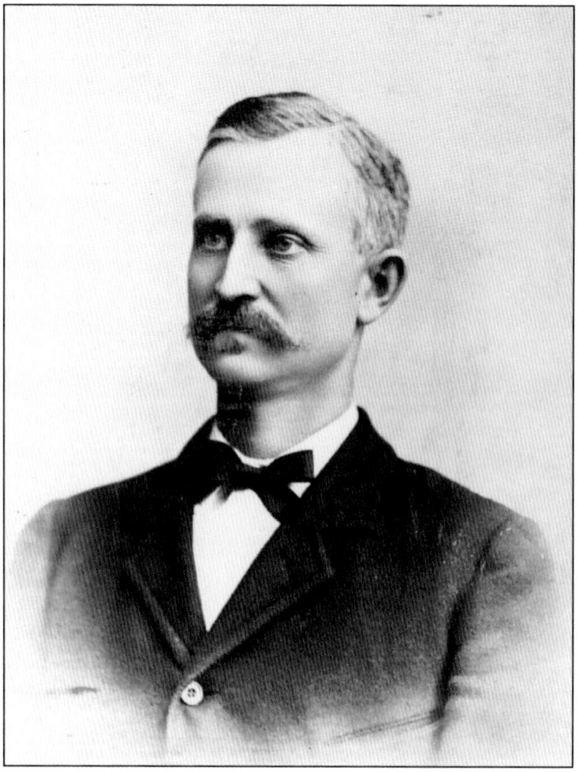

A native of Valley Head, Alabama, George Washington Davenport (1858–1917) came to Chattanooga in 1877 with his brothers Joseph and Rodolph. They formed a wholesale dry goods business, Davenport Brothers. Eventually, George became the president of the Citizens Bank and Trust Company and held interests in textile milling. His *Chattanooga Times* obituary refers to him as a man of "indomitable energy . . . close application to work and thrift characterized him."

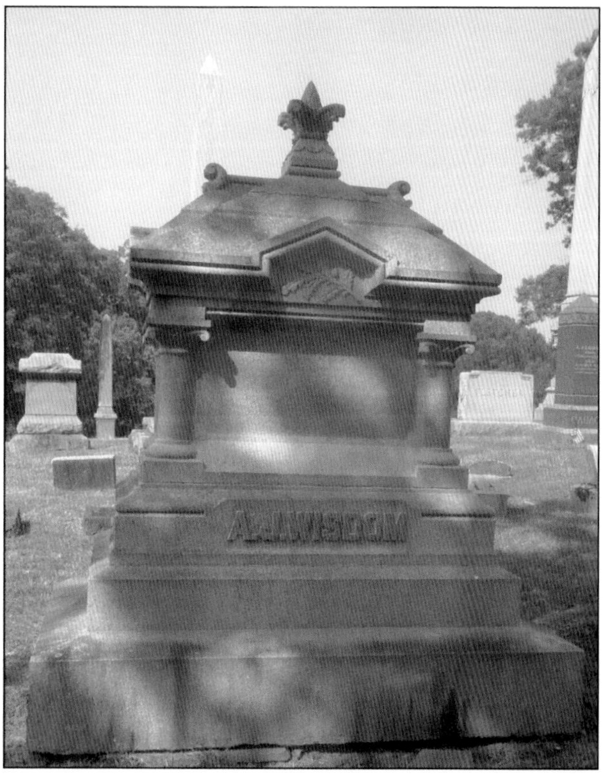

Abner "Ab" Wisdom (1826–1897) came to Chattanooga in 1852 and worked in a livery stable. Joining the Confederacy, he was captured early in the war. He gained his release by promising not to again aid the Confederacy and he returned home. At the conclusion of the war, he purchased a carload of surplus mules to start his successful livery and undertaking business.

Born in Wilna, New York, Zeboim Carter Patten (1840–1925) was a captain in the Union Army. In partnership with other ambitious young men, Patten helped found Volunteer Life Insurance, T. H. Payne Company, Stone Fort Land Company, American Trust and Banking Company, and Title Guarantee and Trust Company. He also built the Patten Hotel, but he is best known for founding the Chattanooga Medicine Company, later known as the Chattem Company. He is pictured here with his first wife, Mary Rawlings (1847–1875).

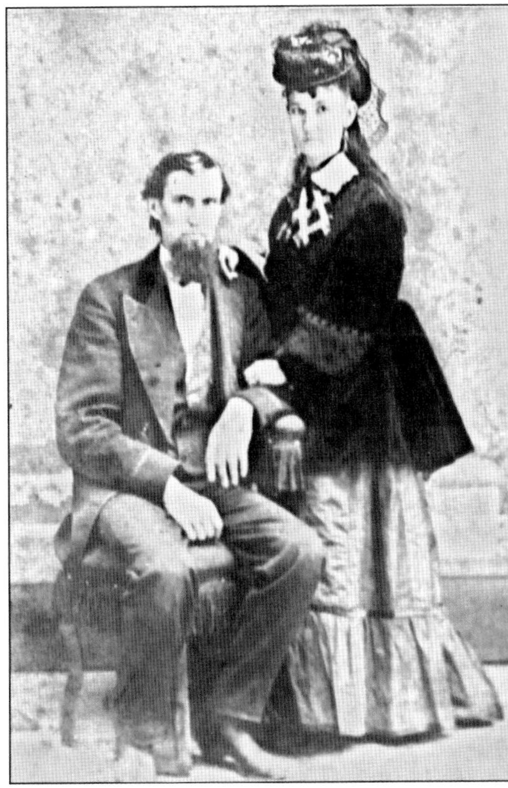

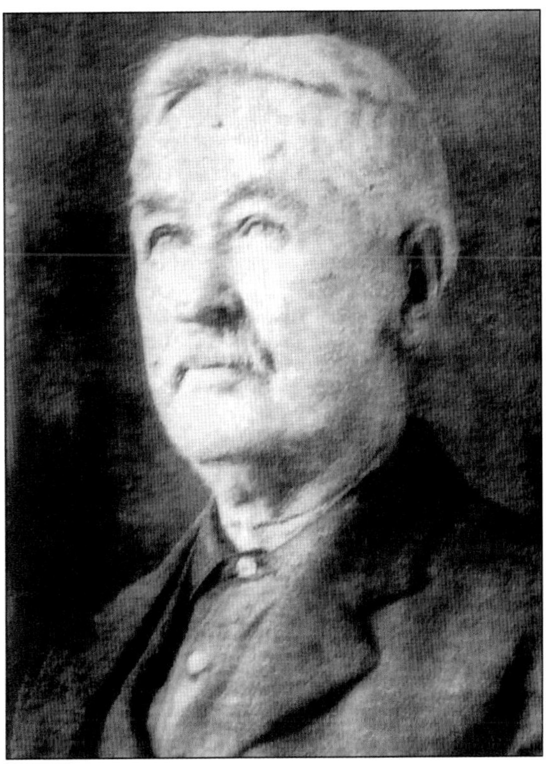

The family of John C. Roberts (1835–1919) came to the area when he was a boy. Having served with distinction in the Confederate Army, he returned to the family farm. Although he preferred to be known as a farmer, he entered the real estate business in 1886. Dividing his farm into town lots, Roberts created Clifton Hills. As a member of the county court, he helped establish the first public school in Chattanooga. (Photograph courtesy of David Scott.)

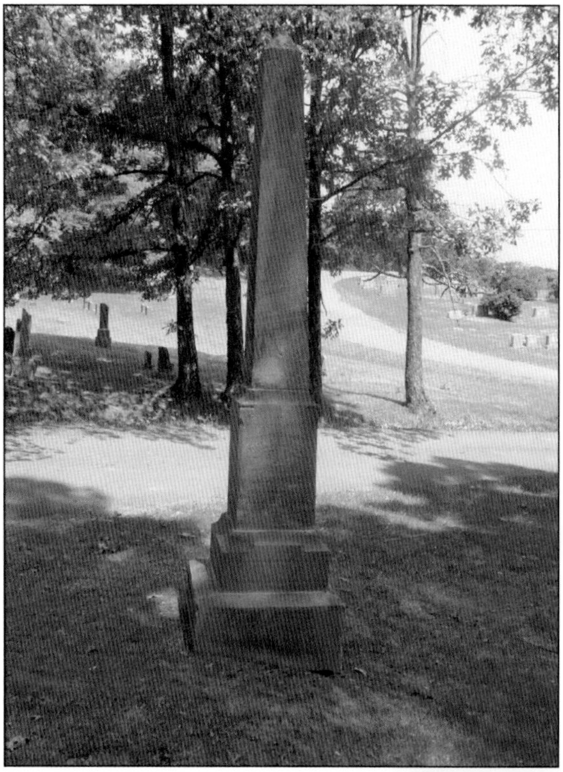

John Lovell (1838–1898), the son of a wealthy white planter and nephew of William Lewis, was a "free born Negro." He arrived in Chattanooga in 1863 with 50¢ in his pocket. He acquired a tent and set up a barbershop. Ambitious and eager to make his fortune, he opened another tent to sell liquor. During the city's postwar boom, he built a block of buildings on Ninth Street and opened the Mahogany Hall, the largest saloon and dance hall in the city. His liquor and prostitution business made him wealthy, but his love was breeding racehorses.

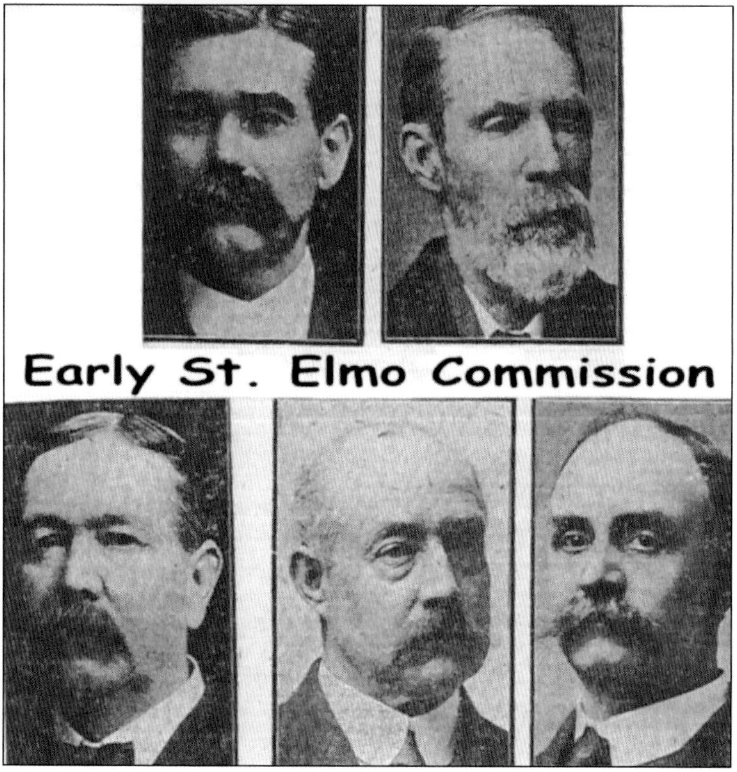

Welshman Reese Thomas (1845–1935) moved to Chattanooga and later St. Elmo after the Civil War to open a general store with his brother. Later, he was the proprietor of the Natural Bridge Hotel on Lookout Mountain. Active in civic affairs, he was an alderman, school board member, and St. Elmo's first mayor. He is pictured here on the bottom left. Other commissioners include, clockwise from upper left, Finley Seagle, L. W. Bates, P. S. Poindexter, and Dr. H. B. Wilson.

German-born Robert Scholze (1843–1907) moved to the St. Elmo area with his wife, Gertrude, in 1870. He operated a dairy for several years, before deciding to go into the tannery business. He had little capital and often carried buckets of water from the creek to fill the vats at the tannery. By 1876, his tannery and saddlery were successful. Scholze was known for his generosity toward his employees and other members of the community.

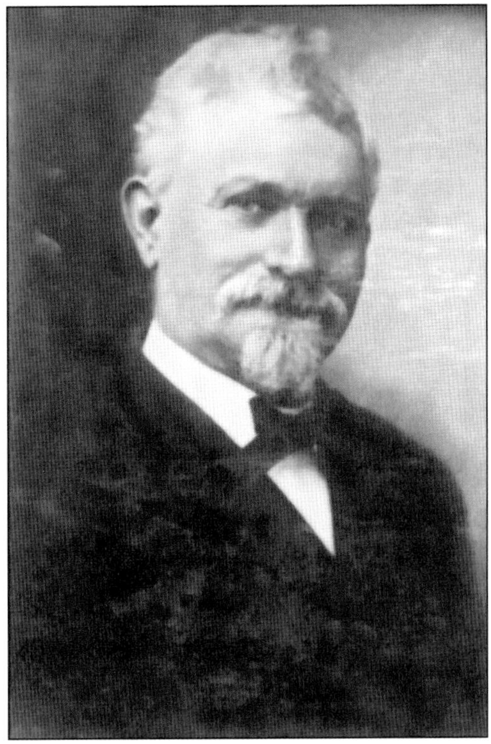

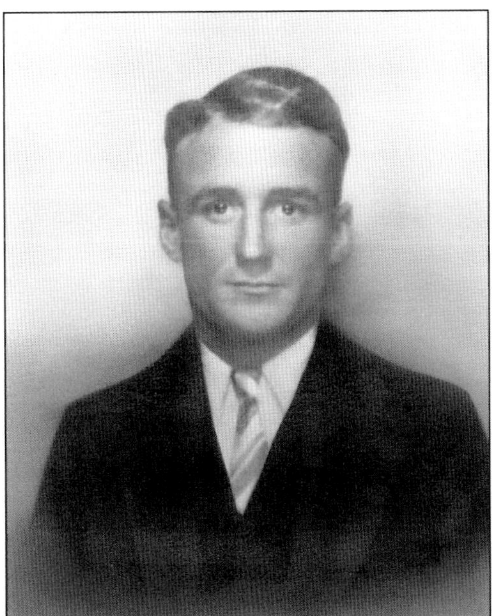

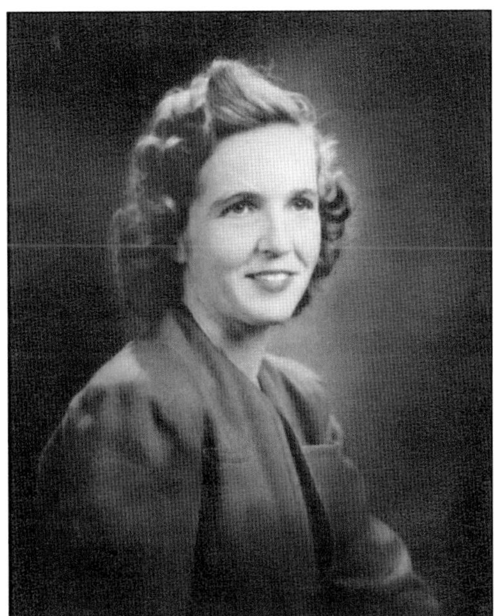

Rob (b. 1907) and Margaret (b. 1915) Eldridge were killed in a head-on collision on December 26, 1948. Their sons, Frank, 7, and James, 4, were not with their parents at the time. Frank is now a physician, and James owns Ledco Construction. His company remodeled the Forest Hills Cemetery office in 2003.

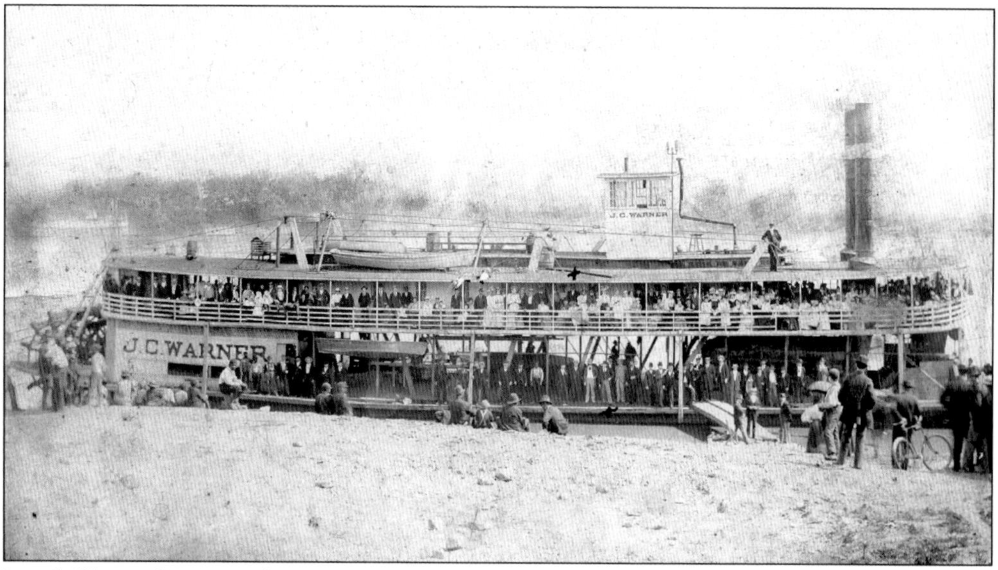

Joseph Warner (1842–1908), a city commissioner and banker, helped found Chattanooga's first public transportation system, which consisted of mules pulling trolley cars back and forth on Market Street. He owned a fleet of riverboats, including the *J. C. Warner*. Warner Park is named for him. He and his wife, Alice, owned the home that remains on the corner of Vine and Palmetto Streets.

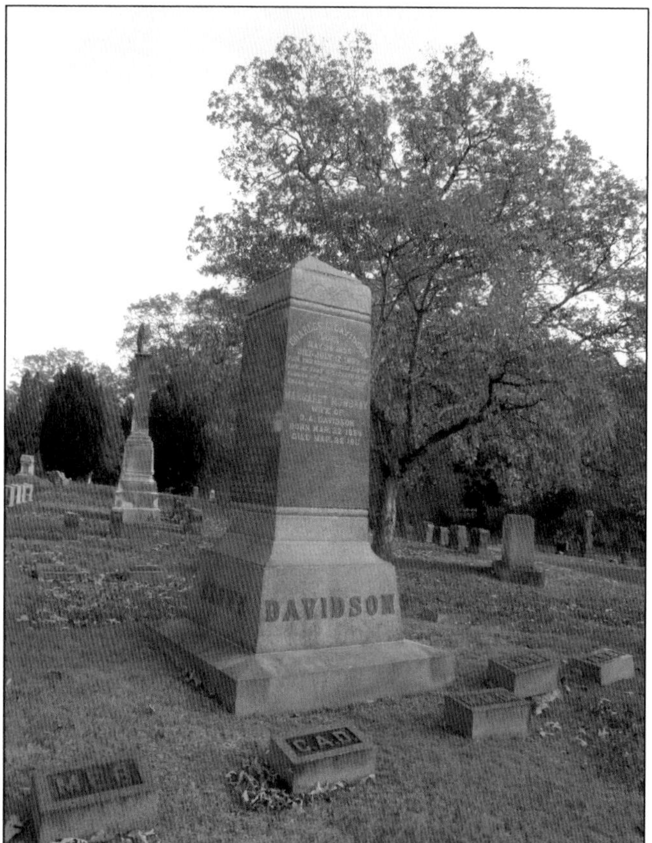

Born in Aberdeen, Scotland, Charles Davidson (1832–1899) arrived in Chattanooga in 1869. He worked as a clerk in William Crutchfield's Dry Goods Store. In 1881, he opened his own clothing store at the corner of Market and Eighth Streets. Davidson's was the first local store to have plate glass display windows that, according to the *Chattanooga Times*, "people came from afar and near to see and admire."

John Thomas Lupton (1862–1933) came to Chattanooga from Virginia in 1887. During his career as a lawyer and businessman, he was associated with Chattanooga Medicine Company, Dixie Mercerizing Company, First National Bank, Stone Fort Land Company, Volunteer Life Insurance, and Patton Hotel. His greatest business achievement, however, was being co-founder and president of the Coca-Cola Bottling Company.

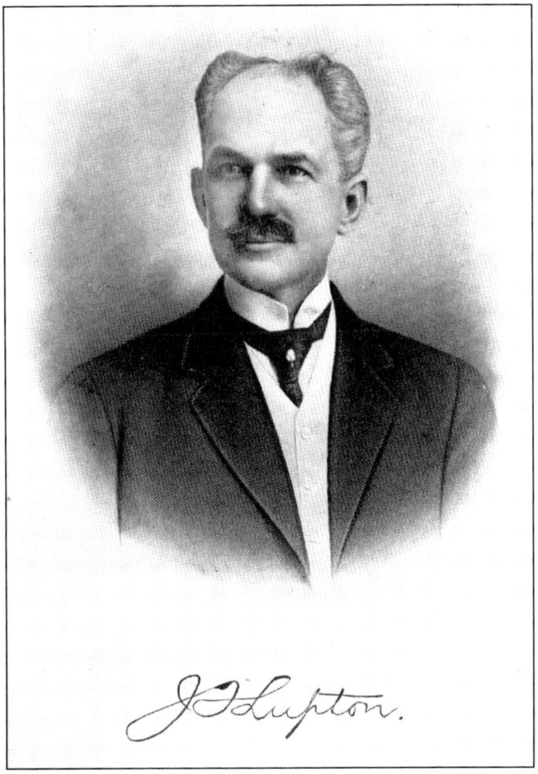

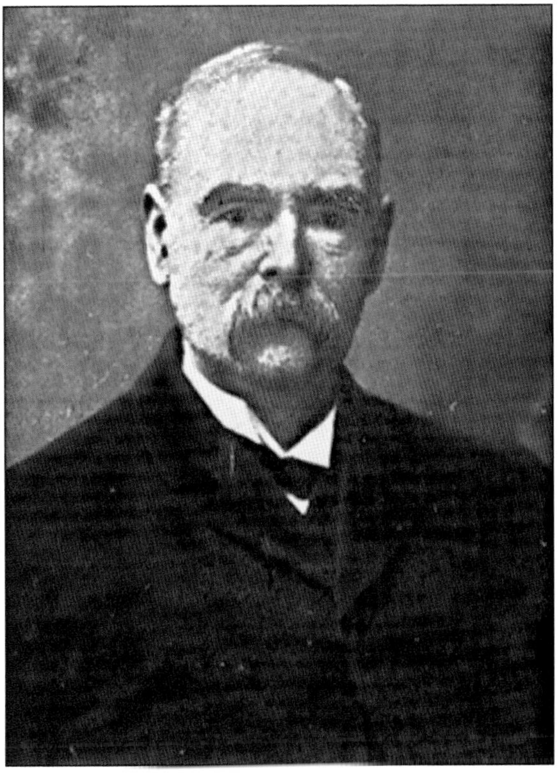

Thomas Webster, an immigrant from England, made cannons for the Confederate Army. Two of his cannons were named for his daughters, Katherine and Lilla (1856–1941). "The Lady Lilla" was mounted at Confederate general Braxton Bragg's headquarters and used at the battle of Missionary Ridge.

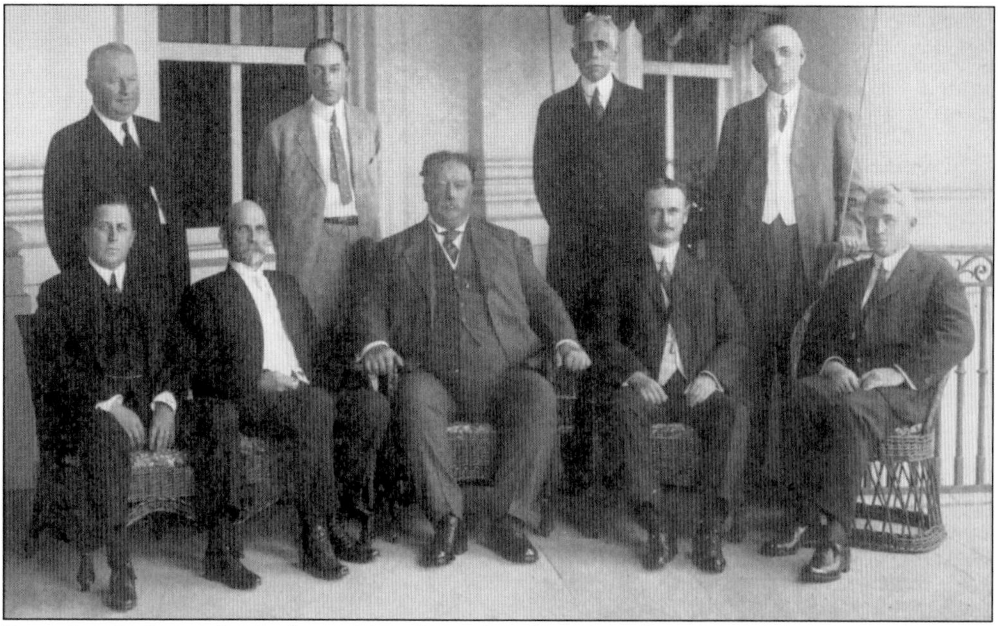

Reared and educated in Indiana, Newell Sanders (1850–1939) founded the Chattanooga Plow Company in 1877. A successful businessman, Sanders eventually had interests in banking, steamboats, and railroads. He entered politics in 1894. In 1912, he was appointed to the U.S. Senate. An advocate of women's suffrage, he was instrumental in Tennessee's ratification of the 19th Amendment. Sanders is on the far right of the second row in this picture. Pres. William Howard Taft is in the center of the first row. (Photograph courtesy of Elizabeth Miller.)

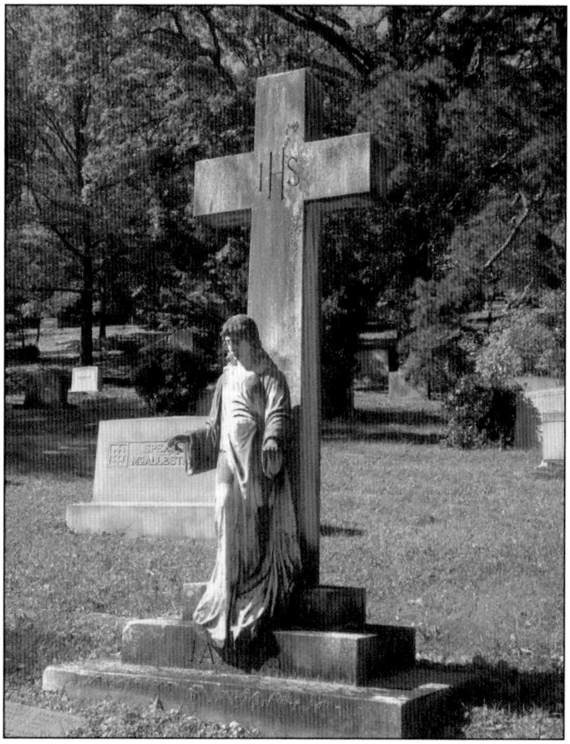

Charles "C. E." James (1851–1939) built railroads in and around Chattanooga, helped establish Chattanooga Gas Company, developed East Lake, and constructed the city's first skyscraper, the handsome James Building on Broad Street. He developed a large section of Walden's Ridge, renaming it Signal Mountain. He built the Signal Mountain Hotel and developed the town of Signal Mountain, of which he was twice elected mayor.

Moving to Lookout Mountain from Alabama in the late 1890s, John (1868–1919) and Josephine Speight (1862–1944) opened the first grocery store on the mountain, located next to their home on East and West Streets. John delivered groceries in his buggy. The Speights donated the northwest corner of Forrest Avenue for the first African American school. The first teacher in the one-room school was the Speights' daughter, Lillie Bell. (Photograph courtesy of the Bessie Smith Cultural Center.)

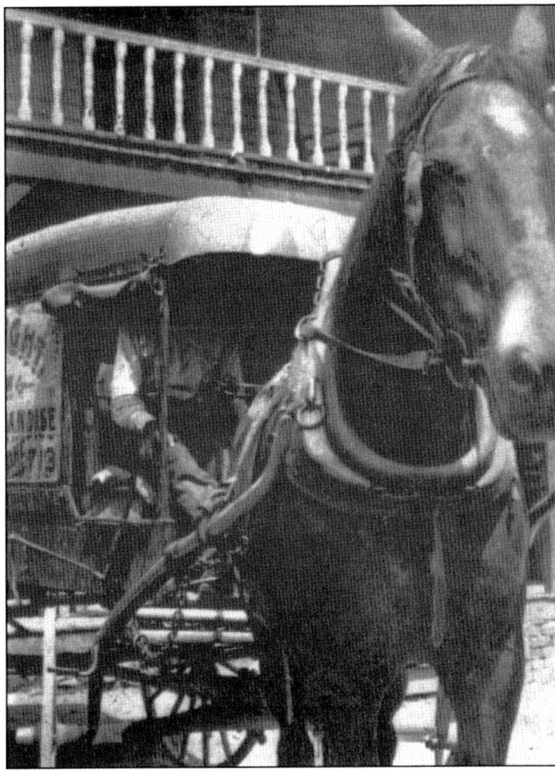

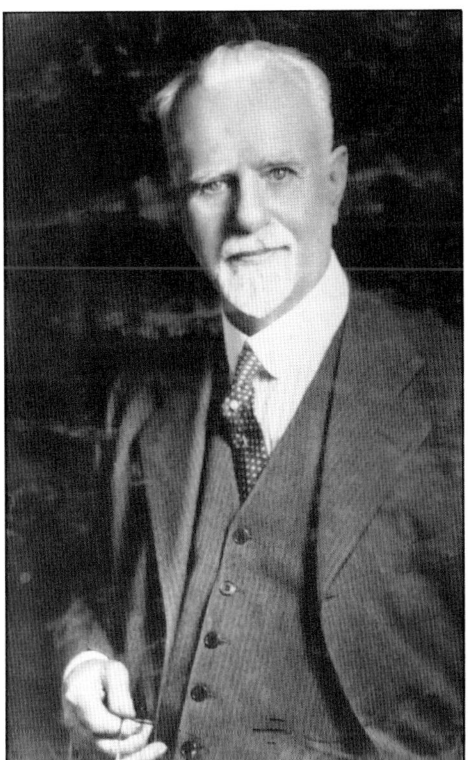

When the Crutchfield House burned in 1867, Thomas Read leased the property and built the Read House. The hotel had three of the first 25 electric lights turned on in the city on May 6, 1882. Samuel Read (1860–1942, pictured here) managed his father's hotel and, upon his death, purchased the block and opened the current Read House Hotel in 1926. Undergoing several modernizations and renovations over the years, the elegant hotel remains a city landmark

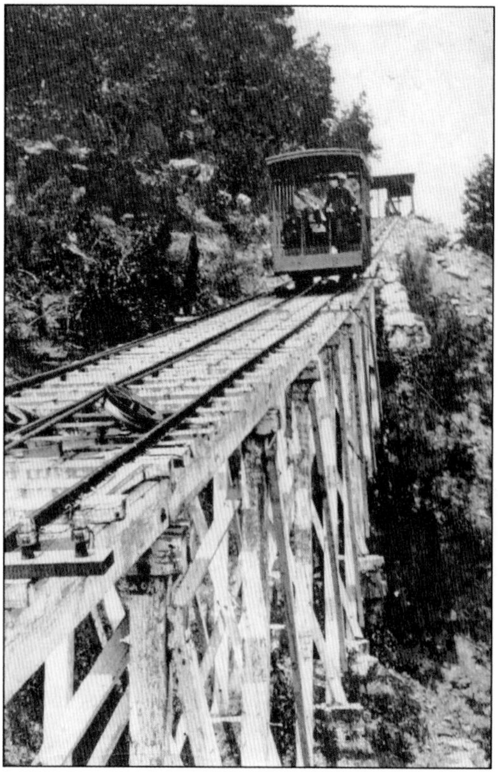

A native of Pennsylvania, Union veteran George Duncan (1834–1918) was the principal contractor of the first incline railway up Lookout Mountain. Opened in 1886, this narrow gauge railroad crossed five trestles and covered 4,360 feet over a 33 percent grade. It ran from Thirty-eighth Street to the Point Hotel, carrying 23 people in open-air wooden cars. It ceased operation in 1899.

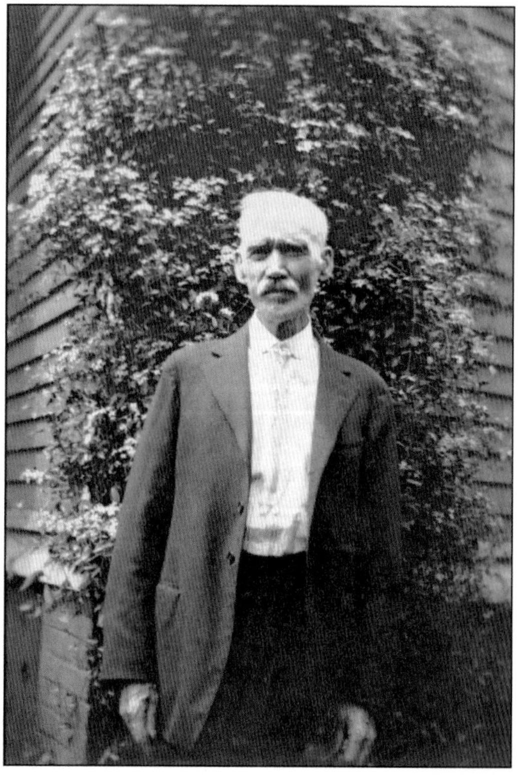

Canadian James Mighton (1858–1928) served in the Royal Canadian Mounted Police before coming to Chattanooga around 1880. As an owner of the McDaniel and Mighton Construction Company, he built the Point Hotel on Lookout Mountain. The hotel served as the terminus for the first incline railway. This incline was built, in part, as a response to public outrage. Harriet Whiteside, who owned much of the top of the mountain, charged visitors, including veterans who had fought there, 25¢ to visit Point Park and $2 to use the only turnpike up the mountain. (Photograph courtesy of John Doyle.)

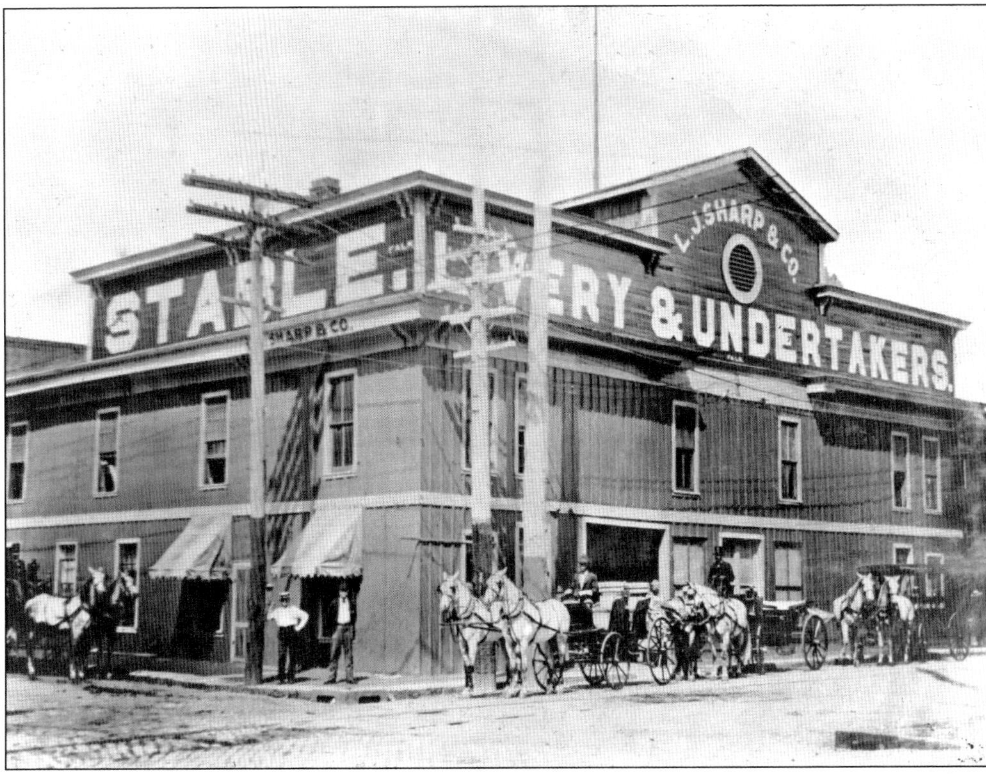

Born in McMinn County to a large landowner and slaveholder, Leonard Japhet "J. B." Sharp (1845–1917) served in the Confederacy for four years. He moved to Chattanooga in 1870, married Nellie Gillespie, and joined his brother-in-law in the livery and undertaking business. Located on Georgia Avenue at the site of the Volunteer Building, it was the largest livery and undertaking establishment in the city.

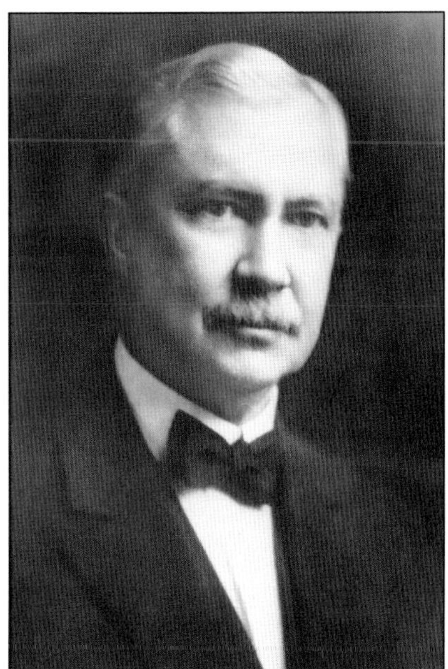
Harry Scott Probasco (1858–1919), like many young businessmen, came to Chattanooga during the boom of the 1880s. In 1885, Probasco founded the Bank of Chattanooga with F. F. Wiehl. In 1910, he became president of the American National Bank. Eventually referred to as the "Coca-Cola Bank," American National was closely identified with the founders of the Coca-Cola Bottling Company, as well as a number of other business enterprises in Chattanooga.

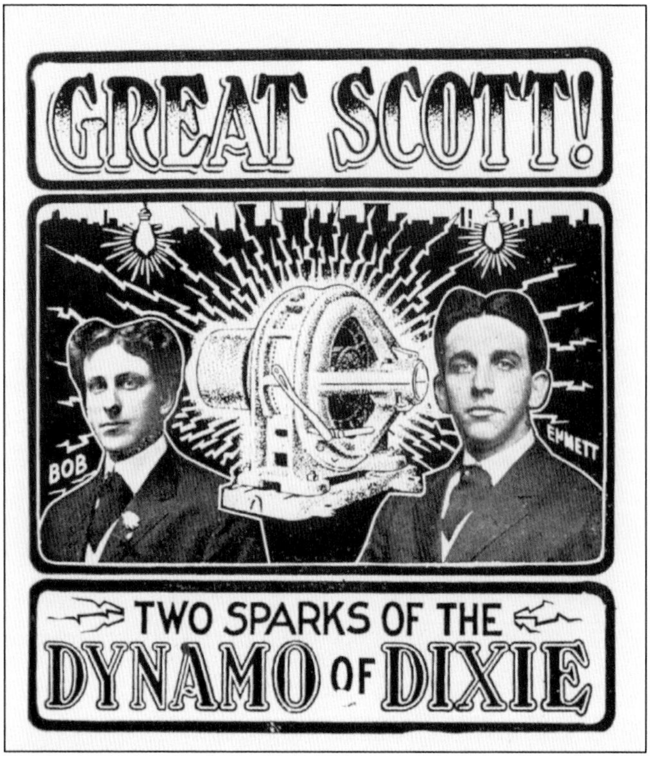

This postcard advertisement is for the Scott Brothers Electrical Company. It features the owners, pioneer electricians Bob (1885–1922) and Emmett Scott (1881–1927).

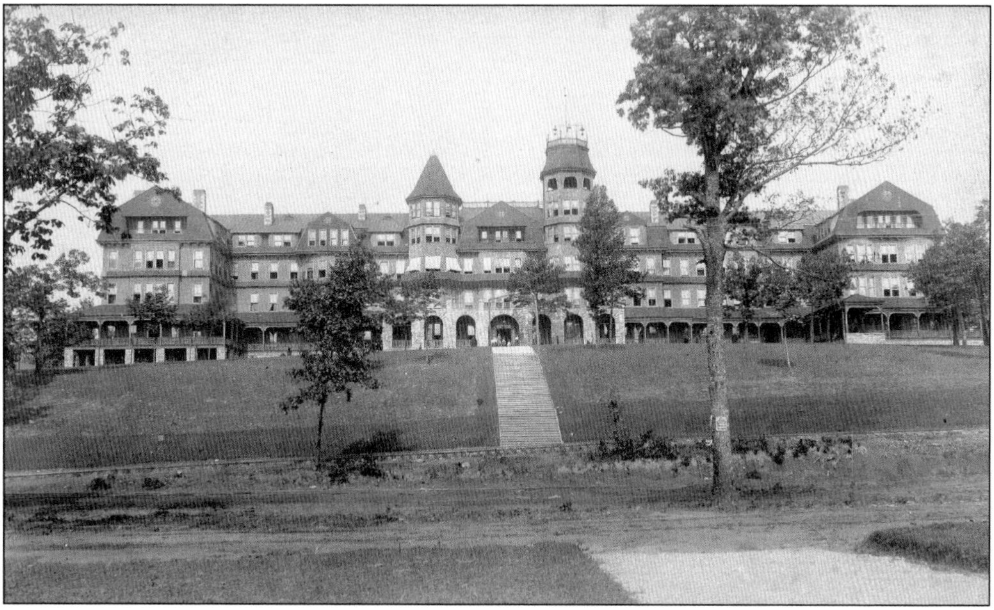

Arriving in Chattanooga at age 20, Ruben Harrison Hunt (1862–1937) worked as a carpenter and studied architecture in his spare time. By 1885, he was working as an architect. Specializing in churches and public buildings, he designed more than 60 churches throughout the southeast, including Chattanooga's First Baptist Church. He also designed the Memorial Auditorium, Federal Courthouse, James Building, Hamilton County Courthouse, and Lookout Mountain Hotel, pictured here.

Born in Blountville, Tennessee, Aleyzana "Alice" Chambers Cooper (1833–1893) was a widowed mother by 1863. Coming to Chattanooga in 1878 or 1879, by 1881 she was listed in the Chattanooga City Directory as "Madame Alice Cooper." As the owner of a successful brothel, she became wealthy. On November 29, 1893, "the most notorious woman in Chattanooga," according to the *Chattanooga Times*, was found in her room with her throat slit and four additional stab wounds to her body. Her death was ruled a suicide.

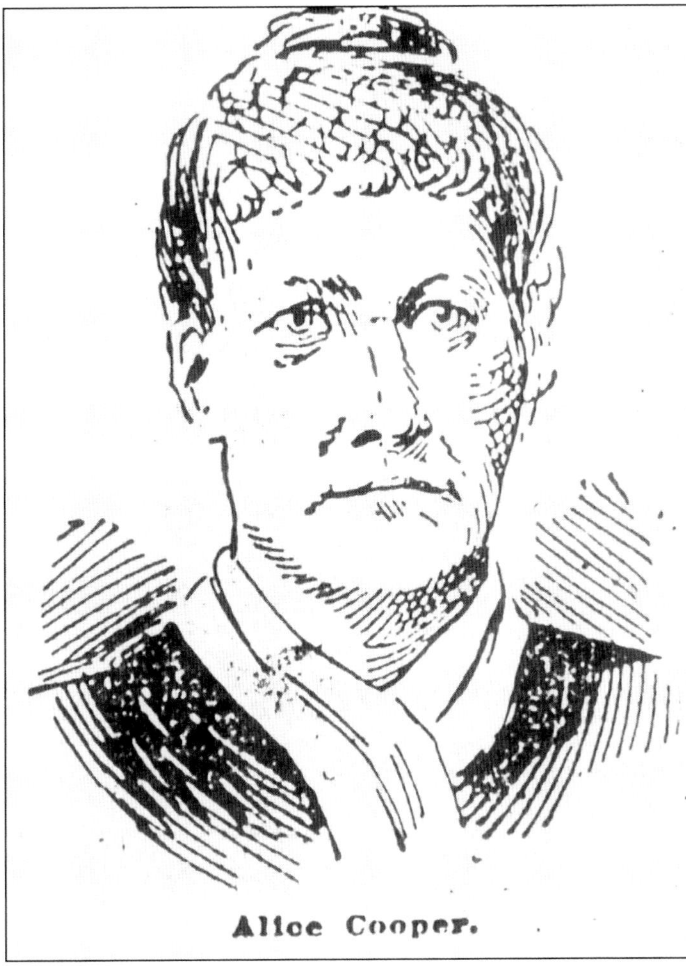

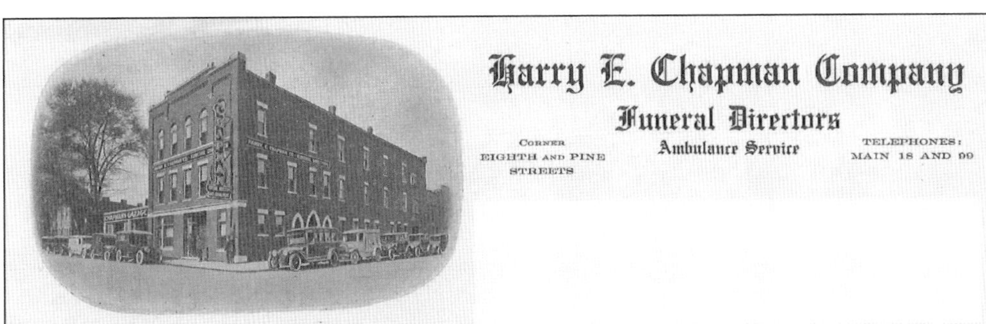

The Harry E. Chapman Company began as a livery business in the late 1880s. A religious man, Chapman (1856–1934) was a member of Centenary Methodist Episcopal Church and supported many charities. Known for his strict observance of the Sabbath, he refused to open his livery business on Sundays except in the case of a dire emergency. Chapman also operated an ambulance service.

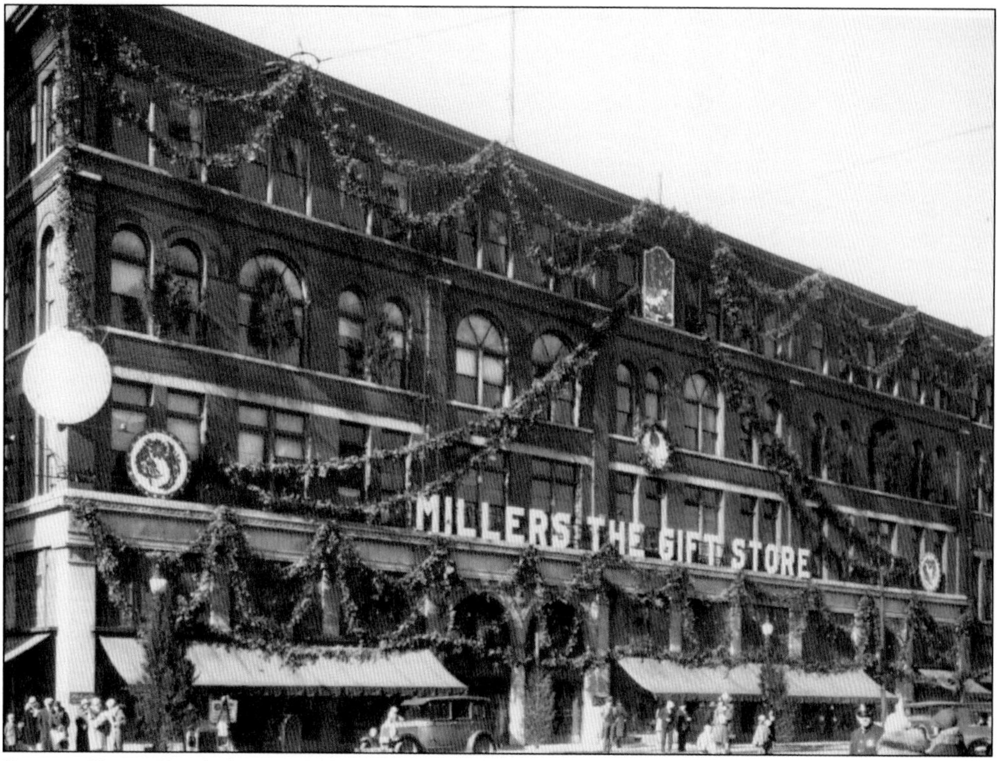

Born in Texas, Frank (1862–1921) and Gustavus (1857–1929) Miller came to Chattanooga in 1889 and opened a small store on Market Street. At a time when every city had its own independently owned department store, Miller Brothers was one of the largest in the South. This postcard shows the store in 1930, shortly after the death of Gustavus, when his estate was valued at more than $1 million. Gustavus also wrote two widely distributed books on biopsychology.

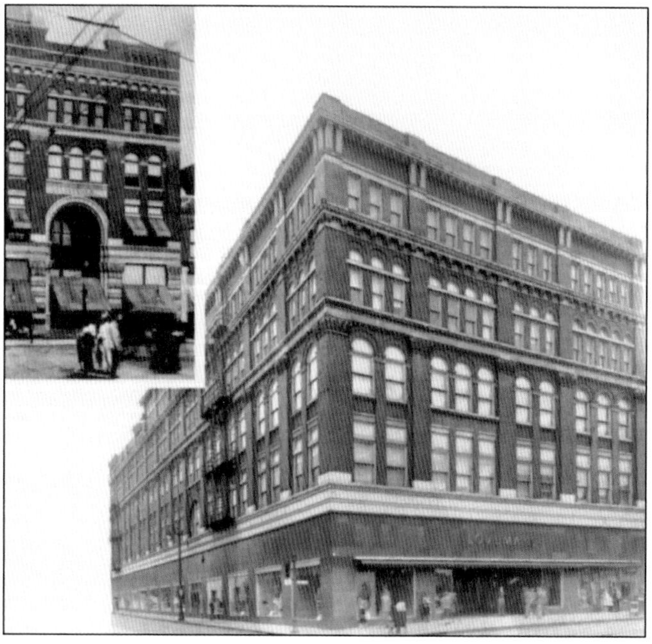

Hungarian born Herman Loveman (1852–1880) came to Chattanooga from Michigan with his brother David in 1875. Together they opened the New Orleans Store at the corner of Eighth and Market Streets. According to the *Chattanooga Times*, they employed the first woman clerk in Chattanooga, but she proved to be "over shy of masculine patrons" and was dismissed. During the yellow fever epidemic of 1878, Herman served on the committee for the "Removal of the Sick to Hospitals and the Removal of the Well to Camp Bell."

In 1884, David Loveman (1884–1926) bought a site across the street from the New Orleans Store for $85,000 from the Centenary Methodist Church in order to build a new department store. When the building was destroyed by fire, he built a more opulent store that continues to occupy the site. Loveman was the first president of the Chattanooga Chamber of Commerce.

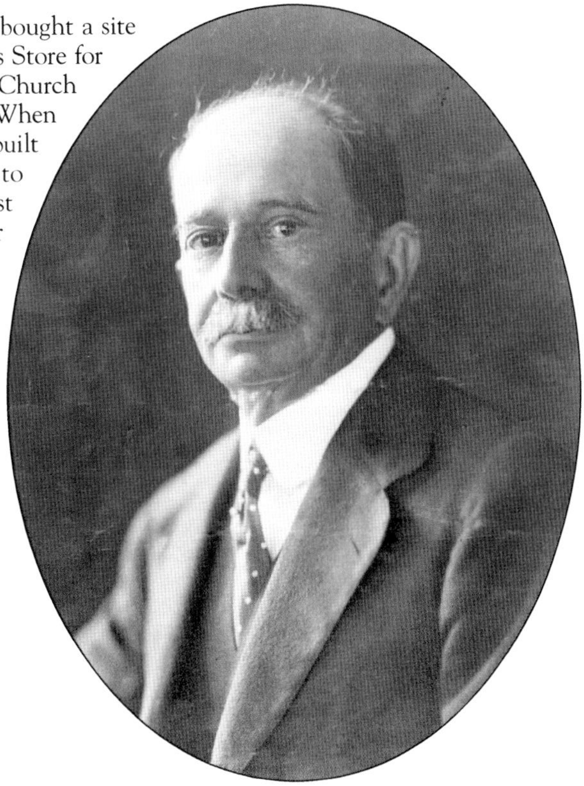

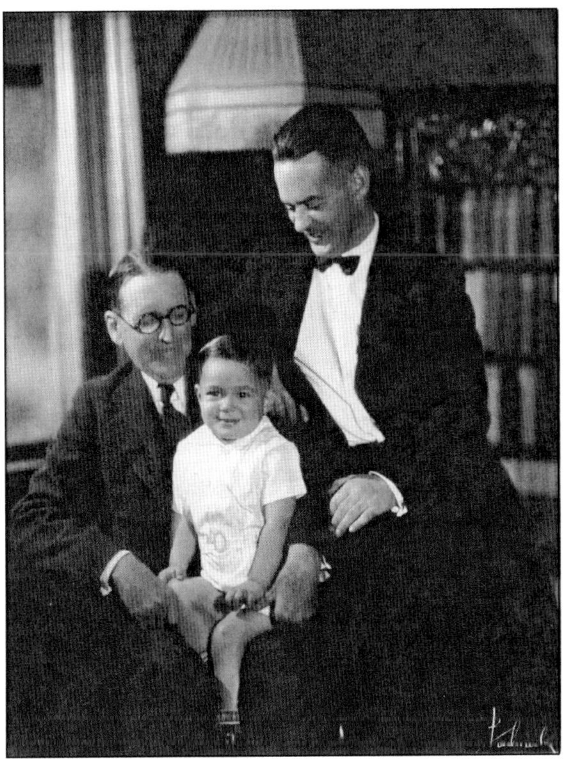

Lawyer James B. Sizer (1861–1938) moved to Chattanooga in 1910 and joined the Alexander Chambliss law firm. In 1911, he tried his most famous case. Termed *The United States vs Forty Barrels and Ten Kegs of Coca-Cola*, it dealt with the claim that Coca-Cola contained the narcotic cocaine. Sizer successfully defended the Coca-Cola Company and elected to receive $30,000 in cash instead of the $30,000 in company stock he was offered. He is pictured here on the left with his son James "Burnett" Sizer (1899–1947) and grandson James B. Sizer III.

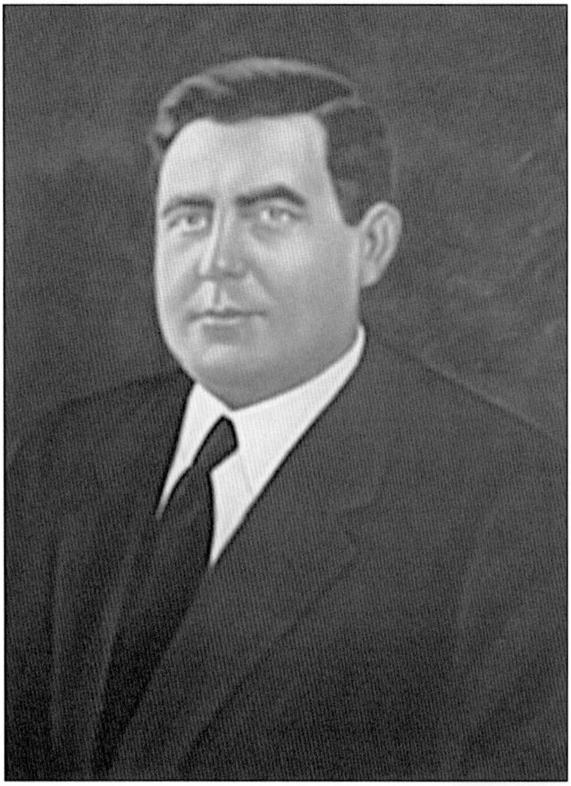

Situated on Tennessee Avenue across from the Forest Hills Cemetery, the Wann Funeral Home was founded by James Wann, who was joined in the business by his son Paul (1888–1928). At that time they also owned a livery stable that housed elaborately decorated horse-drawn hearses. At one time it was one of the largest such businesses in the South.

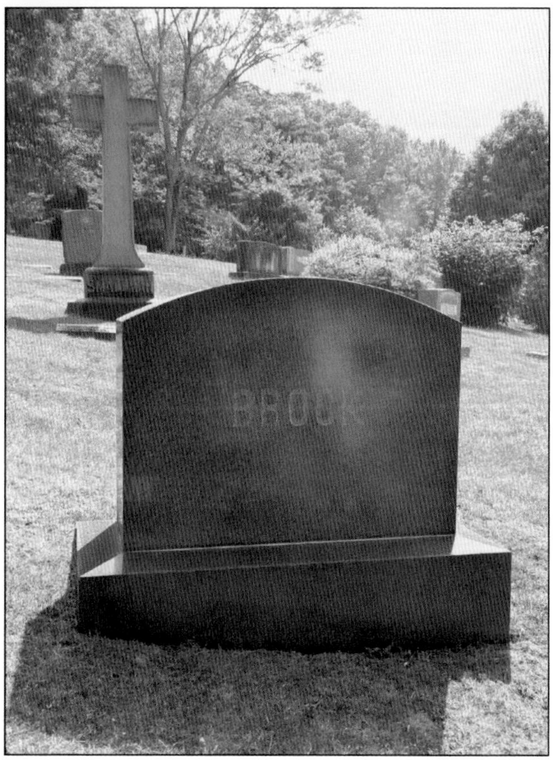

William Brock Sr. (1869–1951) began his career as a salesman for R. J. Reynolds in North Carolina. Eventually settling in Chattanooga, he began making candy by hand. During his long career he founded a bank, served in the U.S. Senate, and was a trustee at the University of Tennessee at Chattanooga, all the while operating his Brock Candy Company until his death.

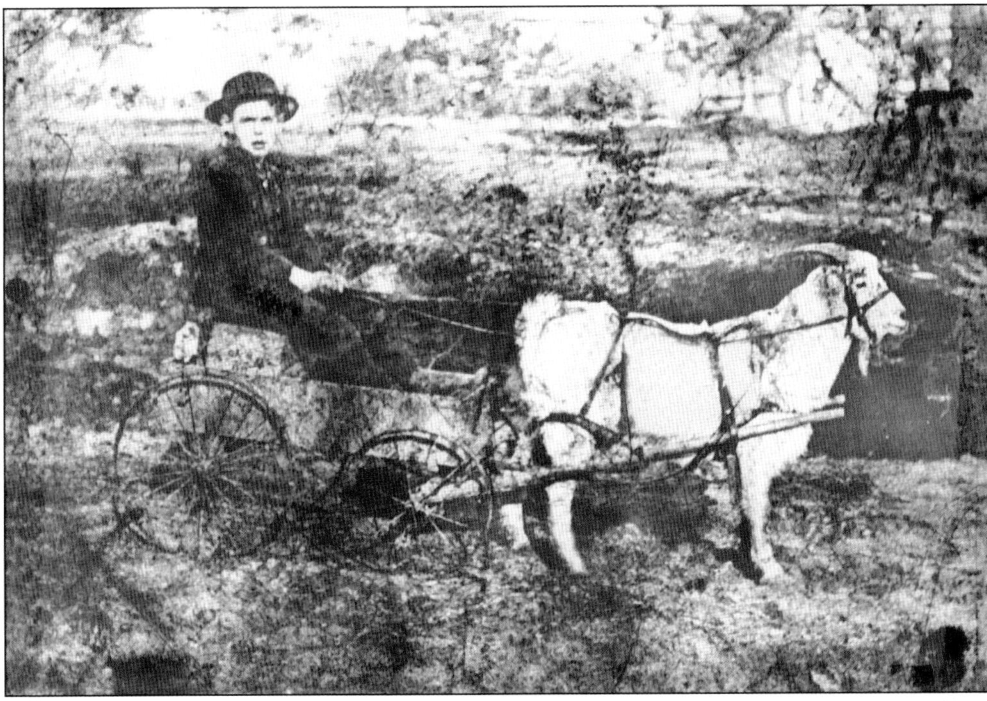

Shown here at age 10 in 1894 with his goat "Dandy Goat, Bill" on Lookout Mountain, William Burton (1884–1954) eventually owned the Burton Silversmith and Plating Company.

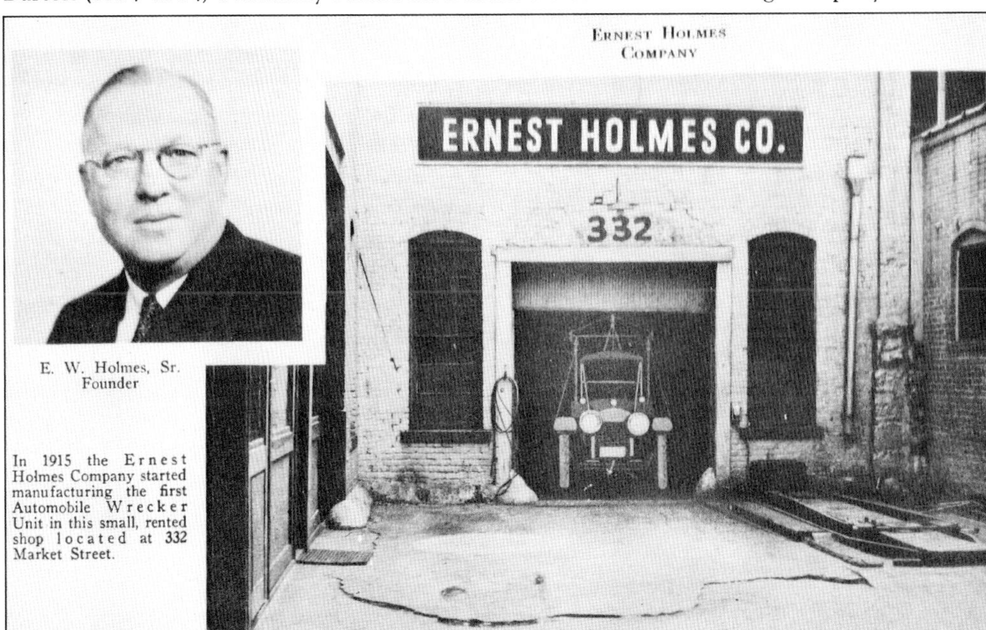

Ernest Holmes (1883–1945) opened an automobile repair business with his brother Curtis in 1915. Following the harrowing rescue of a local businessman and his Model T from a creek, Holmes conceived the idea of a wrecker and patented it in 1920. His invention was sold worldwide. He also invented and patented additional garage and automobile repair equipment. Wreckers with the Holmes name continue to be manufactured in Ooltewah, Tennessee.

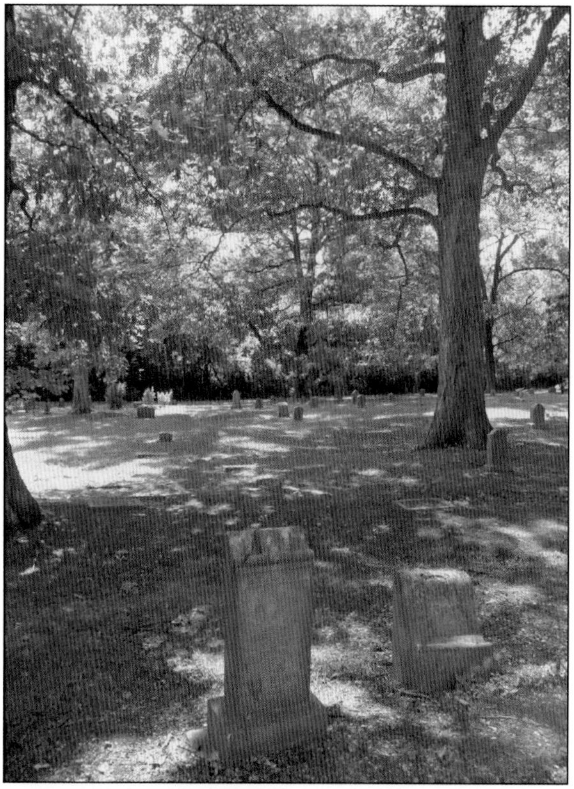

J. W. White (1848–1927) began attending Talladega College shortly after his emancipation. Coming to Chattanooga in 1875, he taught school for 15 years. During this time he opened the Penny Savings Bank. When the bank closed during the Panic of 1903, he entered politics, serving as a justice of the peace, alderman, tax assessor, and commissioner for the care of the poor. At the time of his death he was practicing law with his son, J. Bliss White.

Rodolph "Rody" Davenport Jr. (1906–1943) believed there was a demand for a hamburger and a cup of coffee at 5¢ each. In 1932, he and Glenn Sherrill opened the first Krystal restaurant at the corner of Seventh and Cherry Streets. The business was modeled after the White Castle restaurants located in many northern cities; Davenport agreed not to open any restaurants north of the Mason-Dixon Line.

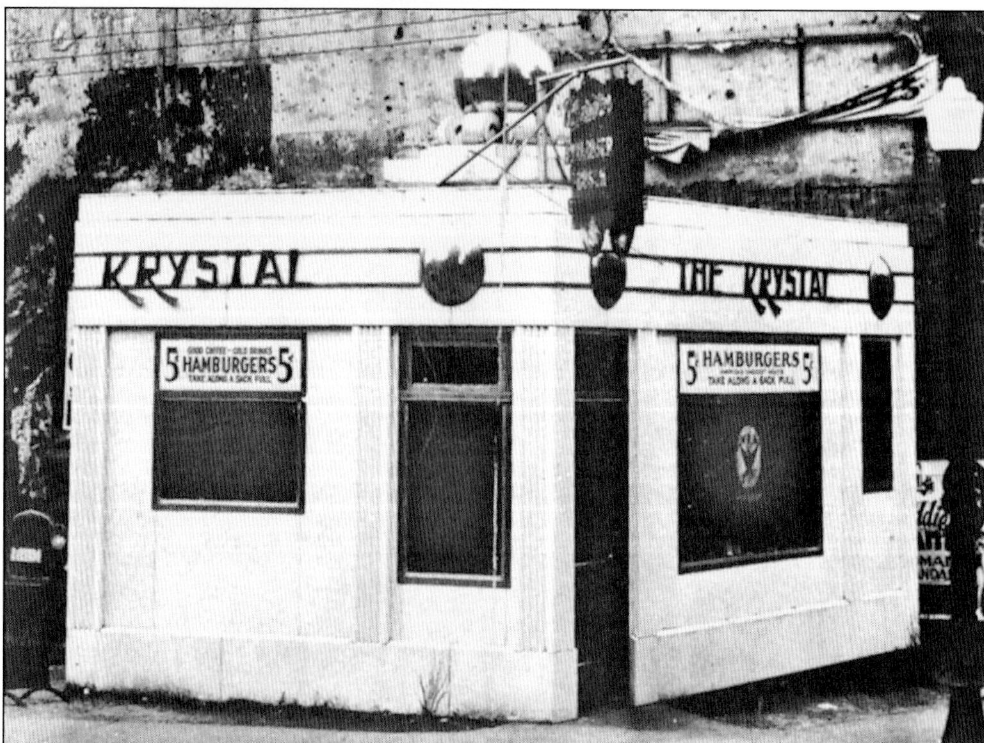

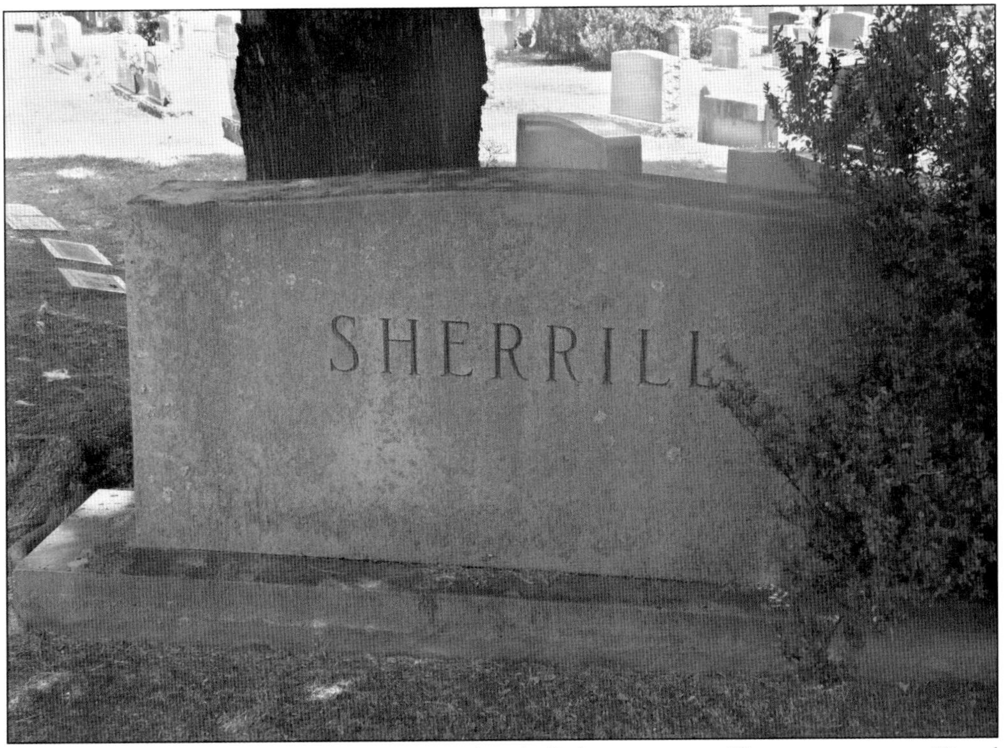

Glenn Sherrill (1905–1961), a former semipro baseball player, came to Chattanooga at age 18 and worked at a pharmacy, where he met Rody Davenport. By 1932, Sherrill was a family man and bank teller when Davenport offered to put up the money if Sherrill would manage the Krystal restaurant business. At the time of Sherrill's death, Krystal Company had 76 restaurants in 19 southeastern cities.

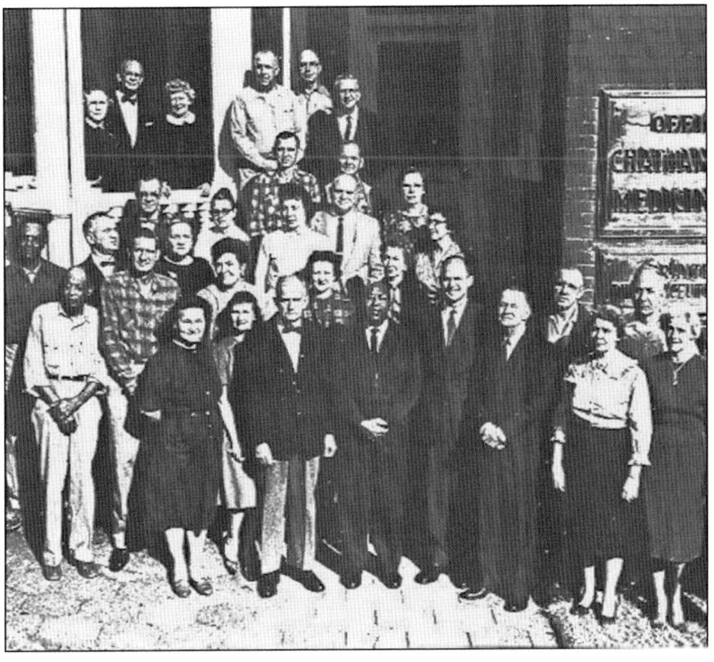

John Henry Dean (1902–1993) retired from Chattem Company in 1985 after 70 years of service. He started with the company at age 15, moving rolls of paper many times his weight. Later he worked as a handyman and typesetter, and supervising the janitorial force. He was a trusted aide to the presidents of the firm for many years. Dean is shown here in the front row with a number of other Chattem employees.

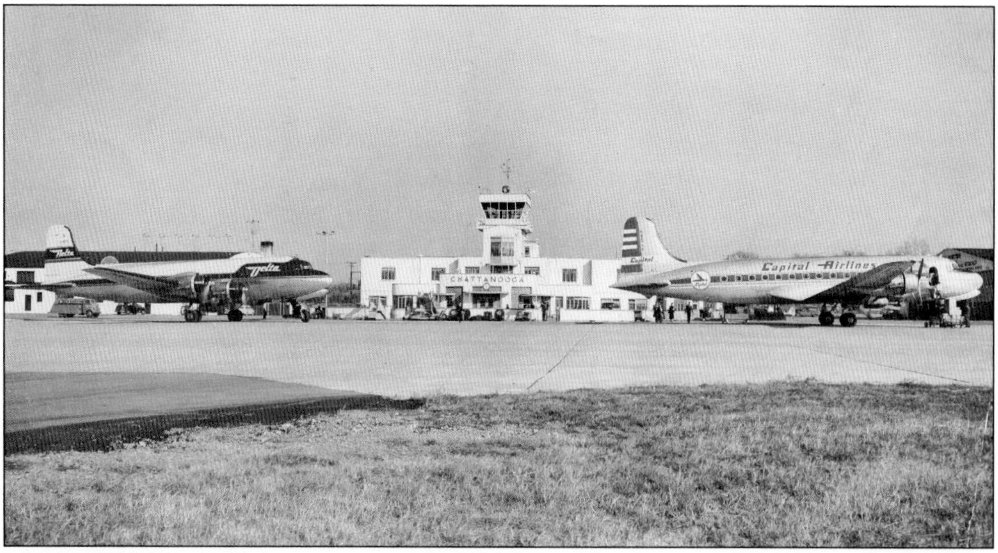

John Lovell (1882–1947), long-term manager of the Hotel Patton, served on the board of directors of the chamber of commerce for more than 30 years. During his time as president of the chamber and president of Dixie Highway Association, he was instrumental in bringing the Dixie Highway—which runs from Chicago to Miami—through Chattanooga. He was also a leader in building the Chickamauga Dam and the airport, which was named Lovell Field in his honor.

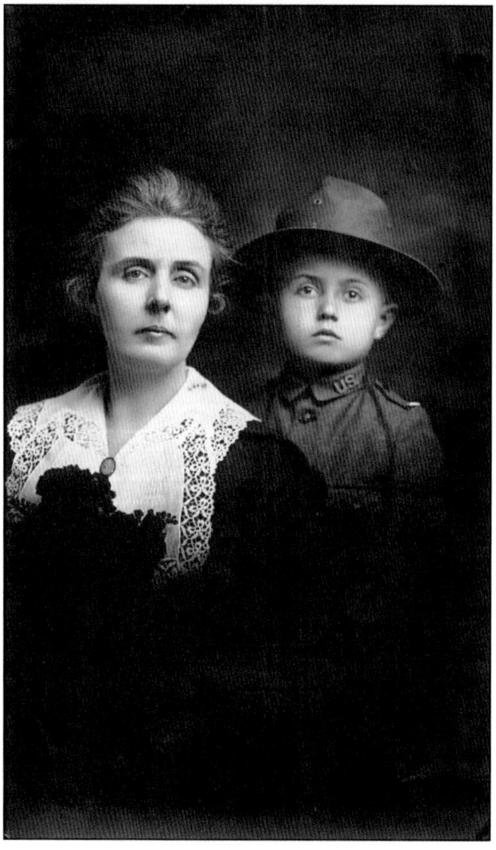

Zerelda "Zee" Ellis Webster (1884–1963), pictured here with her son Billy, 9, around 1918, was a single mother who ran the Kosmos Cottage Boarding House on East Thirty-seventh Street from 1916 to 1939. The boardinghouse catered to the many young women who worked in various businesses in the city. Webster insisted that all of her residents behave in a respectable manner. After her retirement, she devoted herself to rearing Pekingese dogs. (Photograph courtesy of Nancy Webster Diwan.)

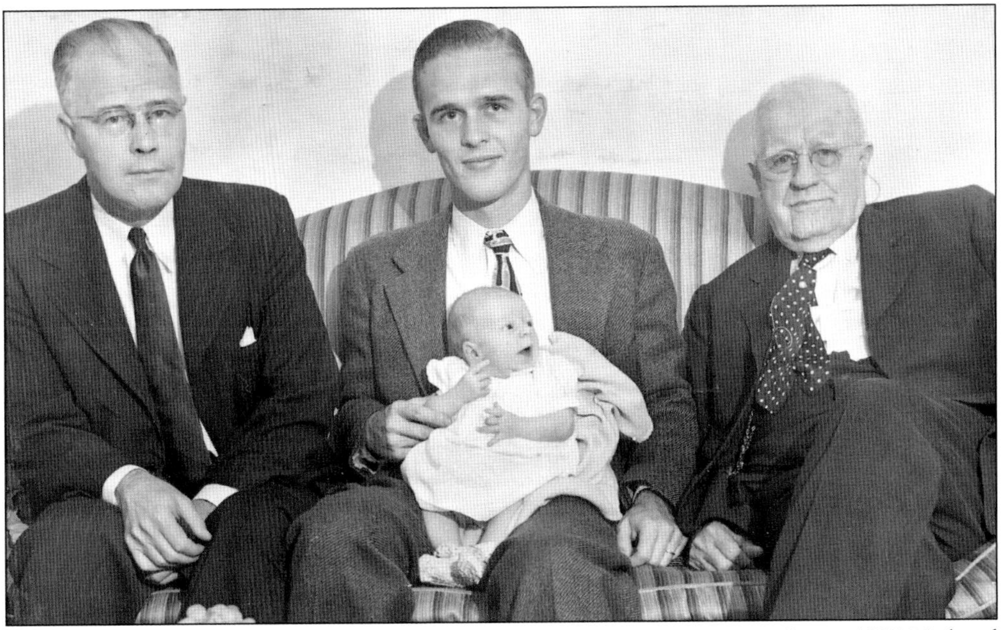

Edward Young "E. Y." Chapin (1865–1954) came to Chattanooga to practice law in 1887. He lived at the Williams sisters' boardinghouse with a number of other young men who where seeking their fortunes. By the early 20th century, Chapin was serving as director or board member of a number of companies, including the Coca-Cola Bottling Company. Chapin also served on the school board and the tuberculosis sanatorium board, and was instrumental in founding the public library. He is pictured here on the far right with three additional generations of E. Y. Chapins.

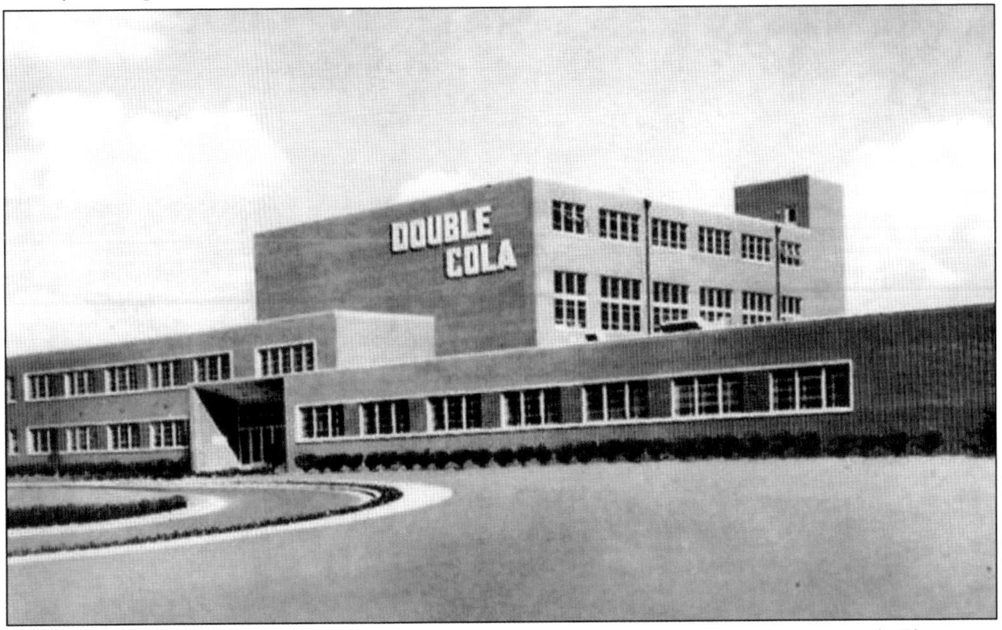

Charles Little (1888–1978) moved to Chattanooga in 1916 and organized the Seminole Flavoring Company in 1928. Introducing Double-Cola in 1934, it became one of the largest bottling businesses in the United States and Mexico. Double-Cola was the first to be sold in embossed, raised-letter bottles. (Photograph courtesy of Jeff Webb.)

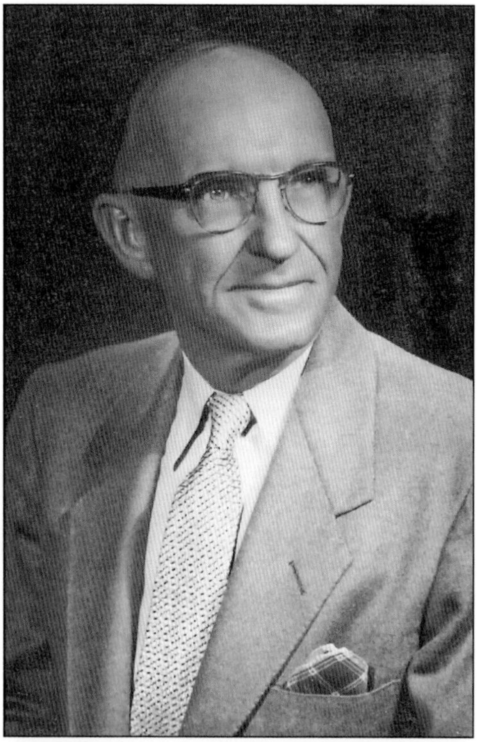

Lee Warlick (1889–1959) was the founder and president of Warlick Construction Company. His company was responsible for the construction of the Jones Observatory, First Christian Church, Ridgeview Baptist Church, American National Bank Building, several additions to Erlanger Hospital, and the old Ridgedale Baptist Church, of which he was a member. (Photograph courtesy of Judy Short.)

In 1945, Gordon Street Sr. (1903–1982) purchased the Wheland Company. Under his leadership, the business became the largest independent supplier of automobile parts in the United States. Interested in civic affairs, he told a *Chattanooga Times* reporter, "We must plan and build to assure better education for our future leaders and generously share with those who are less fortunate." He and his wife, Ruth (1905–2005), donated the stained-glass window in the nave of the Centenary United Methodist Church.

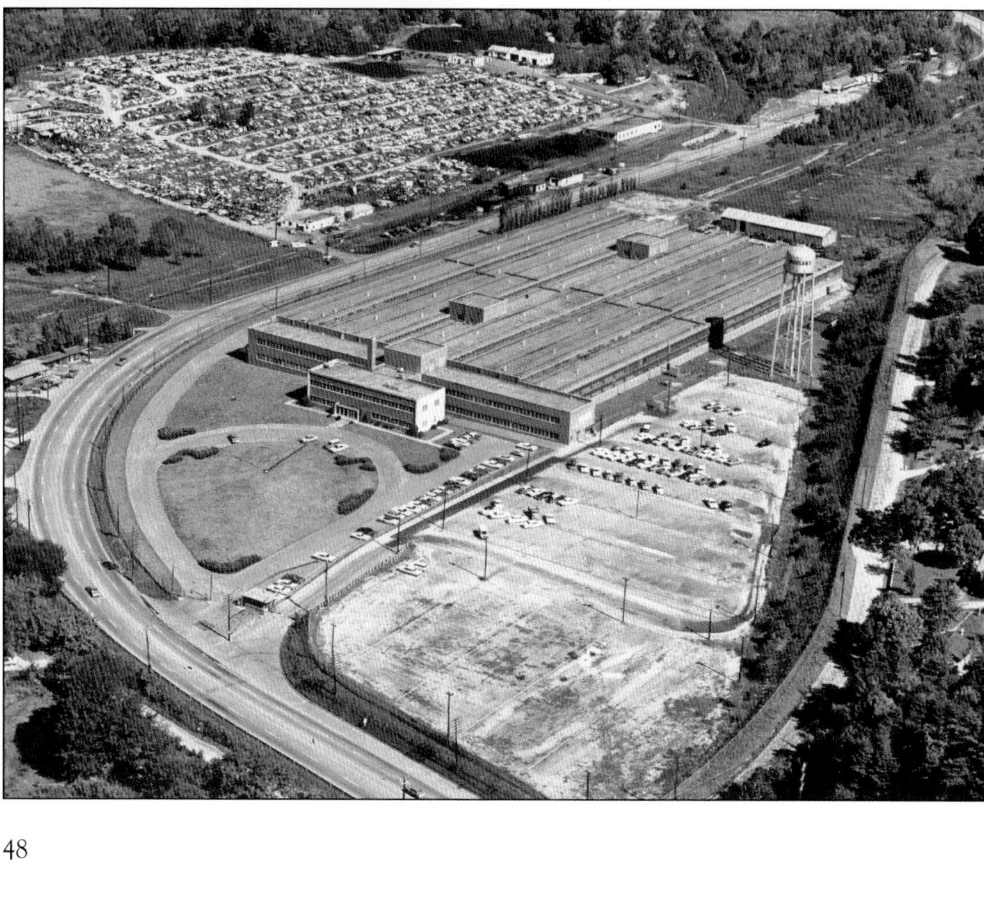

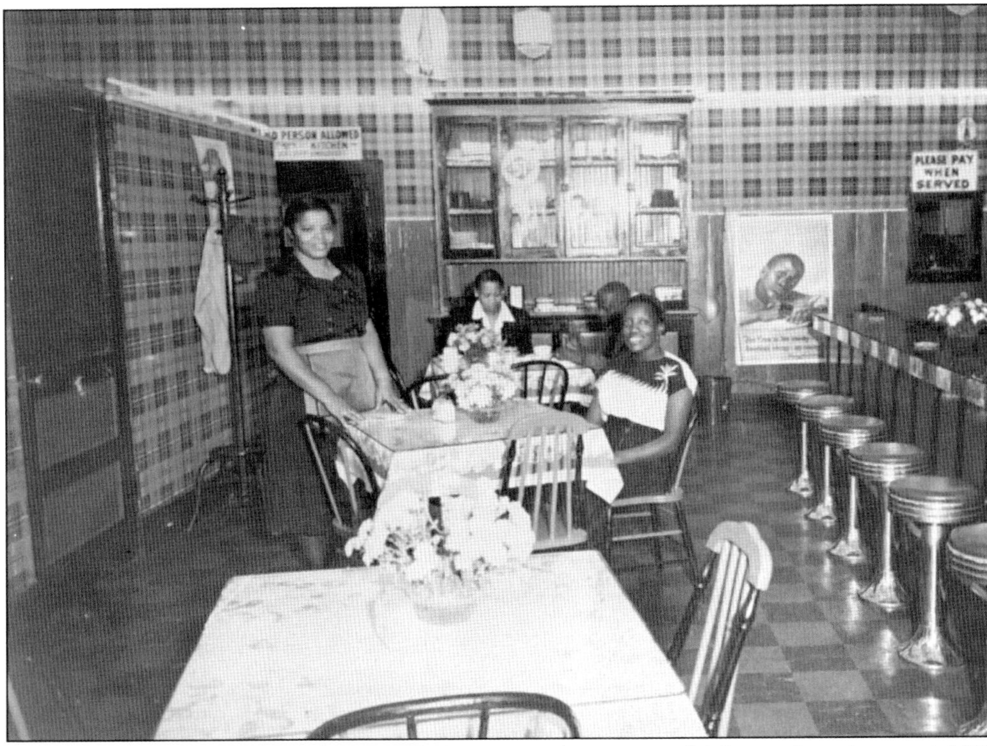

For 61 years, the Martin Hotel on Ninth Street was the center of African American social life and hosted visiting African American performers and athletes. Mayme Martin (1905–1986) gave up her South Carolina teaching position in 1931 to help her uncle manage the hotel restaurant. After his death in 1936, Mayme managed the Martin Hotel until it closed in 1985. A year later she died when a fire broke out in the boarding house she was operating for those who had nowhere to go when the hotel closed.

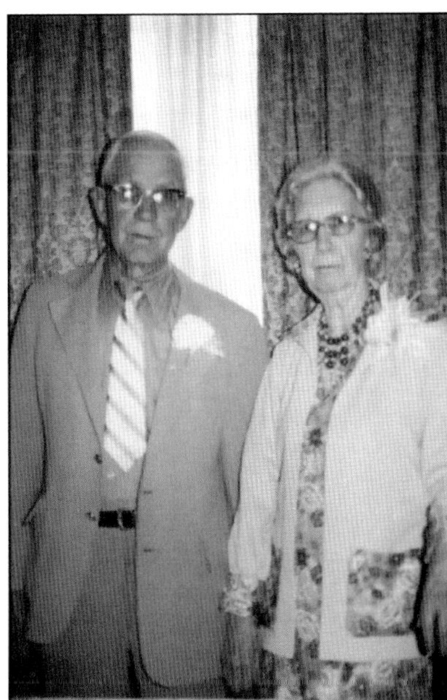

In 1940, Manuel "M. V." Davis (1898–1986) opened the Davis Candy Company in Alton Park. He made peanut brittle, peppermint sticks, bonbons, and Christmas candy. Moving to a larger location on Rossville Boulevard, his wife, Willis (1889–1978), hand-wrapped the peppermint sticks, until he was able to hire more employees. His sons, Clifford, Jack, and Leo, waited on customers in the shop and delivered candy to grocery stores. The family operated the business until Davis's retirement in 1970. (Photograph courtesy of Linda Layman.)

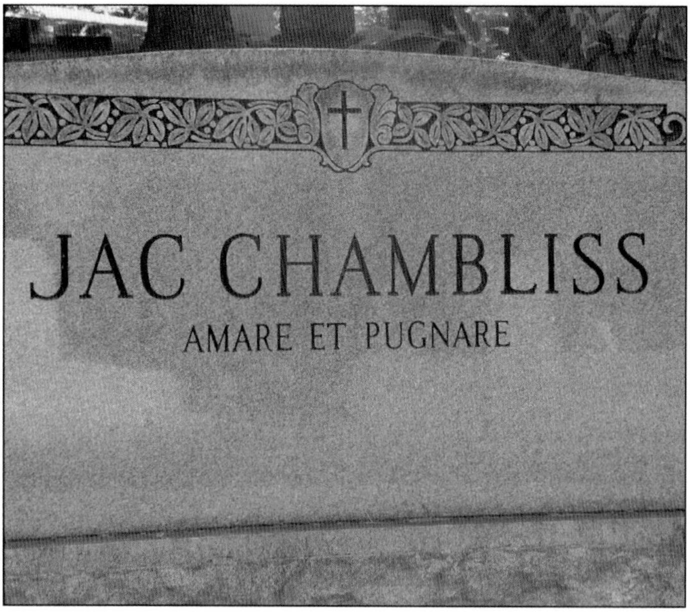

In 1932, Jac Chambliss (1910–2010) joined the law firm founded by his grandfathers, Chief Justice of the Tennessee Supreme Court Alexander Chambliss and Burnett Sizer. Practicing law until his death, he also wrote poetry, contributed columns for the local newspaper, and composed banjo and guitar music for his children, grandchildren, and great-grandchildren. He chose *Amare et Pugnare* as the motto for his tombstone, Latin for "To love and to fight."

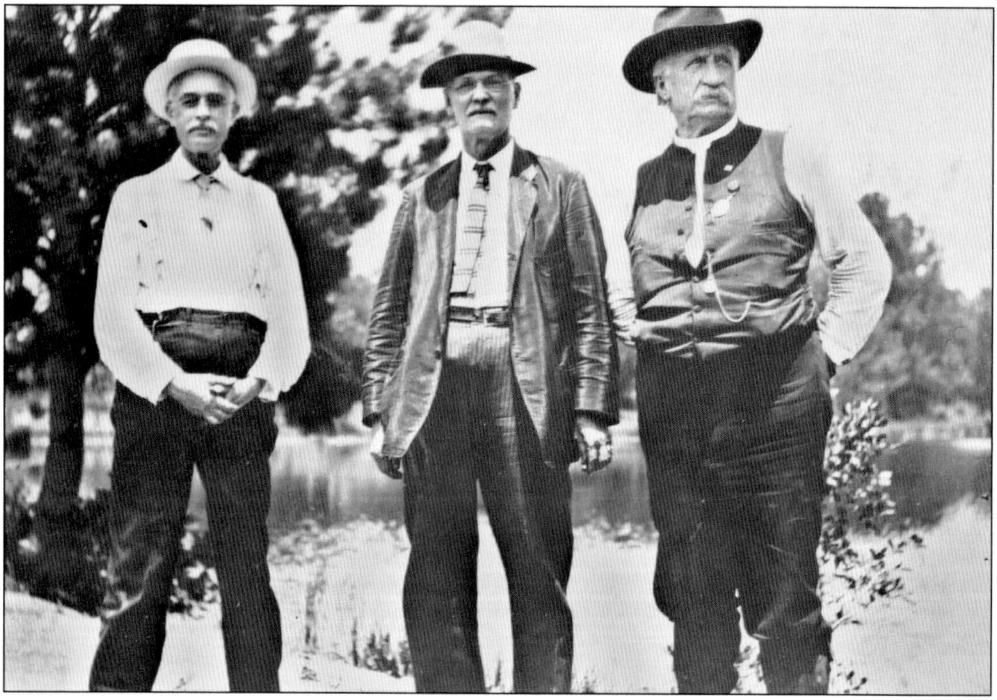

Thomas Henry Payne (1842–1924) first came to Chattanooga as part of the Union Army. Seeing opportunity in the destroyed but strategically placed town, he began business as a bookseller and stationer. He was on the original committee of the Chattanooga Library Association. Payne is pictured here on the right with Joab McCollum and Jonathon Bachman. His business remained in operation until the 1990s.

Three

Newspapers

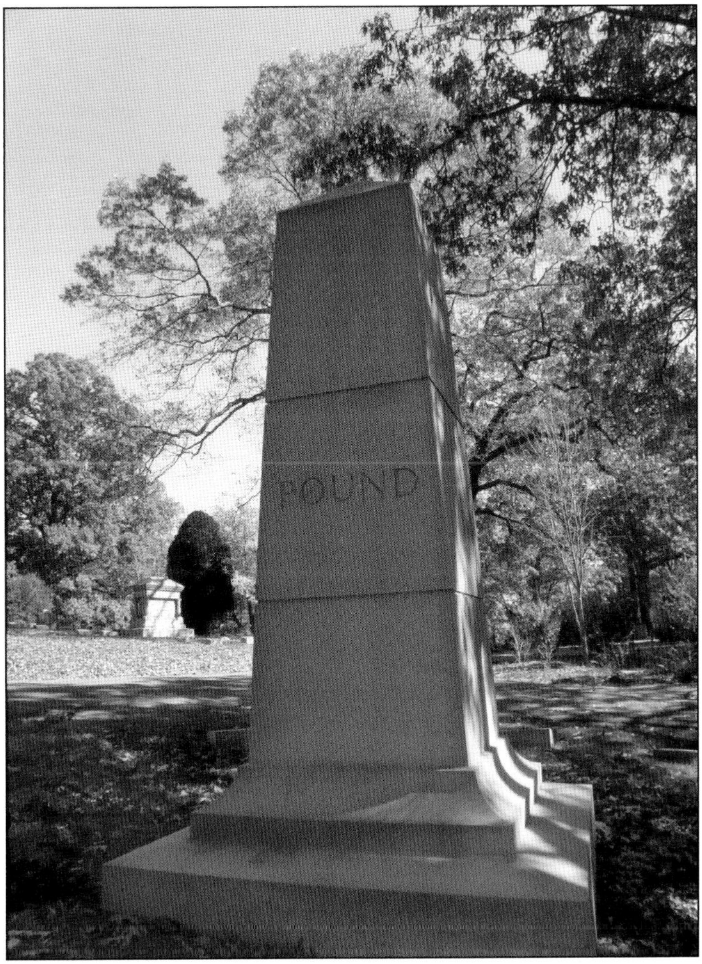

At age 20, Jerome B. Pound (1863–1952) founded the *Chattanooga Evening News*. He later bought the *Knoxville Morning Tribune* and the *News Sentinel*, and founded the *Memphis Morning News*. At age 40, he left the newspaper business and began building hotels throughout the South in cities like Chattanooga, Atlanta, Jacksonville, Savannah, and Louisville. He was on the staffs of three Tennessee governors and served as mayor of Lookout Mountain

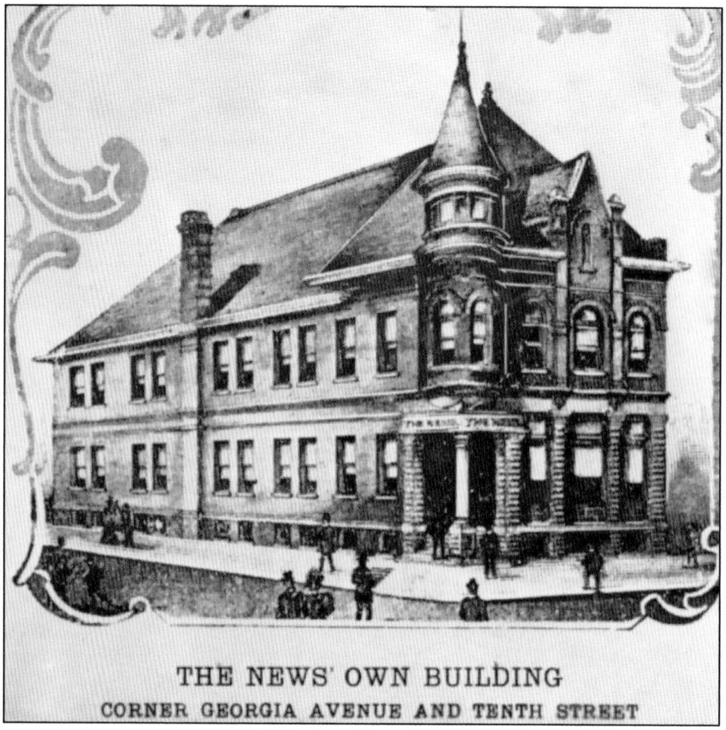

George Fort Milton Sr. (1869–1924) acquired the *Chattanooga News* from Jerome Pound in 1910. The paper continued its liberal positions under the direction of Milton and his wife, Abby, who was active in deciding the editorial policy of the paper. George Milton Jr. continued the paper's progressive editorial policies. Such policies often lost the paper advertising revenue and led to its demise and takeover in 1939 by the more conservative *Chattanooga News-Free Press*.

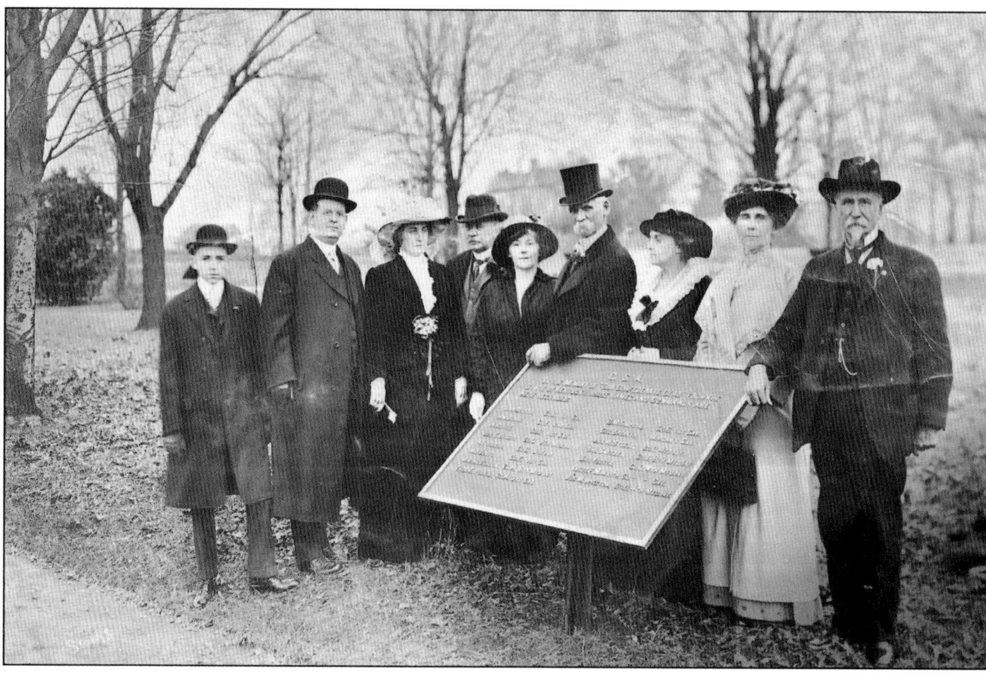

Abby Crawford (1881–1991, fifth from left) met George Milton Jr. (fourth from left) while they were students at the Chattanooga College of Law. Upon their marriage, Abby became part-owner of the *Chattanooga News*. She never practiced law, but used her knowledge to campaign for women's suffrage. Abby was the first president of the Tennessee League of Women Voters. Although there is a headstone with her name next to her husband's grave, her ashes were scattered elsewhere.

Randolph Miller (1842–1916) was born into slavery in Virginia. In Chattanooga, he worked as pressman at the *Chattanooga Gazette* and, later, at the *Chattanooga Times*. He founded his own newspaper, the *Blade*, in 1896. In 1905, Miller and other African American businessmen founded the Omnibus Motor Car Company in response to the laws that forced African Americans to sit at the back of streetcars. The city closed down the company, stating that the cars were unsafe, but Miller continued to publish the *Blade* until 1914.

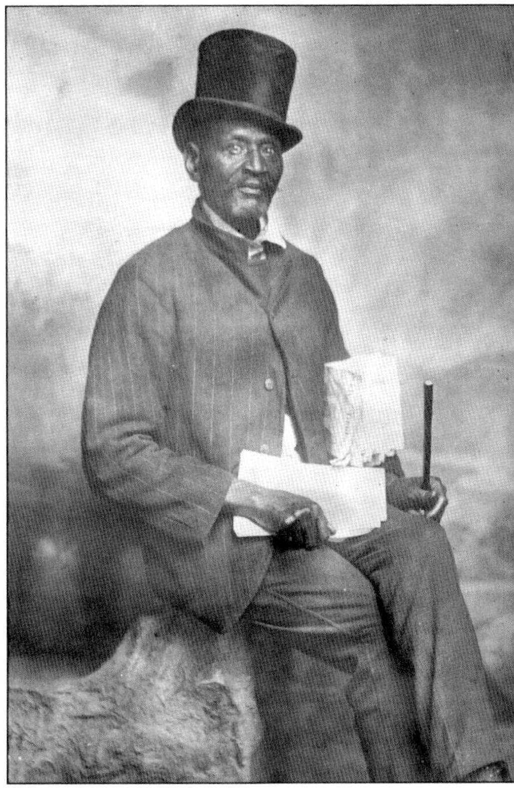

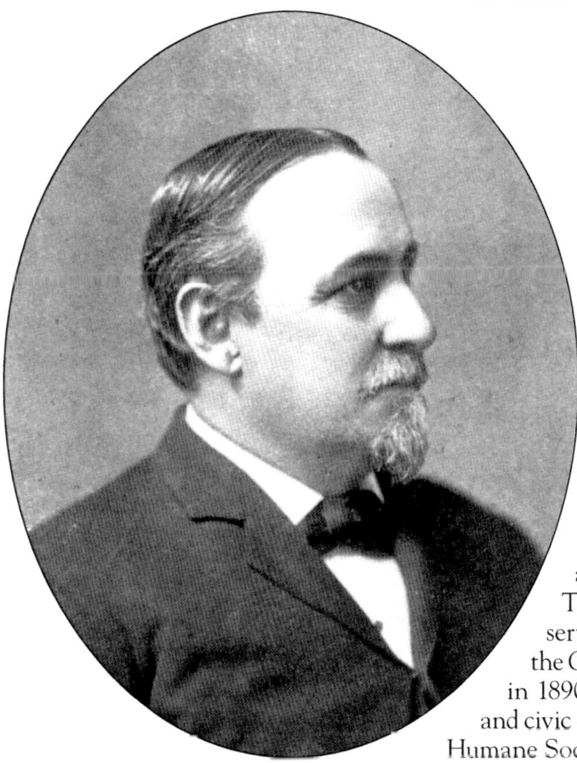

John Wellington Faxon (1840–1918) was a newspaper editor at age 13 and an assistant supervisor of Banks of Tennessee at age 19. During his military service with the Confederacy, he wrote for the *Chattanooga Rebel*. Moving to Chattanooga in 1890, he continued to be active in banking and civic organizations, including the Chattanooga Humane Society he helped to establish.

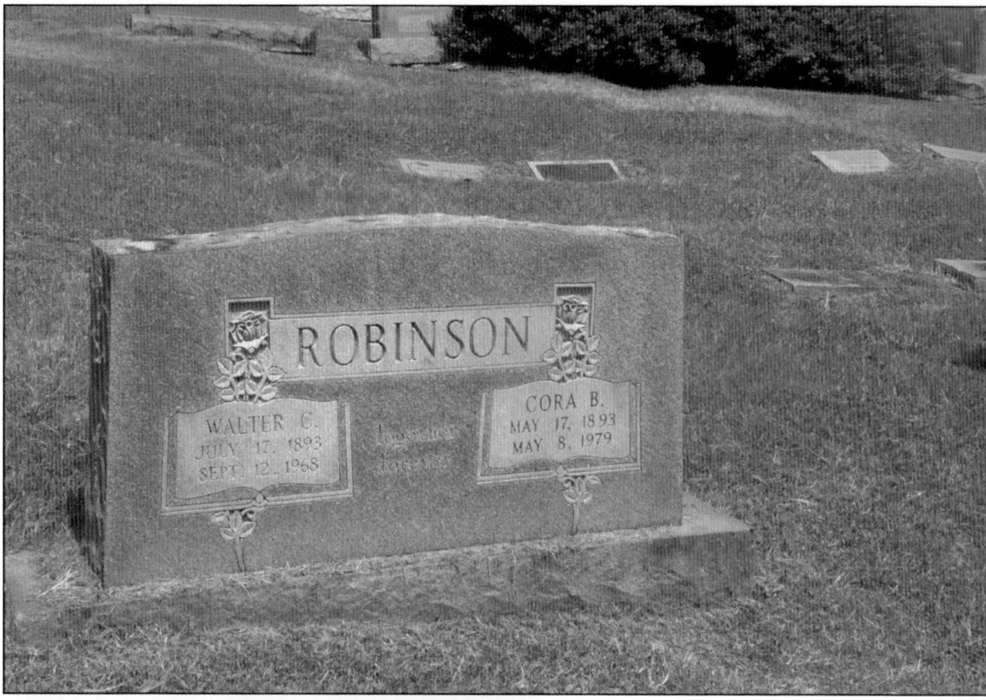

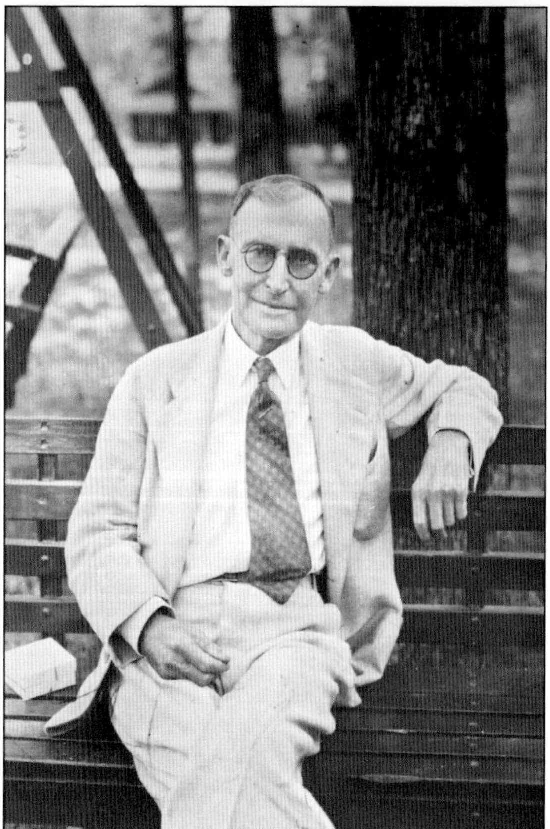

Founder and editor of the *Chattanooga Observer* for 35 years, Walter Robinson (1893–1968) was "regarded by many as the most influential Negro political leader in the city's history," according to *Chattanooga* magazine. A longtime fourth ward chairman, Robinson organized the Colored Voters League of Greater Chattanooga in the 1920s and served as an alternate delegate to the Republican National Convention from 1928 to 1963.

When he was a little boy, Lapsley Greene Walker (1854–1939) rode a mule several miles to warn Confederate friends of a party of Union soldiers. His father, Francis Marion Walker, was killed in the Battle of Atlanta in 1864 and Lapsley went to work in a printing office. Although educated in law at Princeton University, he became a newspaperman and was eventually appointed editor of the *Chattanooga Times*, a post he held for 36 years. He was known for his stand against the Ku Klux Klan and his support for the repeal of Prohibition.

In 1886, the *Chattanooga Times* described the erection of this 16,000-pound, seven-piece Quincy granite monument to William Yonge (1856–1885). Younge, who came to Chattanooga in 1876, partnered with Adolph Ochs in publishing the *Tradesman*, an industrial journal, and the *Rural Record*, an agricultural publication. His obituary describes him as "a man of restless energy" for whom "no obstacles were too great . . . a typical representative of Chattanooga's character."

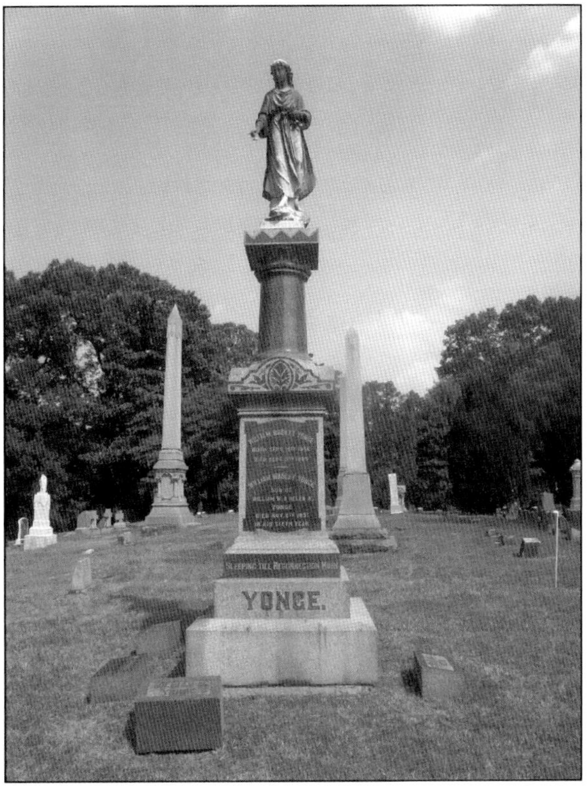

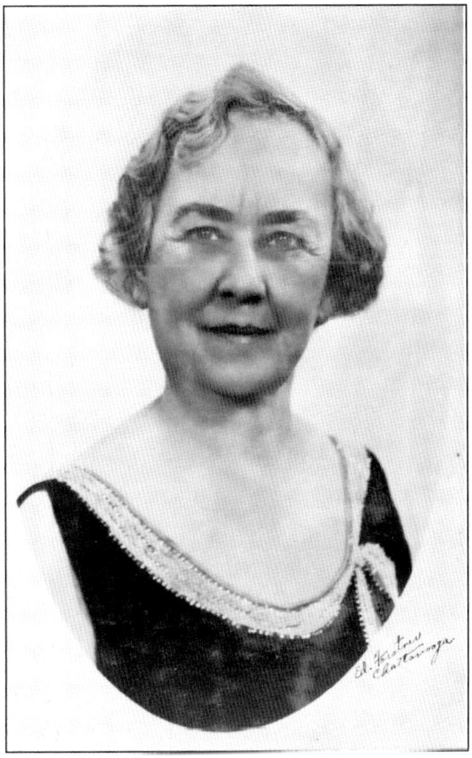

Zella Armstrong (1872–1965) spent her life writing about and promoting Chattanooga. "Miss Zella," as she was widely known, was a columnist for the *Chattanooga Free Press*, publisher of the society magazine the *Lookout*, and author of the two-volume *History of Hamilton County and Chattanooga* and several other history books. She was also a three-term president of the Tennessee Woman's Press and Author's Club, a member of the Tennessee Historical Commission, and founder of the Cotton Ball.

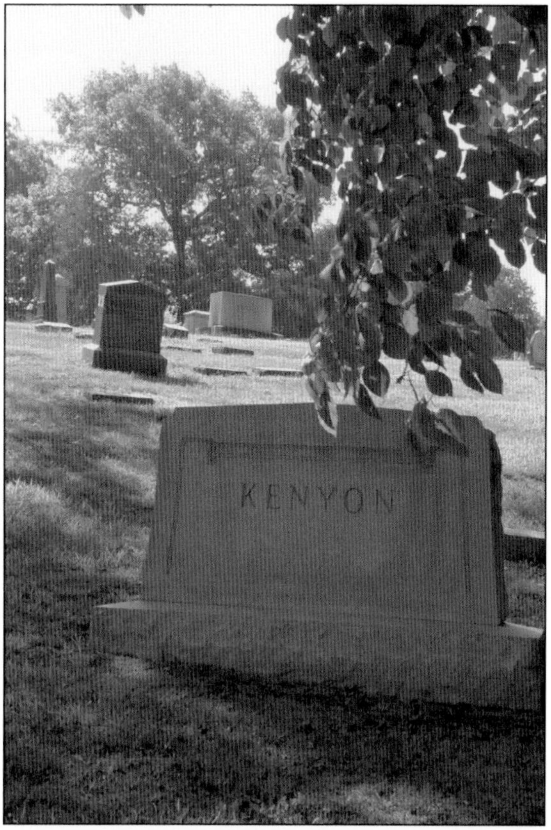

At a time when few women were news reporters, Nellie Kenyon (1900–1982) was widely respected as "tenacious," "accurate," "honest," and "very, very good at what she did." Starting at the *Chattanooga News*, she went on to cover the Scopes Trial and the Jimmy Hoffa Trial in Chattanooga for the Nashville *Tennessean*. She was instrumental in breaking up a statewide baby-selling scheme. In 1932, she interviewed Al Capone while he was en route by train to federal prison.

Moving to Chattanooga in 1925 when his father joined the faculty of the University of Chattanooga, Stanton Palmer (1920–2010) played the trumpet in the Chattanooga Symphony Orchestra for 35 years. He also formed his own band and played at local events, as well as in a number of touring road shows. A U.S. Navy ordnance officer during World War II, he was employed with the *News Free Press* for 49 years, where he served as news editor.

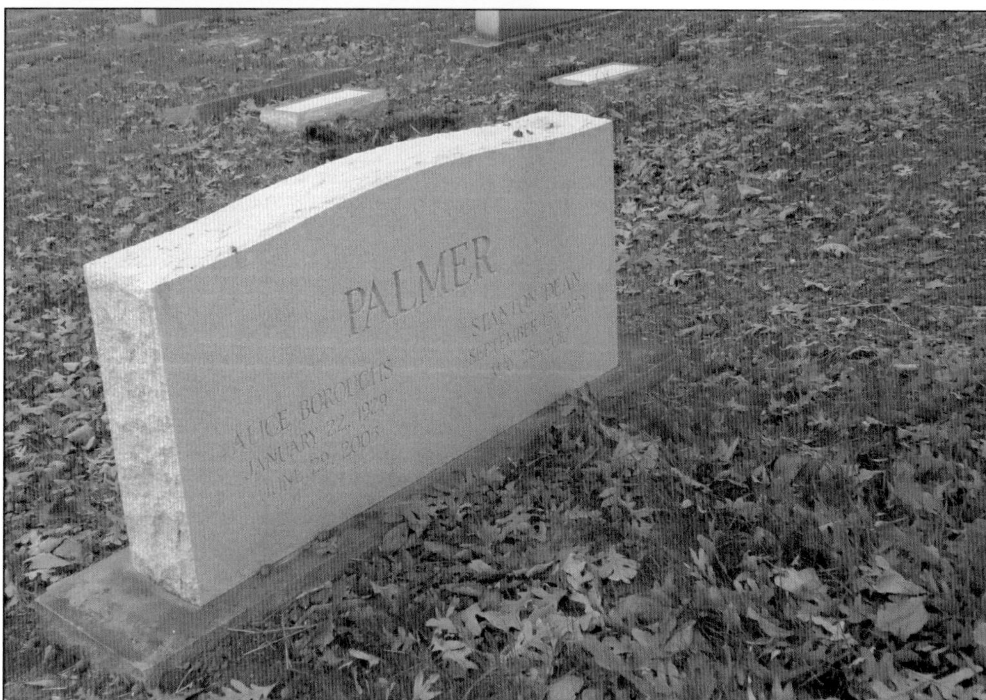

Four

Civil Servants

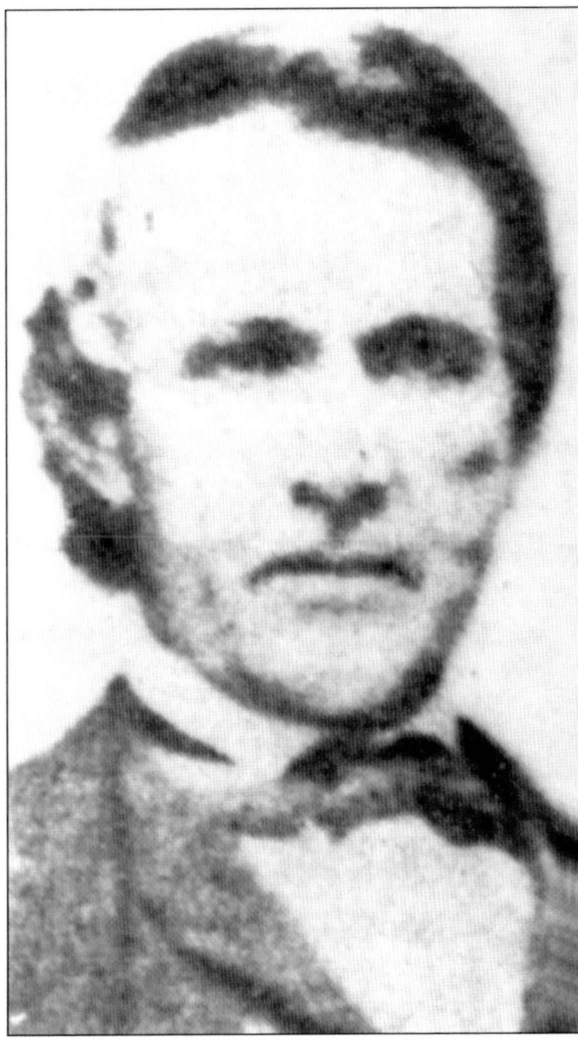

James B. Frazier (1856–1937) is the only Chattanoogan elected governor. A Democrat and, reputedly, the last gubernatorial candidate to campaign from a horse-drawn carriage, he was elected in 1902 and re-elected for a second term in 1904. He resigned as governor in 1905, when he was appointed to the U.S. Senate. He was not reappointed for an additional term and returned to Chattanooga to practice law.

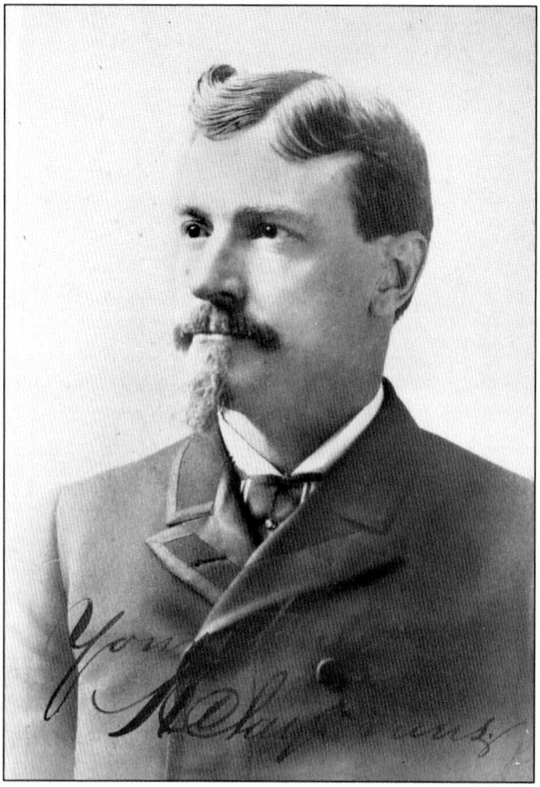

Henry Clay Evans (1843–1921) was elected governor in 1894; however, the election was overturned due to voting irregularities. He was appointed by Pres. Benjamin Harrison as assistant postmaster general, after Evans removed his name from contention as a vice presidential nominee. He was later appointed commissioner of pensions by Pres. William McKinley and consul general to London by Pres. Theodore Roosevelt.

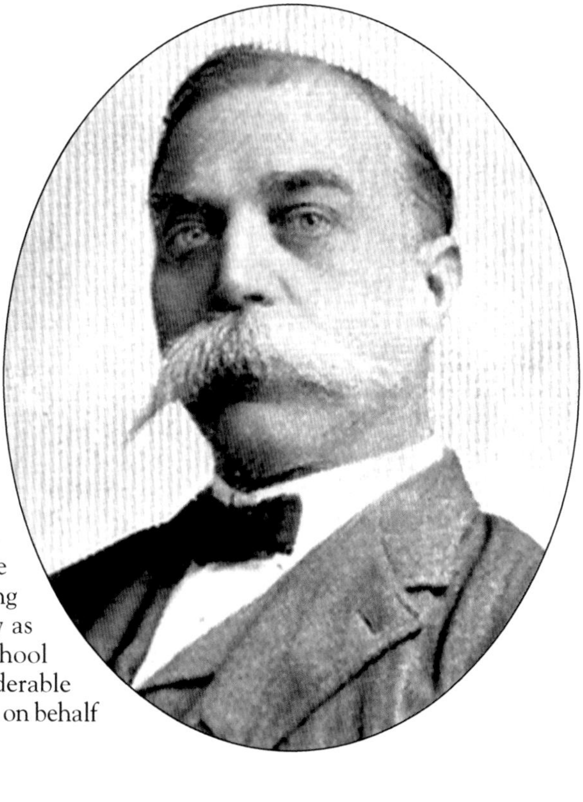

Born into slavery in Richmond, Virginia, Hyram Tyree (1848–1926) came to Chattanooga in 1867. Employed with the railroad, he retired after losing his leg in an accident. He entered politics in 1882 and became chairman of the Republican Executive Committee. During the next 40 years he served alternately as alderman of the fourth ward and school commissioner. He accumulated considerable real estate and was known for his activism on behalf of his constituents.

A lifelong public servant, David Key (1824–1900) graduated form Hiwassee College in 1850, studied law, and moved to Hamilton County in 1853. He served in the 43rd Tennessee Infantry, rising to the rank of lieutenant colonel. A Democrat, he was appointed to the U.S. Senate and served as postmaster general under Pres. Grover Cleveland. He ended his career as a U.S. district court judge.

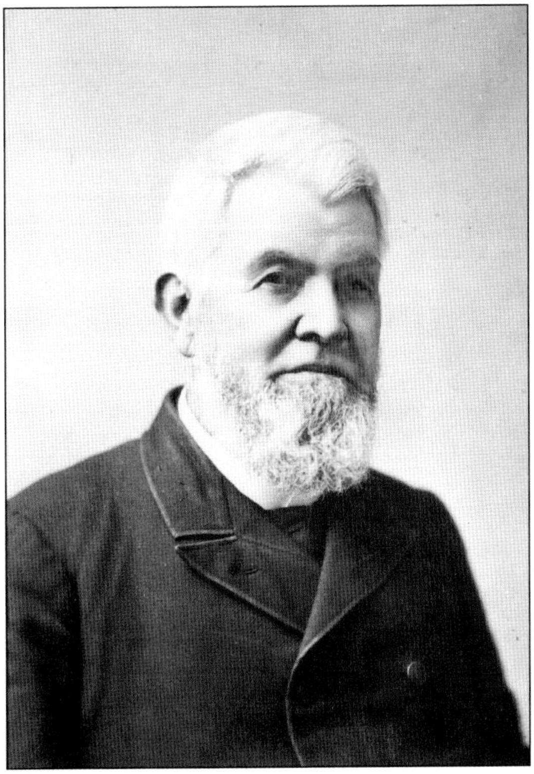

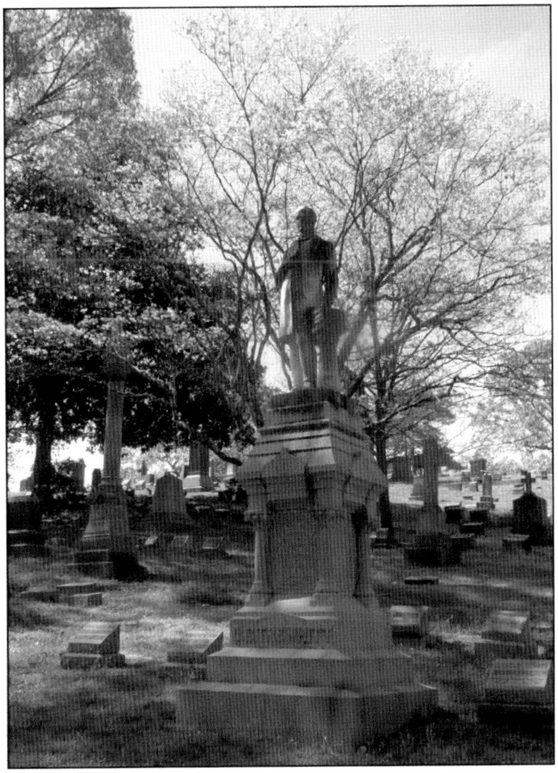

Daniel Trewhitt (1823–1891) has one of the few monuments in Forest Hills Cemetery that is actually a likeness. He was practicing law in Harrison County when the Civil War broke out. An ardent anti-secessionist, he joined the Union Army, rising to the rank of lieutenant colonel. He returned to Chattanooga about 1863. In 1864, he was appointed chancellor and was later elected circuit court judge.

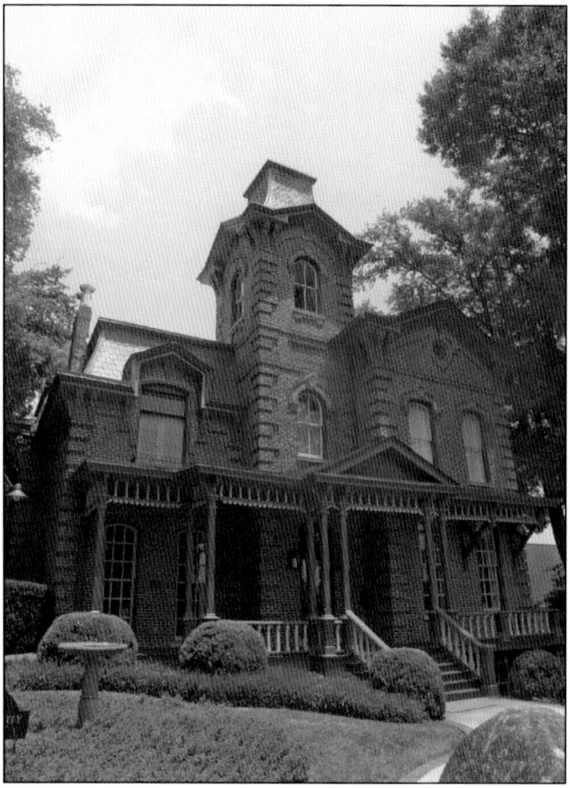

Captured at Fort Donelson and exchanged at Vicksburg in 1862, Capt. Thomas McConnell (1831–1915) joined the staff of Gen. John C. Vaughan as adjutant inspector general and was promoted to major. He came to Chattanooga in 1875 to practice law and was Hamilton County clerk and later chancellor. McConnell ran for governor twice. His home on Fifth Street currently serves as the home of the Lyndhurst Foundation.

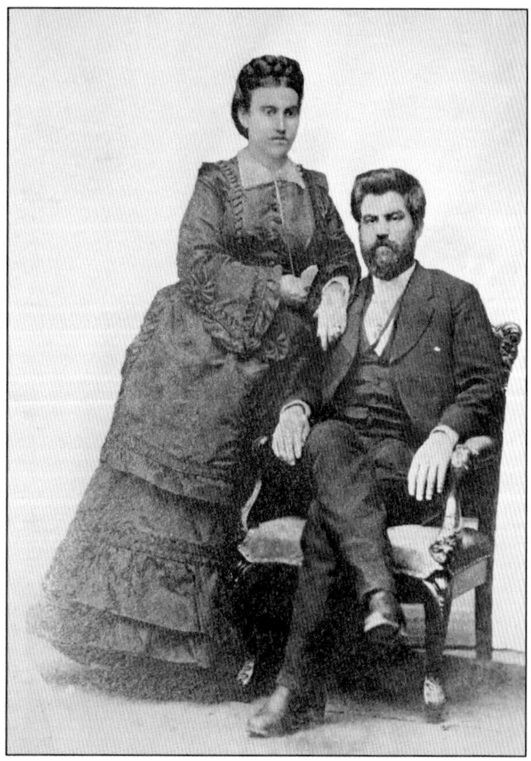

Lt. Summerfield Armitage Key (1834–1891) joined the Confederate 43rd Infantry. Serving at Vicksburg and the Shenandoah Valley, he distinguished himself at Darksville, Virginia, where he was credited with keeping his entire command from capture. Returning home, he studied law and became an attorney and chancellor, and represented Hamilton County in the General Assembly. In 1871, he married Mary Divine, daughter of Chattanooga pioneers John and Elizabeth Divine.

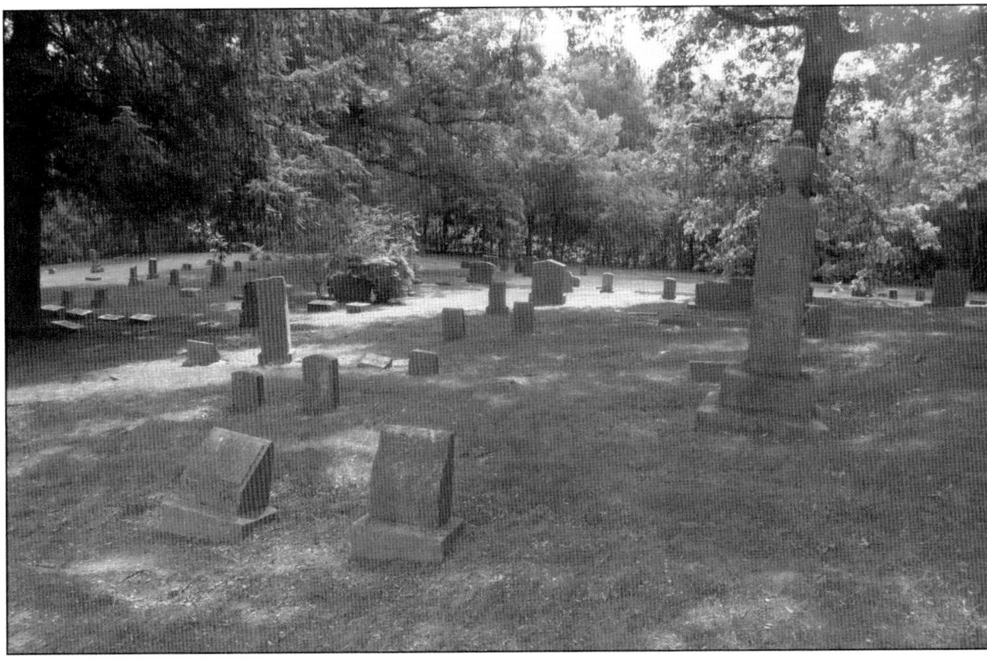

In October 1882, A. A. Elkins (1854–1883) was appointed as the first African American assistant stamping and delivery clerk in the Chattanooga Post Office. According to the *Chattanooga Times*, there was "surprise" and much "general discussion on the streets," as well as indignation among his fellow clerks. Despite "public outrage," postmaster Griscom "stated that he regarded Elkins as a well educated and industrious man, and had no explanations to offer in the matter."

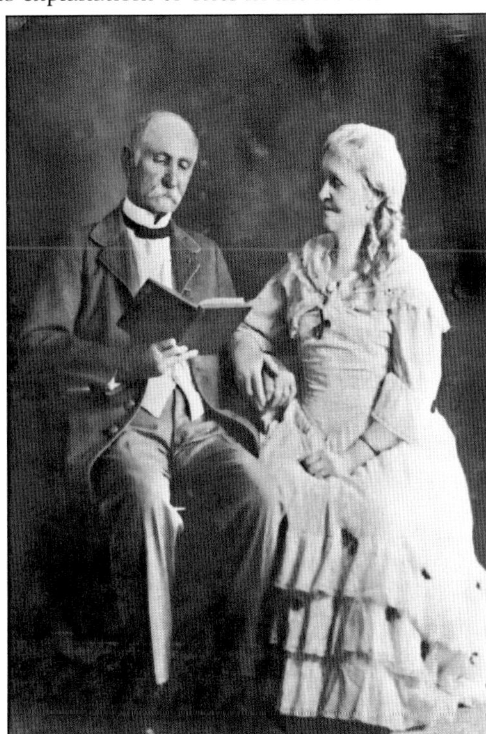

Capt. Joseph Shipp (1841–1925) rose from private to captain in the 4th Georgia Infantry. Following the war, he went into manufacturing. In 1904, he was elected county sheriff. On March 19, 1906, he was mysteriously absent from his post when a mob broke into the jail and lynched Ed Johnson, an African American man accused of rape. Shipp, found guilty of contempt by the U.S. Supreme Court, served 60 days in prison. When he returned to Chattanooga, he was greeted as a hero.

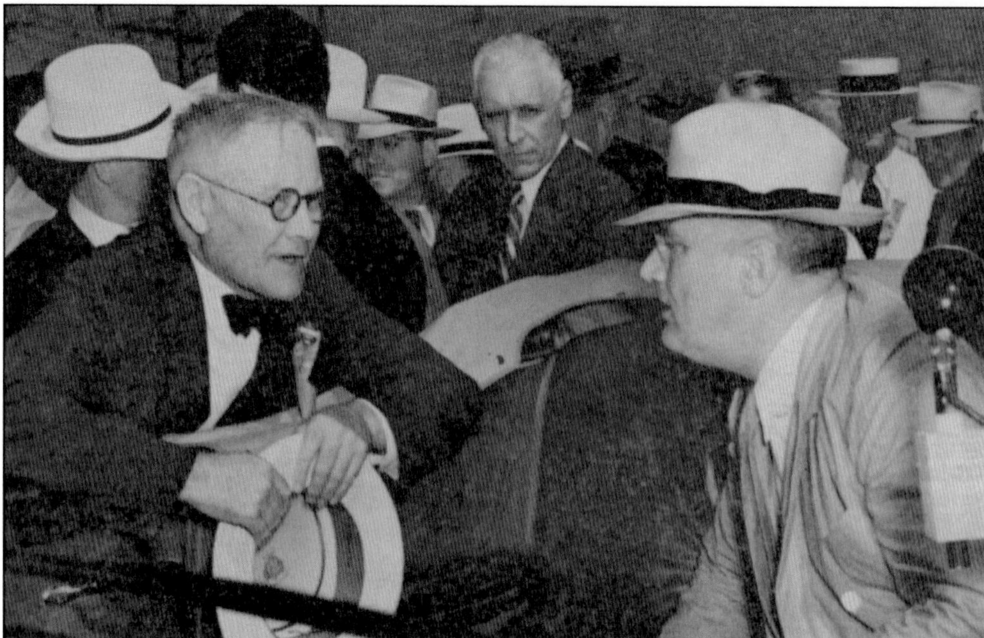

President Roosevelt chats with Judge Cummings at the Cummings' farm.

Will Cummings (1872–1963) was born in Wauhatcie, Tennessee. First elected to the Hamilton County Court at age 24, Cummings was instrumental in building the Market Street Bridge and the highway at the base of Lookout Mountain that bears his name. Seen here with Pres. Franklin Roosevelt, Cummings was a strong proponent of the Tennessee Valley Authority and an advocate for improved public education. (Photograph courtesy of Elizabeth Miller.)

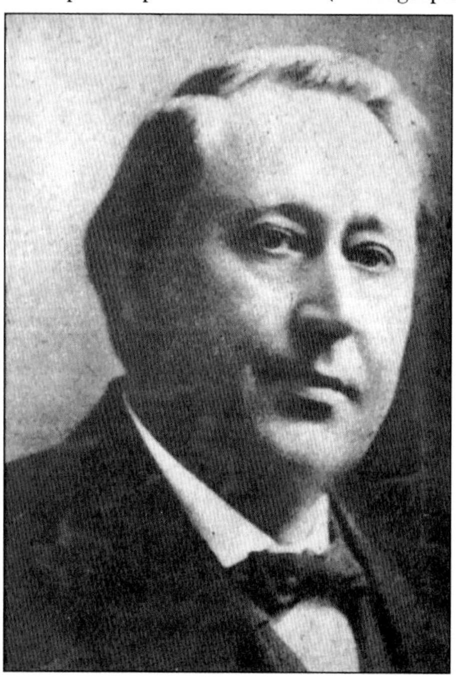

Democratic congressman John Austin Moon (1855–1921) was first elected to public office as the city attorney at age 26. Later, he served several years as a circuit court judge. In 1896, he was elected to Congress. Serving as the chairman of the House Committee on Post Offices and Post Roads, he was instrumental in establishing free rural mail delivery and was called the "Father of Parcel Post."

From 1840 until 1911, Chattanooga was governed by a mayor and elected aldermen. After 1866, African Americans were elected as aldermen. In 1911, the state legislature approved a mayor and city commissioner form of government. All were elected at large and each commissioner served as an administrative head of a department. This law effectively eliminated African Americans from local government. With the exception of T. C. Thompson, who is buried in the National Cemetery, all of these men were eventually interred at Forest Hills Cemetery.

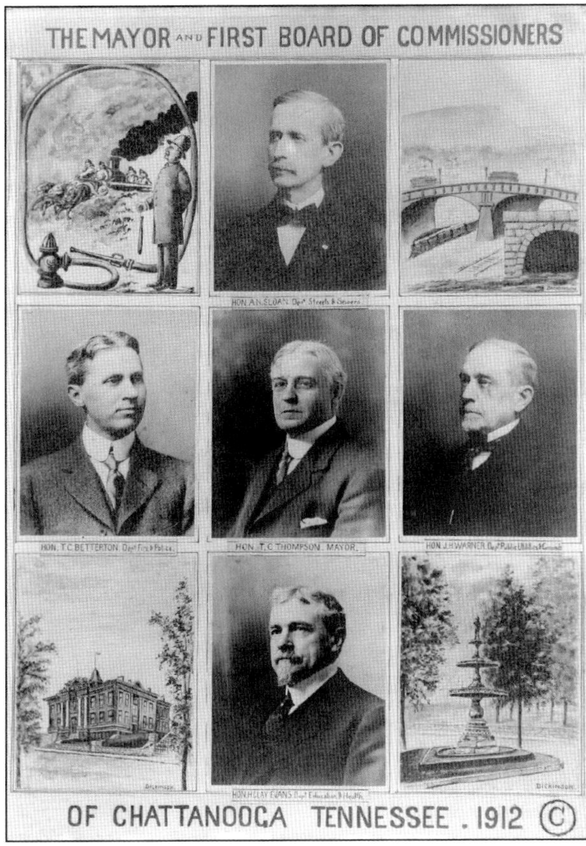

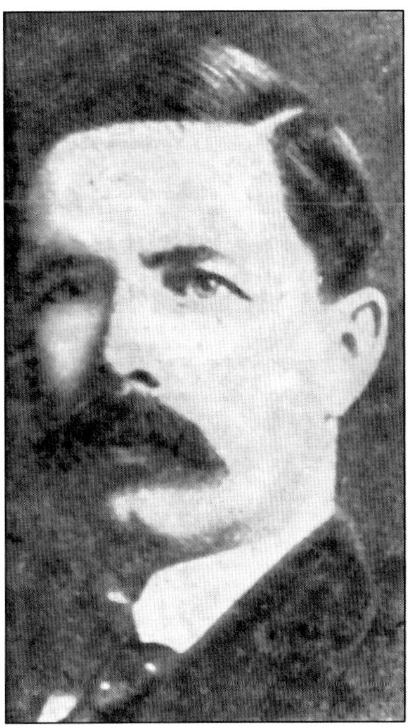

William L. Frierson (1868–1953) came to Chattanooga in 1890 as a young lawyer. By 1916, he was appointed to the state supreme court. Appointed U.S. assistant attorney general by Pres. Woodrow Wilson in 1917 and solicitor general in 1920, during his tenure at the justice department, he argued 116 cases before the U.S. Supreme Court. He presented the government's case in defense of the 18th (Prohibition), the 16th (income tax), and the 19th (women's suffrage) Amendments.

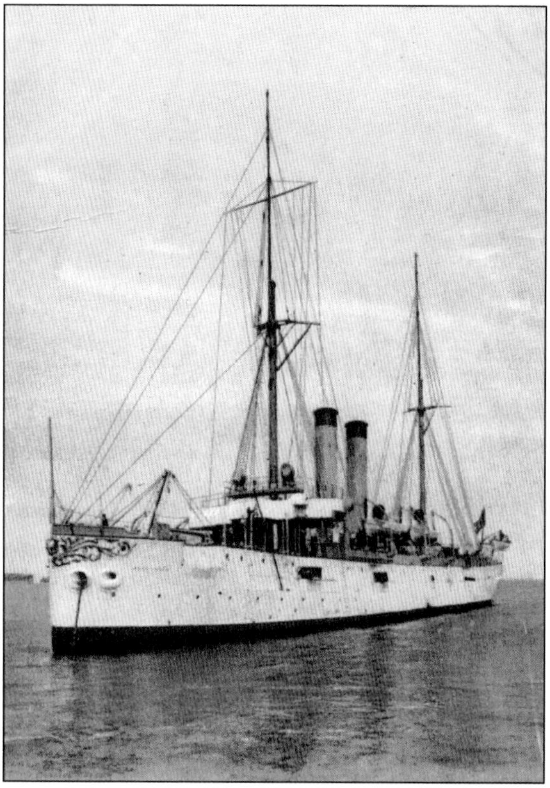

Lillian Nelson Chambliss (1859–1932) sponsored the USS *Chattanooga* when it was launched from Elizabethport, New Jersey, on March 7, 1903. The Denver-class protected cruiser was in service throughout World War I. Alexander Wilds Chambliss (1864–1947) was a lawyer, state senator, mayor of Chattanooga, and eventually chief justice of the Tennessee Supreme Court. He was also instrumental in adding Point Park on Lookout Mountain to the Chickamauga Chattanooga Military Park.

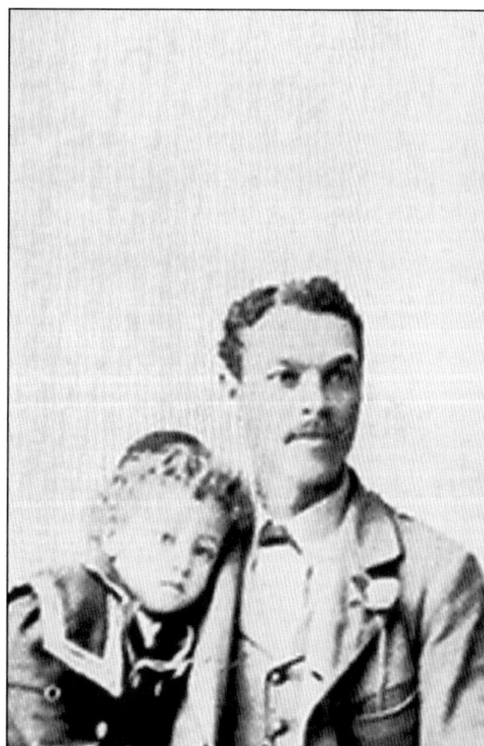

H. B. Lewis (1865–1931), a son of William Lewis, was educated at Howard University in Washington, D.C. He returned to Chattanooga where he taught school for a number of years. He left teaching and joined the postal service to become a letter carrier.

Mayor of Chattanooga from 1927 until 1947, Edward Bass (1873–1960) served throughout the Depression and World War II. During his tenure, he kept the city operating without issuing scrip to city employees or raising taxes. Although he cut many city services, the housing authority was established and the College Hill and East Lake Courts projects were completed. He annexed large areas, including the Brainerd area, into the city.

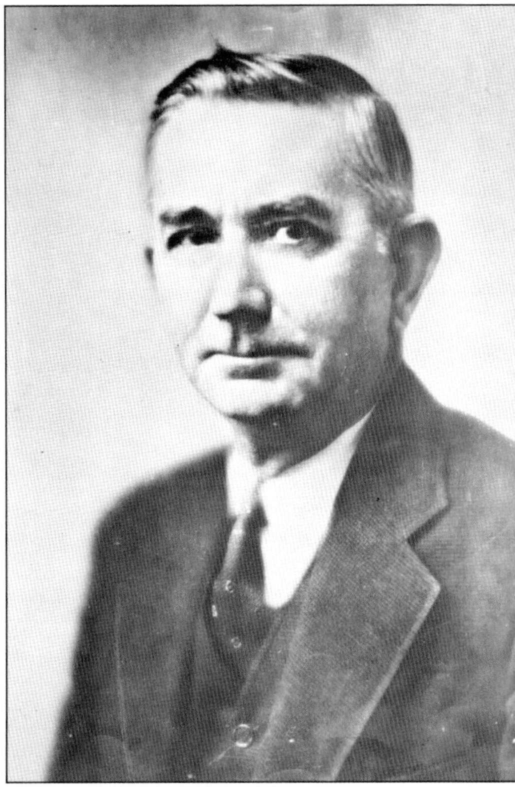

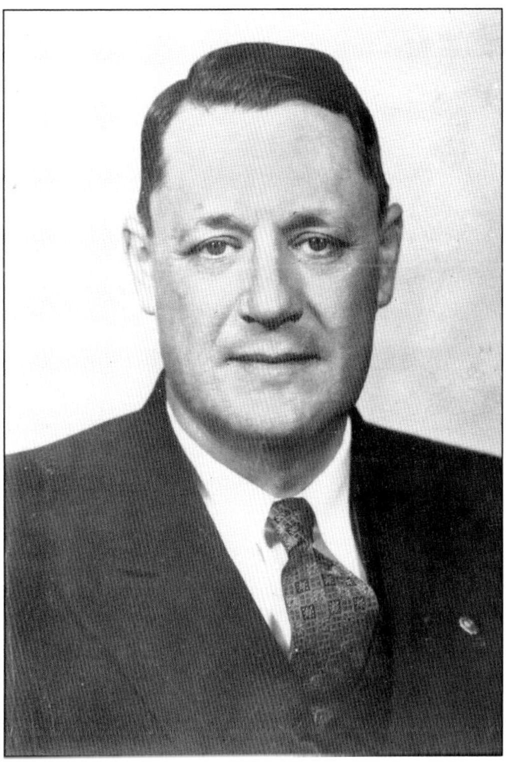

Peter Rudolph "Rudy" Olgiati (1901–1989) was the mayor of Chattanooga from 1951 until 1963. Olgiati helped route a spur of the interstate highway through downtown, necessitating the bridge that bears his name. Spearheading a massive urban renewal project, the Golden Gateway Redevelopment Project led to the revitalization of the west side. In the process, Cameron Hill was lowered, 1,170 buildings were razed, and 1,400 families were relocated.

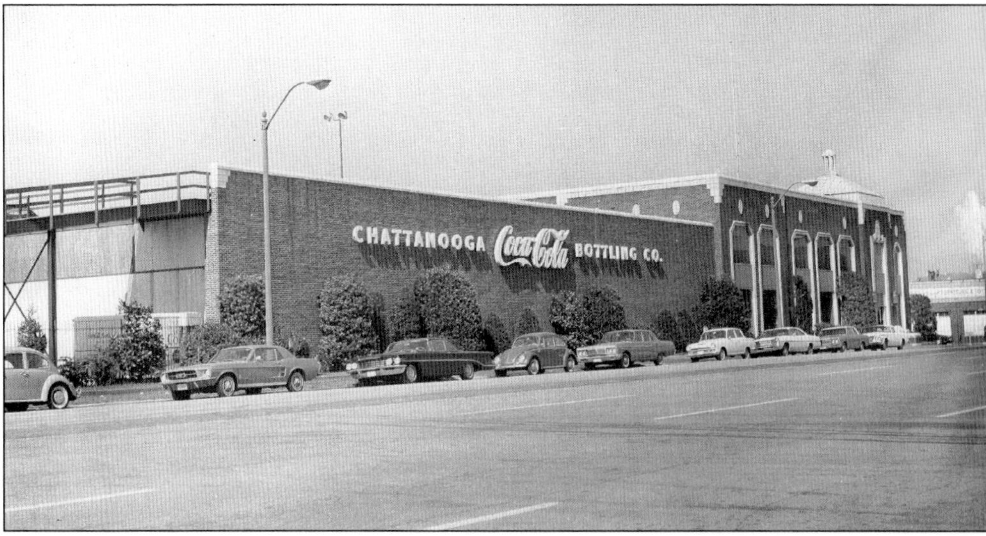

When he was 17, Sam Erwin (1867–1948) was a cowboy in Texas. Settling in Chattanooga, he first owned a clothing store and later became the clerk and master for Hamilton County. In 1899, he agreed to travel to Atlanta to introduce his cousin, Asa Chandler, to Ben Thomas. Chandler was reluctant to sell the bottling franchise for Coca-Cola, but this meeting eventually resulted in the sale of the franchise to Thomas and others. Erwin never profited from his key role.

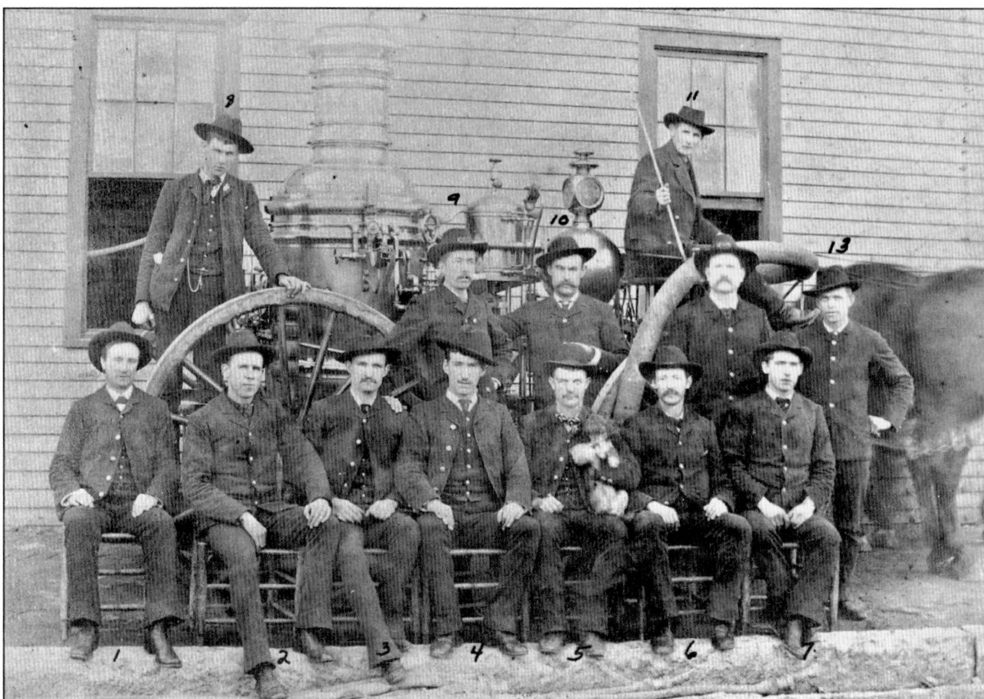

An area of Forest Hills Cemetery was set aside for firemen and policemen after the 1887 Bee Hive Department Store fire. The fire took the lives of firemen Henry Iler (first row, second from left) and Matthew Peek (first row, second from right). Chief Charles Whiteside (second row, second from left) was badly burned while attempting to rescue Iler and Peek. Whiteside was later buried in this section of the cemetery, as he requested.

Fire captain Charles Werner (1857–1891) died while fighting a fire at the European Hotel at the corner of Cherry and Ninth Streets. Despite warnings, he climbed a ladder with a fire hose and came in contact with an electric wire. He was apparently knocked unconscious by the shock and fell to his death.

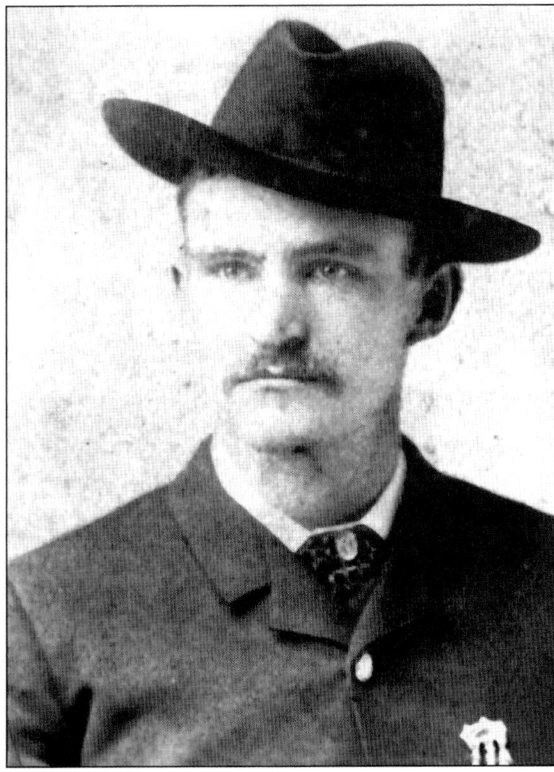

Clarence and Monnie Livingston and their children lived in St. Elmo. Clarence (1881–1912), a mounted policeman, interrupted a robbery at a Main Street saloon and was mortally wounded. In response to his murder, the citizens of Chattanooga raised money to purchase a home in St. Elmo for his widow and children. Livingston is on the far right of this photograph of Chattanooga's first motorized unit.

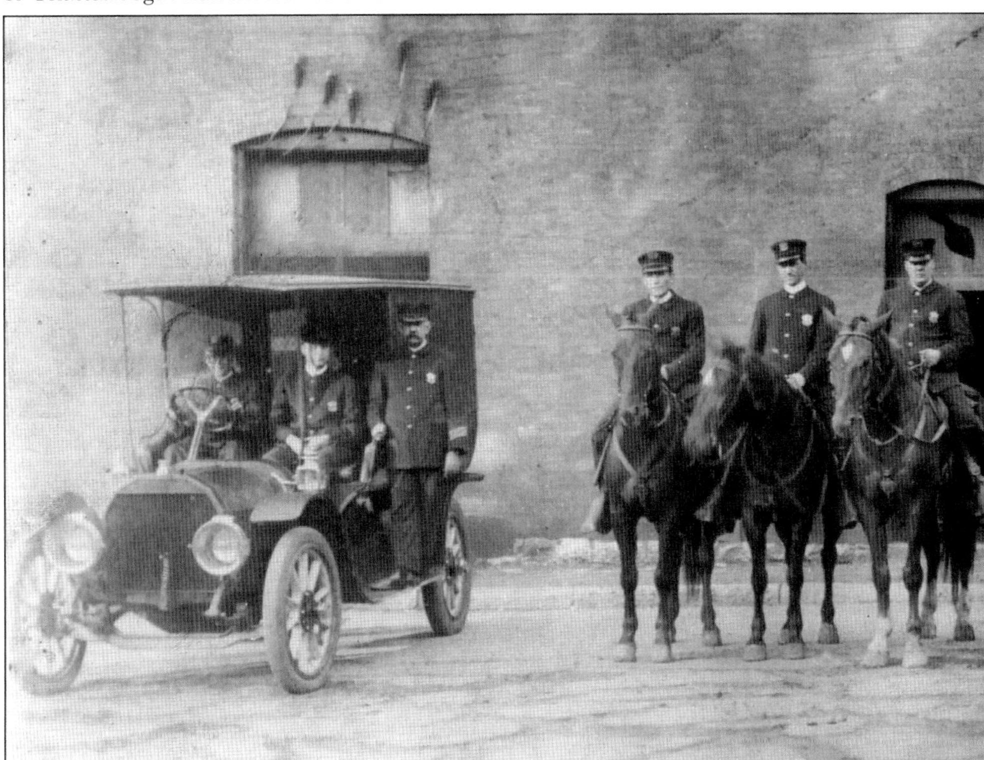

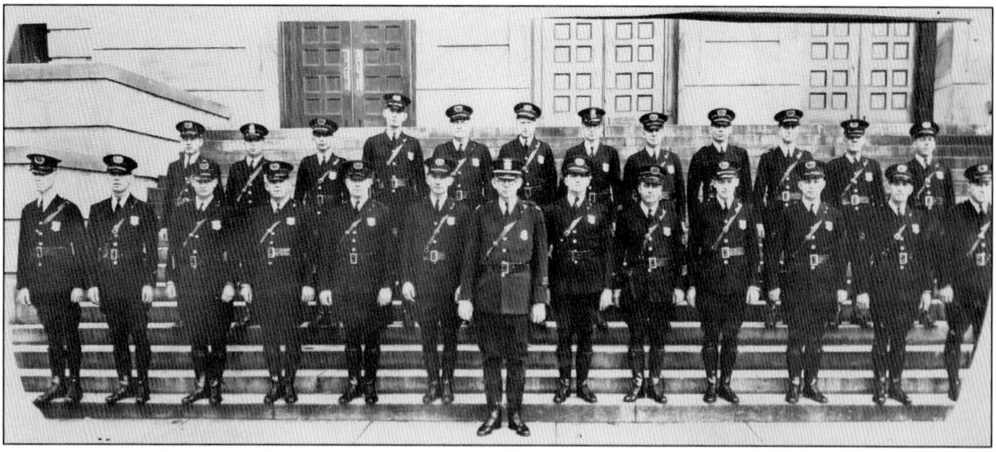

In November 1931, two Chattanooga police officers were killed in the line of duty. The first, J. H. Cornett (1890–1931), died on November 4 while attempting to arrest Elmer Carter. The second officer, Jessie Shirley (1891–1931), died on November 8 when he attempted to arrest a man for drunkenness. Shirley's fellow officer killed the assailant. The funeral included an honor guard of the city's motorcycle policemen, pictured here.

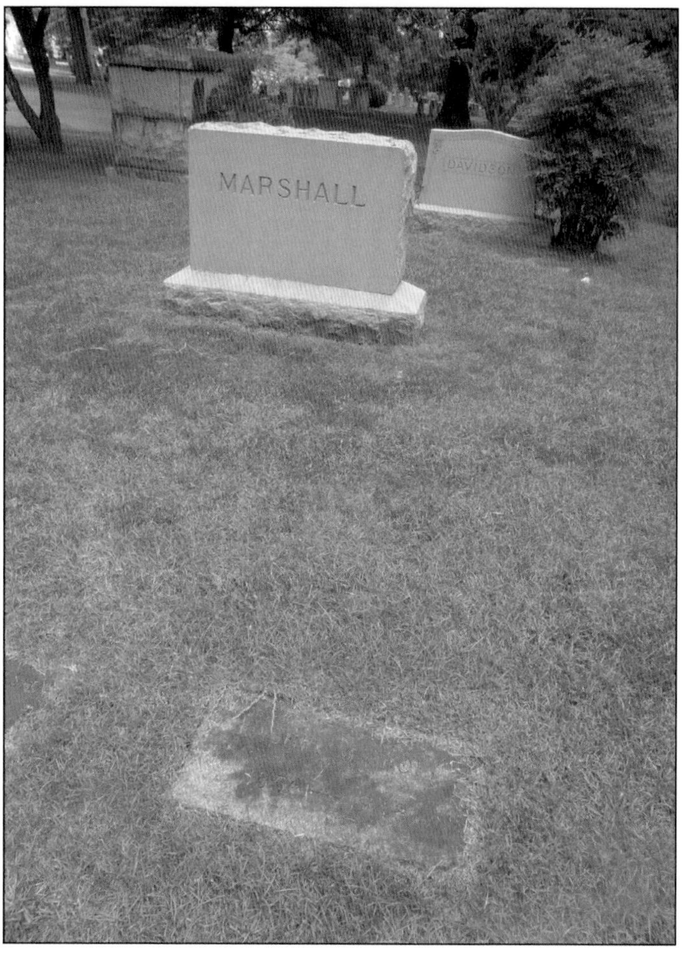

Rachel Marshall Croft (1860–1948) served as city police matron for 38 years. As matron she was in charge of female prisoners and aided many men, women, and children who were in distress. Upon her retirement, the woman called the "angel of the police" stated that of the many women she has overseen, "Some are good and some bad, but they all have souls and I have done my best with them . . . and I am glad I have had the opportunity to be of service."

Five

Community Leaders and the Clergy

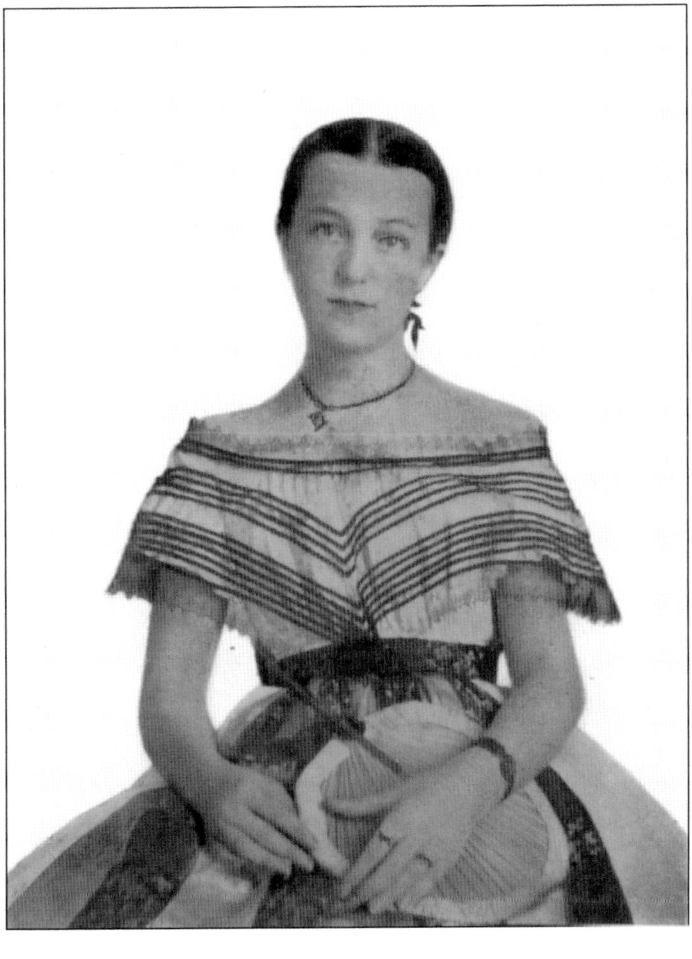

Ellen Jarnagin McCallie (1841–1915) helped establish a number of organizations in Chattanooga, including the Vine Street Orphanage and the Florence Crittenden Home. One of the original founders of the Woman's Christian Association, she is also listed among the nurses who tended to the wounded during the Civil War. A Presbyterian, she was the first woman in Chattanooga to wear the white ribbon of the Women's Christian Temperance Union. (Photograph courtesy of Kathy McCallie Gardner.)

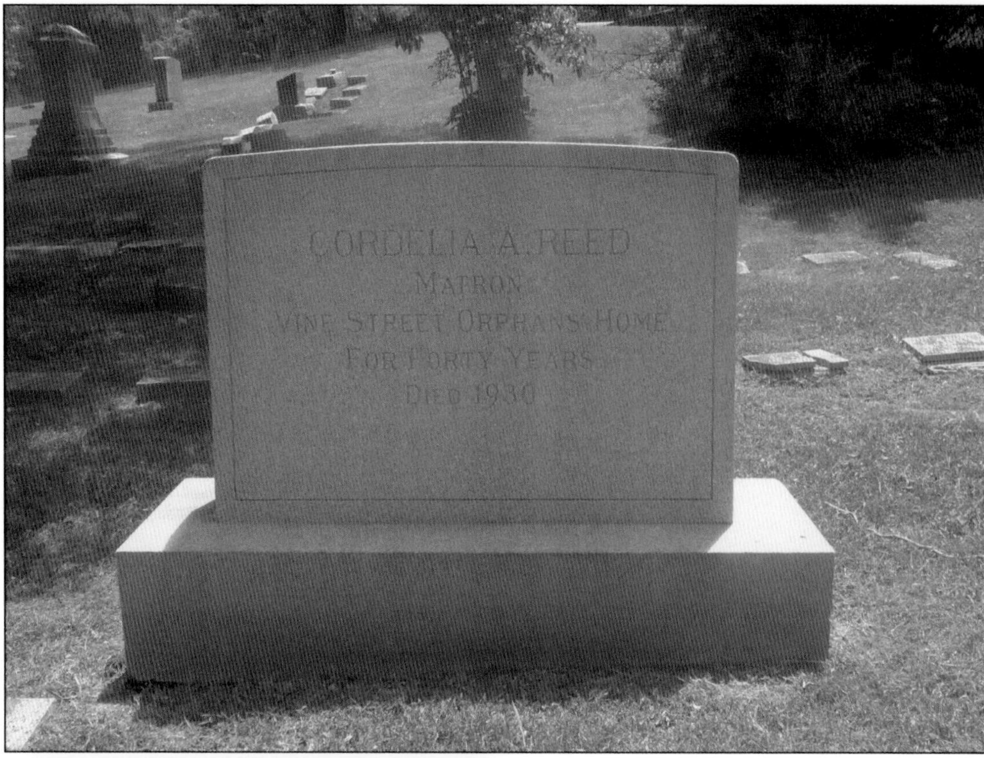

Known as "Mother Reed," Cordelia Reed (1853–1930) was the matron of the Vine Street Orphanage for 33 years from 1886 until 1919. At her retirement, she said, "I am proud of the children who have gone out into the world and made good, but I am prouder of the grandchildren of the home; for there, after all is the biggest proof of the good of our work."

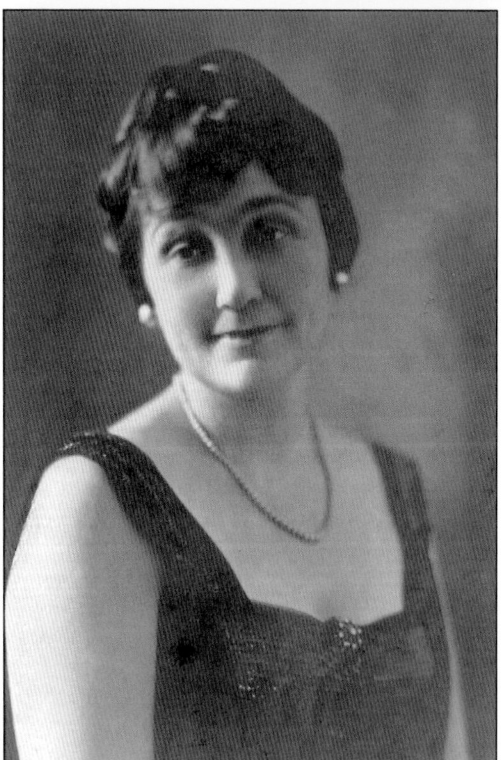

Minnie Newman Wheland (1887–1941) was descended from a long line of distinguished educators. Active in the religious, educational, civic, and cultural life of Chattanooga, she was the first woman elected to the Hamilton County School Board. While out of town, her friends put her name up for election as mayor of St. Elmo. Returning home, she declined the honor. (Photograph courtesy of Margaret Cate.)

Coming to Chattanooga from Ohio in 1880, Capt. William R. Frye (1836–1910) established a successful business. Having grown up under difficult circumstances, he was particularly sensitive to the struggles of working people. When he died, Frye left most of his fortune to establish the Frye Institute. The institute provided working people and their families with "good moral amusements," including a library, gymnasium, auditorium, and dance hall.

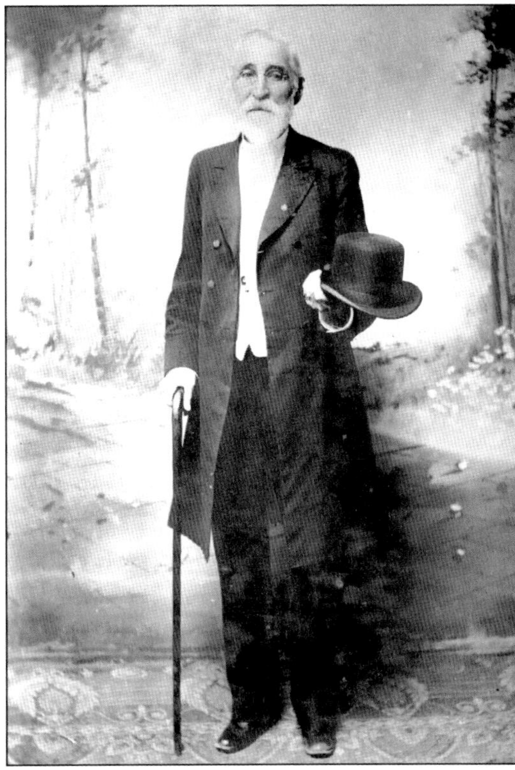

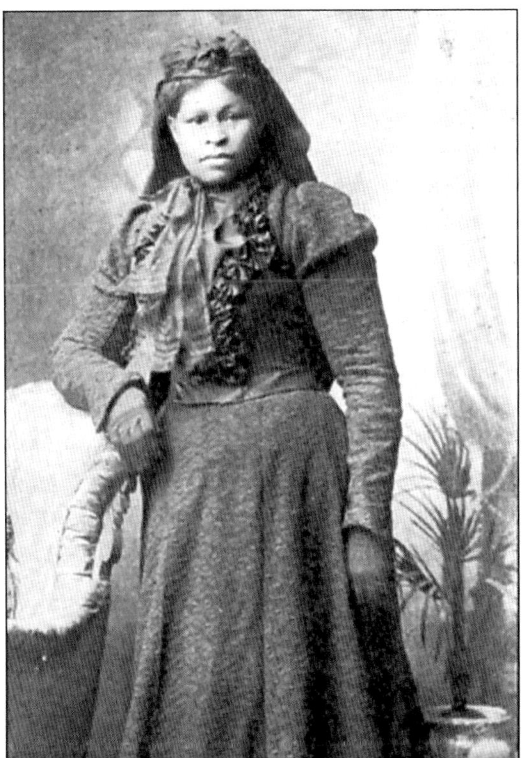

Nancy Barge (1855–1907) came to Chattanooga in 1882 from Huntsville, Alabama. In 1886, she joined the Knights of the Wise Men. Over the years she held a number of high ranking local and state offices in the Ladies' Pleidades Chamber, helping to found or reorganize a number of additional chambers. Such lodges were extremely important in the African American community. They provided many charitable and social services, as well as fun and friendship.

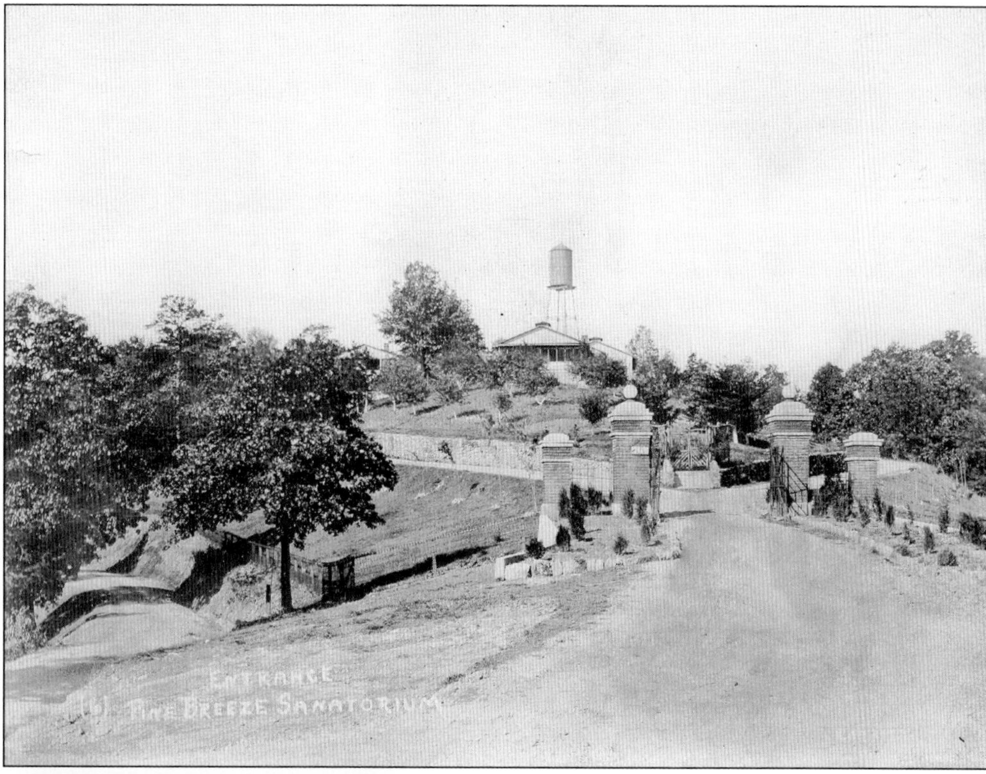

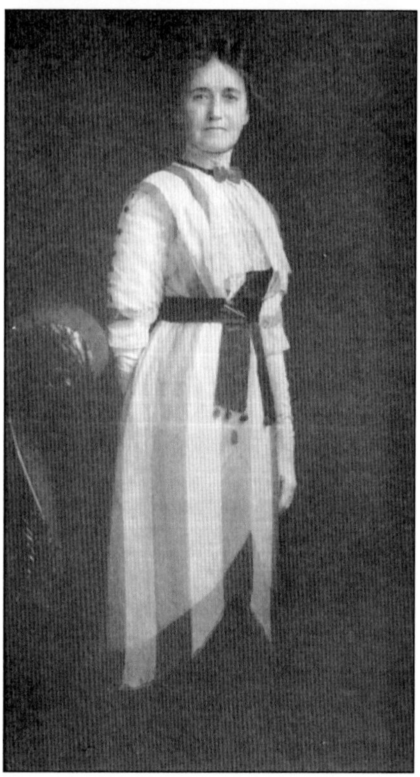

German immigrant Gertrude King Scholze (1846–1932) was known for her desire to help children. In 1918, she gave her Lookout Mountain home, Three Oaks, to the Vine Street Orphanage as a summer home. She wanted the children "who had no parents to take them to the mountain for the summer to enjoy the same advantages that her own children had." At her death, she provided for a building at the Pine Breeze Hospital, pictured here, with the stipulation that it be used for children.

A member of the first coeducational class at Indiana University, Corinne Dodd (1852–1929) married Newell Sanders in 1873. A leader in the League of Women voters, she maintained a desk in her husband's Senate office. According to Tennessee law, municipalities could allow women to vote in local elections. The Sanderses pushed the city of Lookout Mountain to pass such a law, and in 1917 Corinne became the first woman to vote in Tennessee. (Photograph courtesy of Elizabeth Miller.)

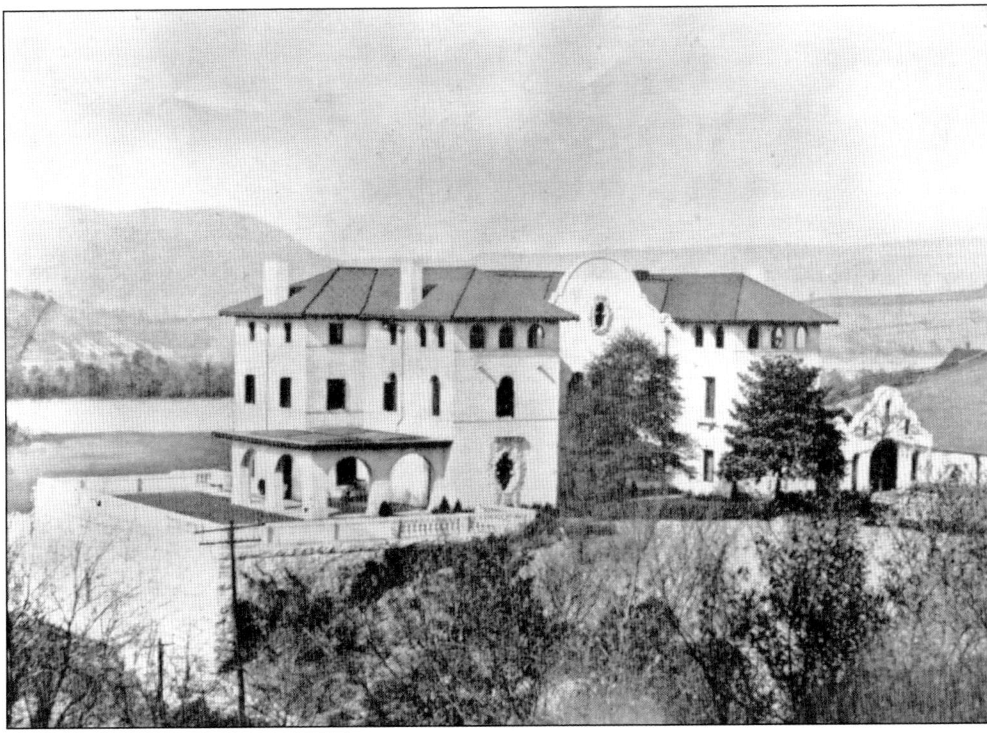

Cincinnati-born Genevieve Allan Montague (1857–1941), promoted the arts in Chattanooga and designed the city flag. She helped found Pine Breeze Sanatorium and served as board president for many years. She organized the Women's Service League and helped establish recreation and health facilities for soldiers at Fort Oglethorpe. During World War I, she recorded personal information on each Hamilton County soldier. Her Cameron Hill home is pictured here.

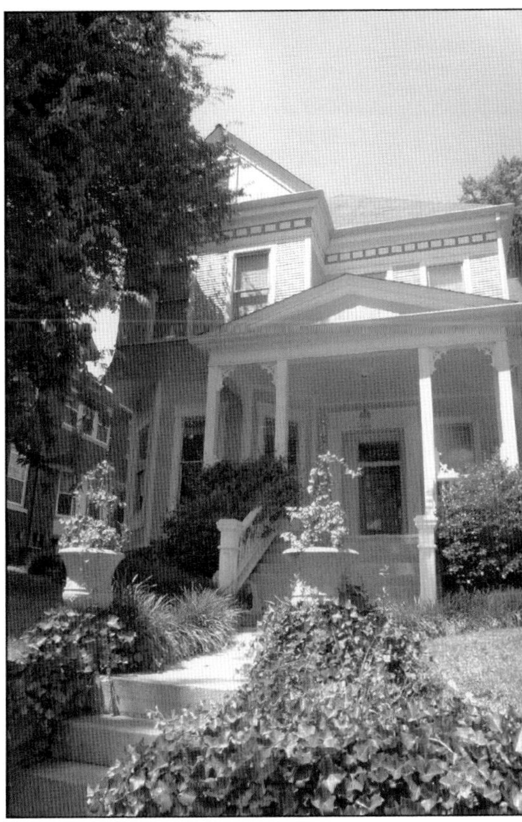

When Sarah Holtclaw Thompson (1892–1968) was named "Woman of the Week" by the *Chattanooga Times* in November 1944, the newspaper asked her to pose in her Red Cross uniform. A member of the Girls' Preparatory School's first graduating class, she was on the board of directors of the Salvation Army and the Vine Street Orphanage. She was in charge of the Red Cross Railroad Canteen for five years during World War II. She and her husband, Mayor T. C. Thompson, lived in this Fort Wood home.

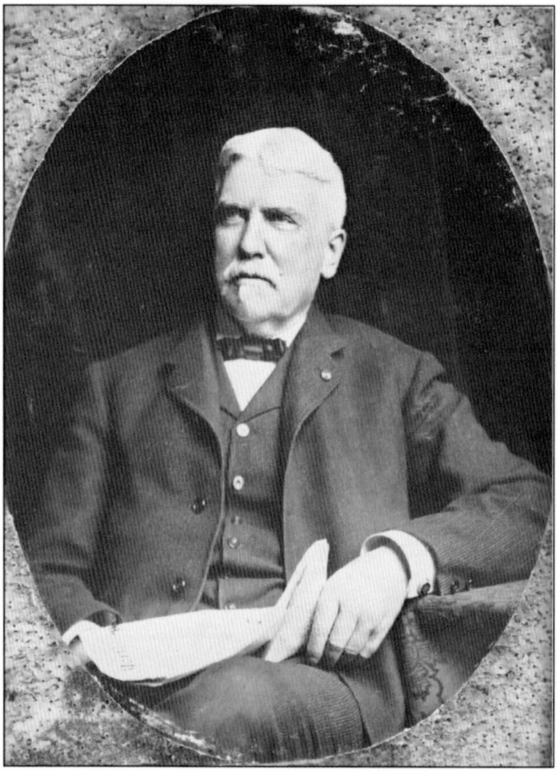

Former Union Army officer Xenophen Wheeler (1835–1914) was attracted to Chattanooga in 1865, "because I thought a place so strategically important in war ought to become a large and important place in time of peace." He practiced law for many years and was appointed U.S. district attorney. Wheeler was the president of the first public library board, a trustee of the University of Tennessee, and fourth president of the Tennessee Bar Association.

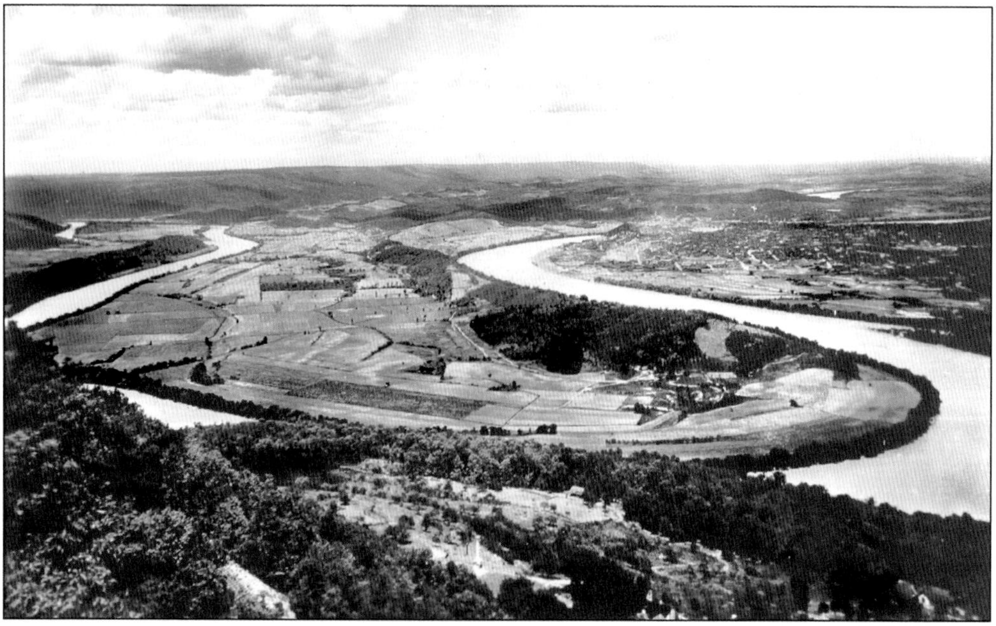

Sophia Scholze Long (1881–1970) fought to preserve the historic landmarks and beauty of Chattanooga and the surrounding area. Although the battle to preserve Cameron Hill was lost, she was a leader in the successful effort to preserve Moccasin Bend from industrialization. She was presented the deed to the property by the county judge, which she accepted on behalf of the citizens of Hamilton County.

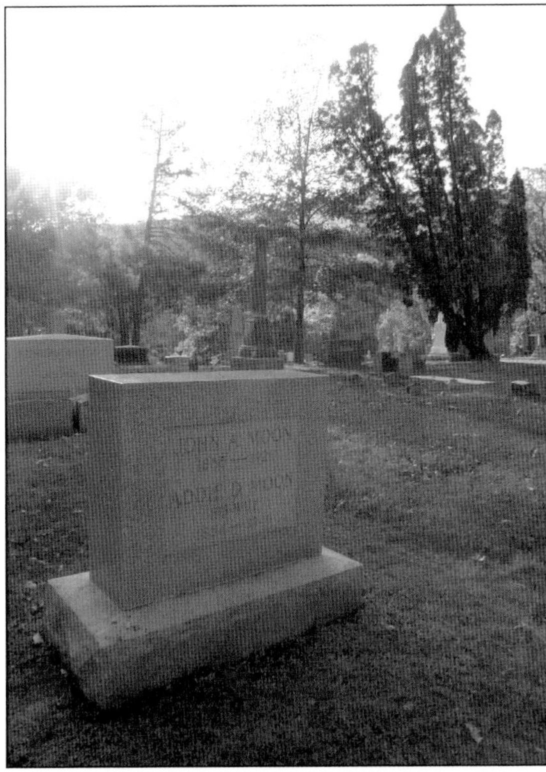

Adeline Deadrick Moon (1854–1948) was the daughter of a Tennessee Supreme Court justice and the wife of a U.S. congressman. At her death, Milton Ochs wrote in tribute, "Mrs. Moon's greatest accomplishment was living her years . . . as a good woman should live. She was all a wife and mother should be. She was without cant or hypocrisy; a true gentlewoman, but with rugged strength for righteous causes. Her simplicity of manner was the badge of her great soul."

People called Sheila Marie Jennings (1965–2008) "the mayor of Westside." Helping to lay down the foundation for the Westside Development Corporation, she was instrumental in the creation of the Grove Street Center. She was the owner of the Home Girls Restaurant, the first resident-owned business to occupy the center. The Sheila Jennings Health and Wellness Center is named in her honor.

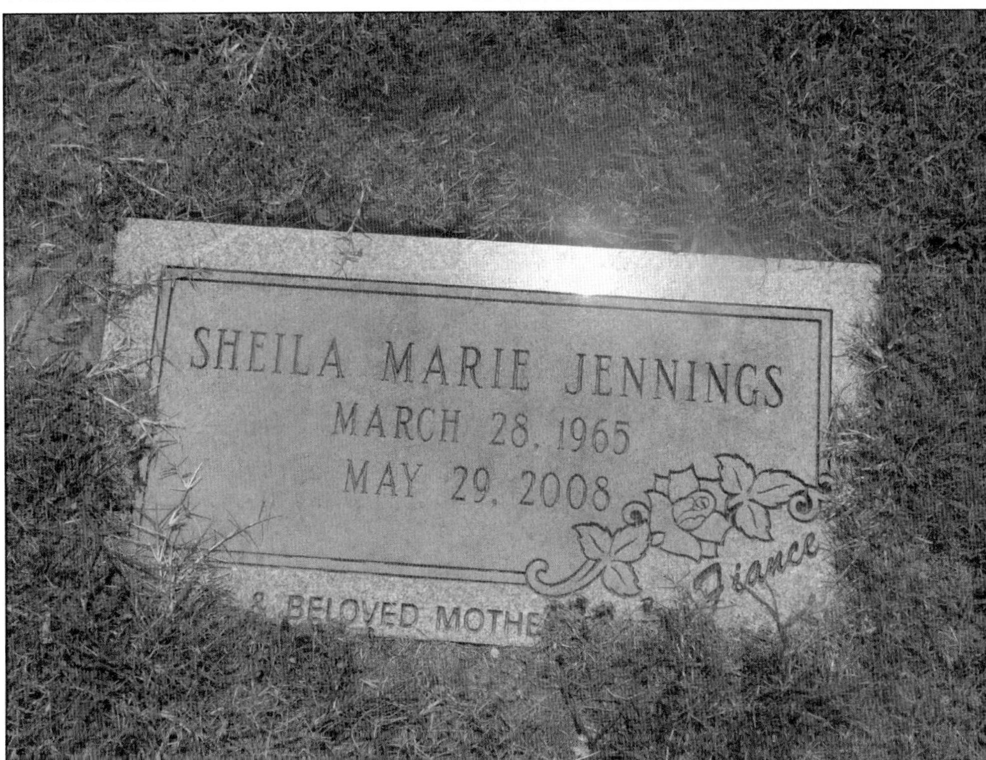

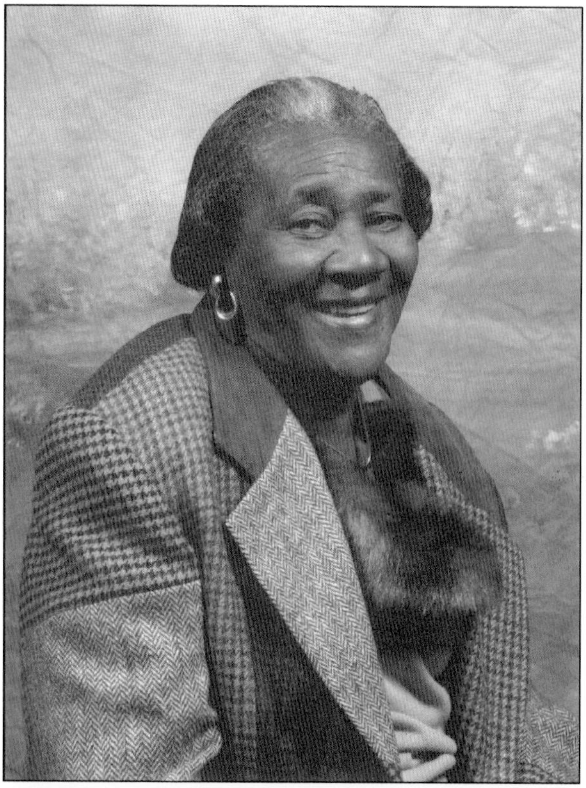

Known as the "Mayor of Alton Park" Elizabeth Dixon (1928–2008) was a community and political activist who sought to improve the living conditions and image of public housing. Serving as president of the City Wide Tenant Association and the McCallie Homes Tenant Association, on her 70th birthday she was honored by the Chattanooga mayor's office for her work.

In 1904, Rev. E. H. Dial (1867–1940) moved to Lookout Mountain and became the first pastor of the First Baptist Church. Originally located at the corner of Scenic Highway and Forrest Avenue, the church remains active. Dial occupied the pulpit for 24 years. He was also an expert in preparing barbeque and cooked for many celebrations and picnics.

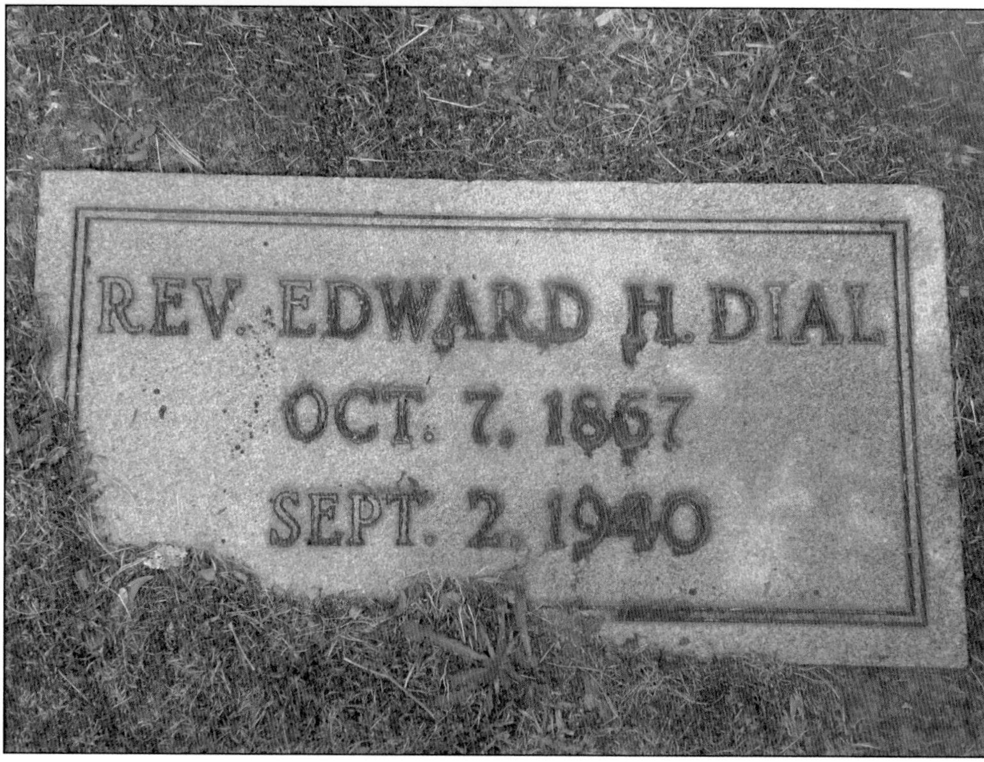

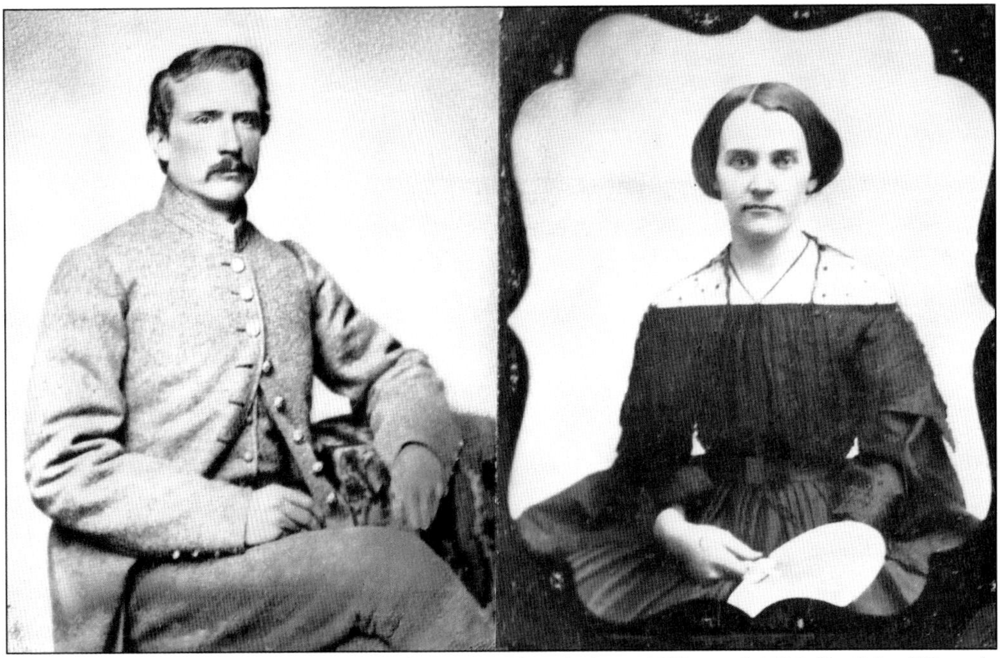

The pastor of Chattanooga's First Presbyterian Church from 1873 until 1924, Dr. John Waverly Bachman (1837–1924) served as chaplain to Gen. Robert E. Lee and Gen. Thomas J. "Stonewall" Jackson. Pastor to many of Chattanooga's families, he also served the wider community. During the yellow fever epidemic of 1878, he nursed the sick, read over services, and helped bury the deceased. Unofficially known as the "Bishop of Chattanooga," he was officially named the "Chaplin of Chattanooga" by the board of commissioners. He is pictured here with his wife, Evalina Dulaney Bachman (1836–1898), at the time of their marriage.

In 1832, Thomas McFarland (1803–1887) and his brother surveyed the area that is now Rossville, Georgia. After the Cherokee removal, the brothers purchased the John Ross home, where McFarland made his home for many years. He acquired large tracts of land, which he divided among his children several years before his death. Two of them, John and Mattie, donated land for the Methodist church named in honor of their parents.

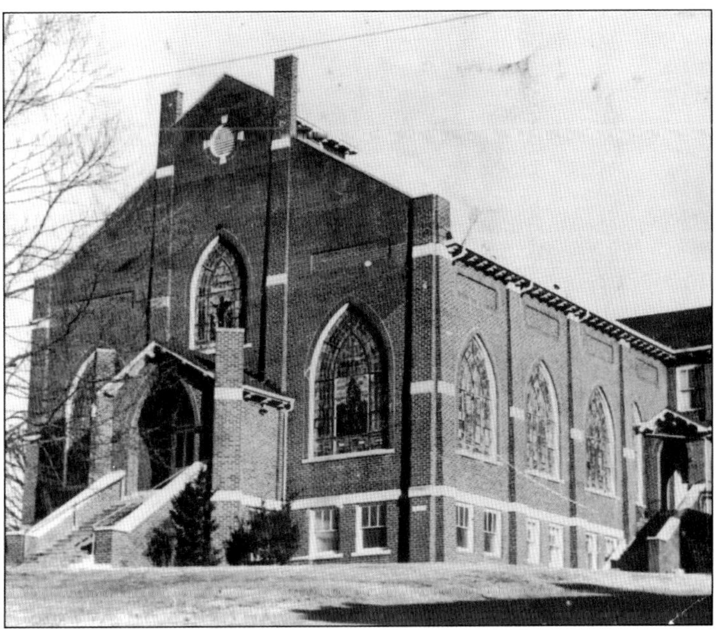

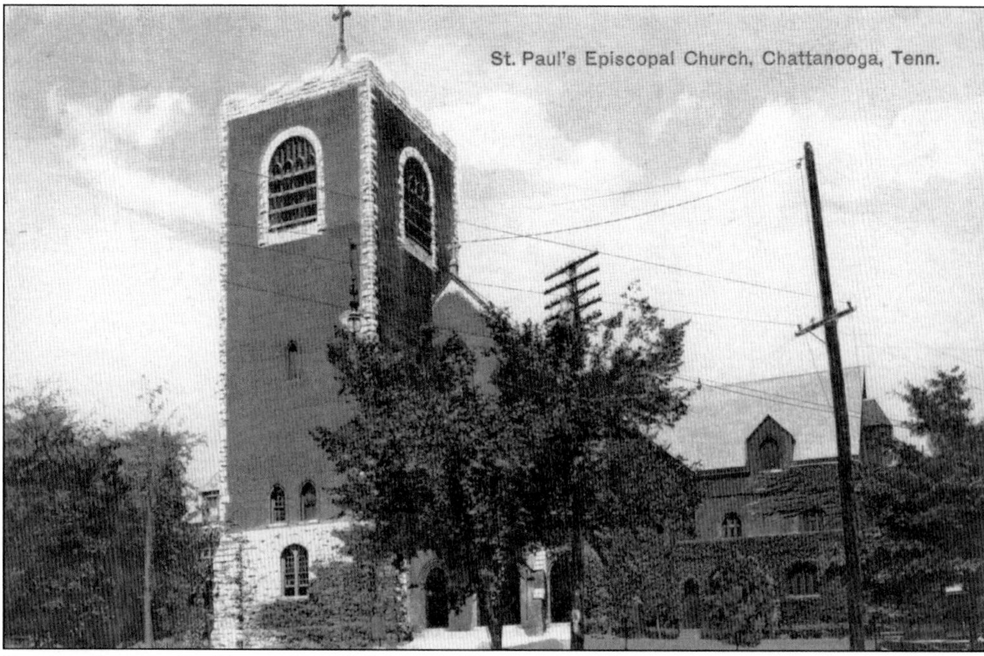

Episcopal priest Fr. Henry Sneed (1841–1927) came to Chattanooga in 1872 to establish the Female Institute, the first attempt to provide a high school education to girls in the city. In 1873, he became the rector of St. Paul's Church. Under his leadership, stained-glass windows, gaslights, and an organ were installed. During the yellow fever epidemic of 1878, Sneed and three other ministers remained in the city to tend the 1,800 residents who did not flee.

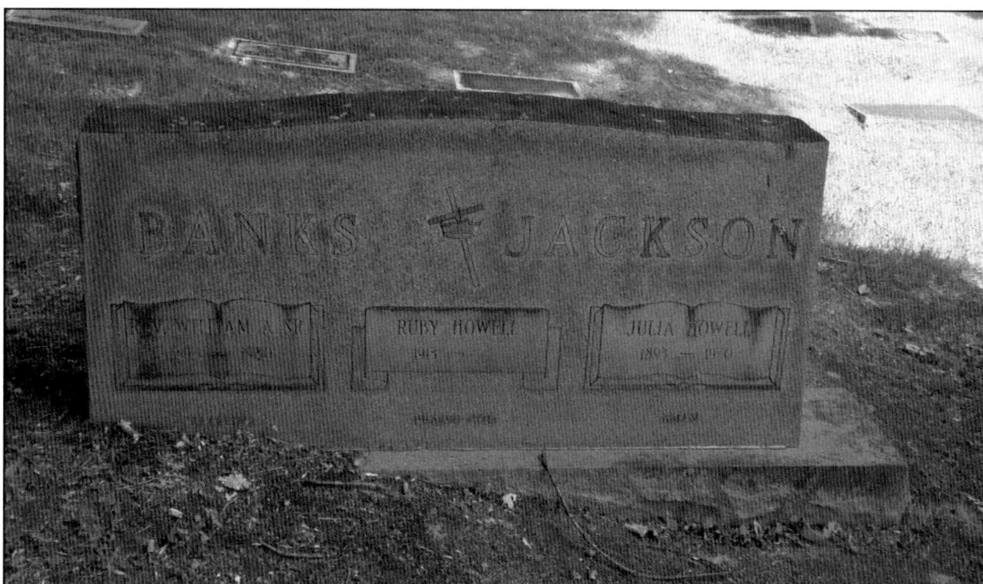

A member of the Antioch Baptist Church, Rev. William Amos Banks (1894–1980) retired after 60 years in the ministry. According to his obituary, he "served in many capacities during an active life of service to God and humanity." At his request, there was "no listing of his many affiliations and achievements." Those who knew him were "aware of services rendered to God's glory along the way."

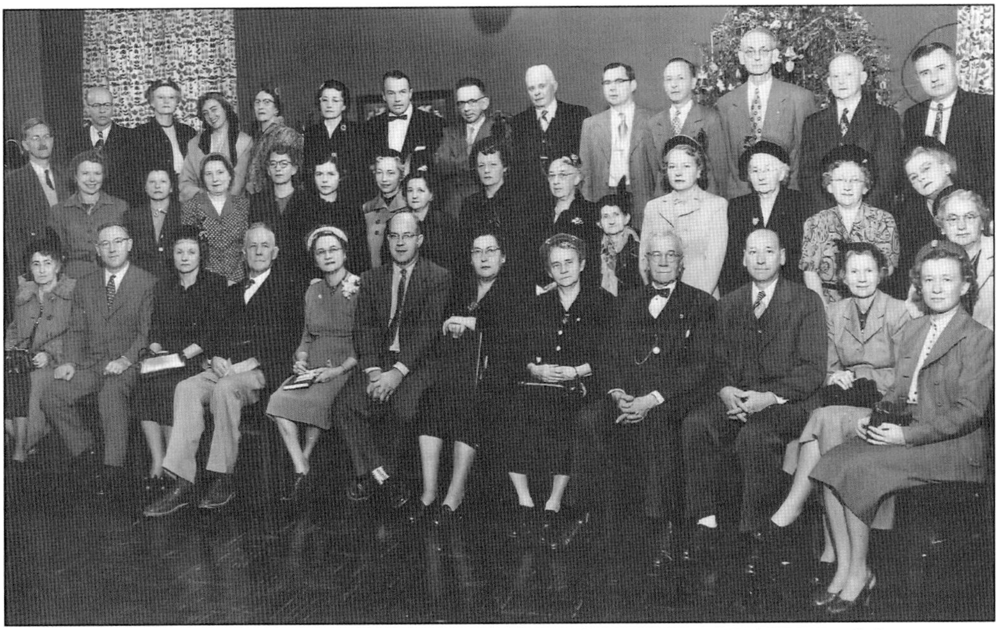

Dr. William Keese (1873–1968) began his career as an educator. In 1907, he entered the ministry at the First Baptist Church in Chattanooga. In 1925, he accepted a position as superintendent of the Bonny Oaks School. He and his wife, Lucy, served the school for 27 years. He stated, "this was the most rewarding and happiest work of their lives." Shown here with his Sunday school class, he is in the bottom row, fourth from left. (Photograph courtesy of Pilgrim Congregational Church.)

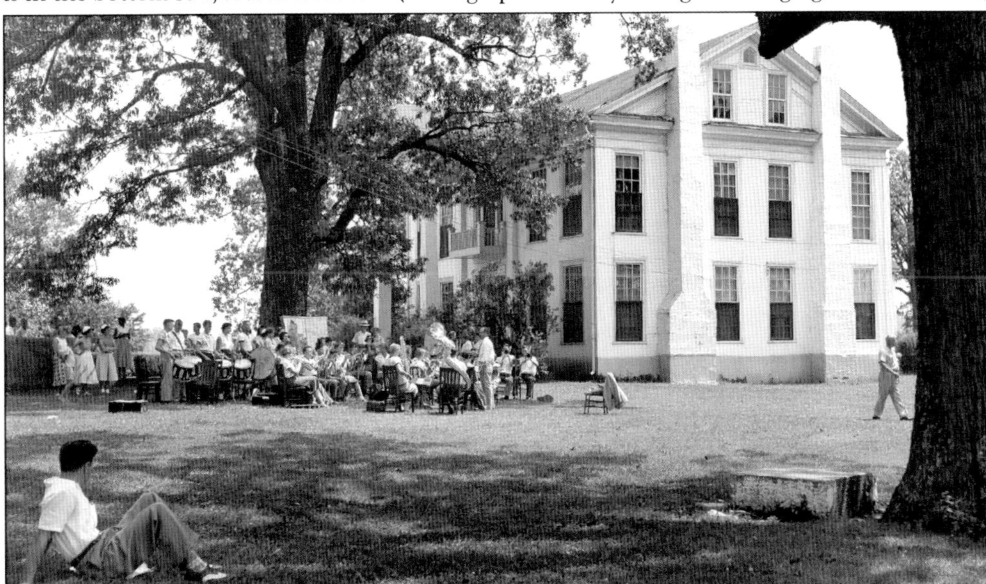

An accomplished musician and teacher, when Lucy Beall (1876–1959) married William Keese, she became a partner in his ministry. As the wife of the Bonny Oaks School superintendent, she was hostess, musician, and "mother" to the children who lived there. The couple lived on the school grounds, shown here during a summer concert. Lucy worked for the construction of the stone church located at the front gate of the school. She taught Sunday school and played the piano at the Pilgrim Congregational Church until shortly before her death.

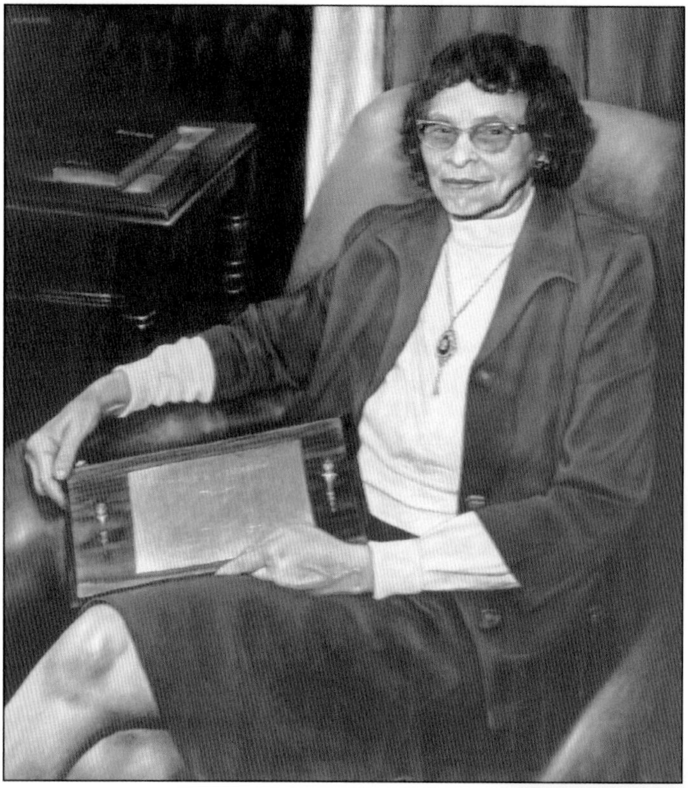

A former missionary to African American coal miners in West Virginia, Sallie Crenshaw (1900–1986) formed the St. Elmo Mission in 1947 to provide day care and help to needy families. She was the first African American female Methodist minster in the Holston Conference, pastoring 10 churches during her career. The Sally Crenshaw Bethlehem Center continues its work in the community in her honor. (Photograph courtesy of the Bessie Smith Cultural Center.)

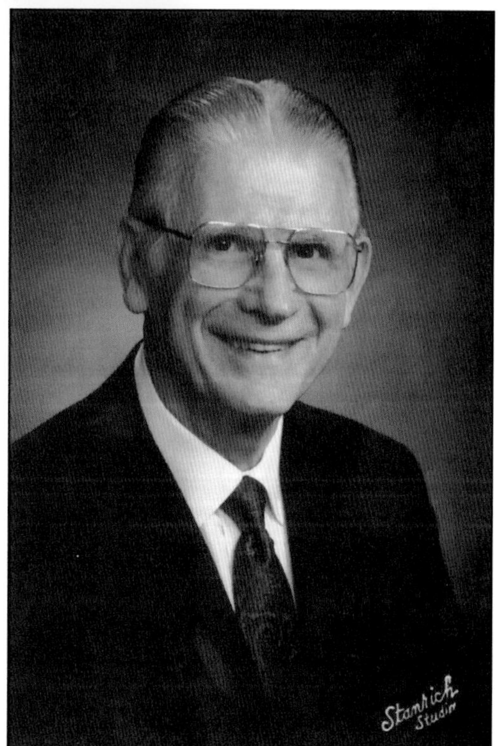

Dr. Ralph Mohney (1918–2008), pastor of First-Centenary United Methodist Church, believed there should be a strong Methodist presence in the center of the city. Merging with First Methodist (Stone Church), Centenary United Methodist Church built its current site under his leadership. According to Methodist bishop James Swanson, Mohney had "skills and abilities to lead congregations in growth and development and . . . inspiring people to put their money where their mouth is." (Photograph courtesy of Centenary Methodist Church.)

Six

Educators

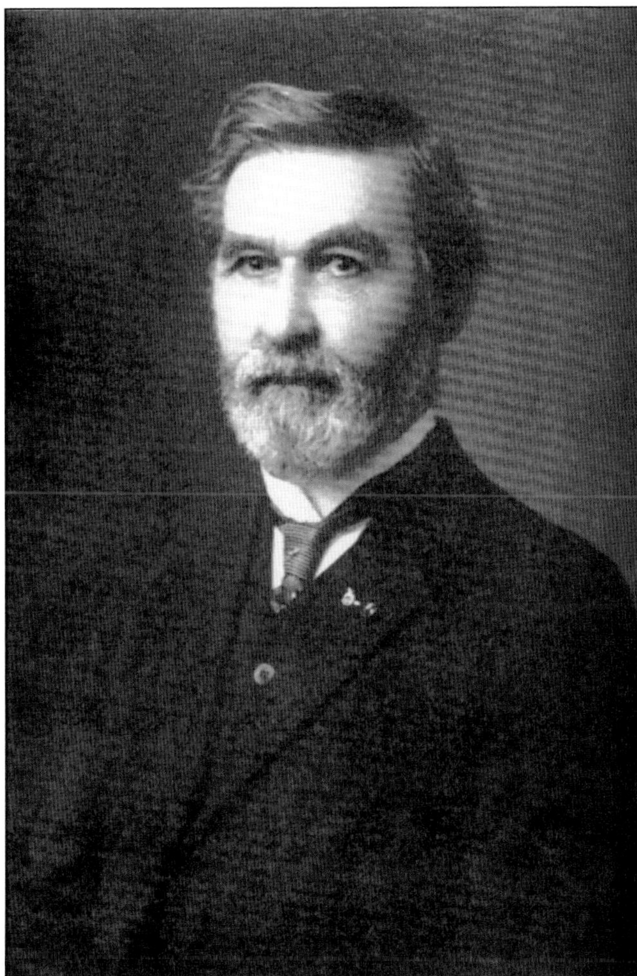

John J. Manker D. D. (1839–1916) was a Union infantry captain, minister, university president, and journal editor. Coming to Tennessee in 1866, he pastored several Methodist churches. He was instrumental in the founding of the University of Chattanooga (then Grant University) and was the dean of the School of Theology. (Photograph courtesy of the University of Tennessee-Chattanooga.)

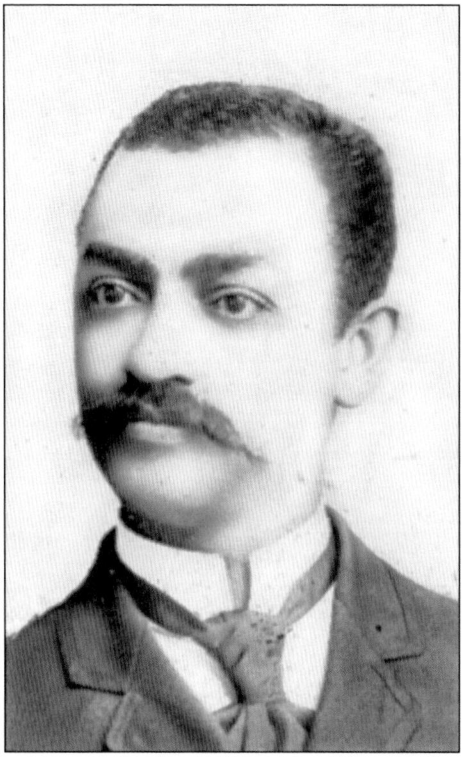

Born in Buffalo, New York, James A. Henry (1859–1914) graduated with a bachelor of arts degree from Atlanta University in 1883. Beginning as a teacher at Howard High School, he became Chattanooga's first African American principal. Serving the Chattanooga city schools for 31 years, he was known throughout the South and lectured widely on improved methods of education. (Photograph courtesy of the Bessie Smith Cultural Center.)

Pictured with her students and two unidentified women at East Lake Park, Annie Arnold (1872–1930) ran a private school at 510 McCallie Avenue. She married Fletcher Lively and the couple had three daughters. The family belonged to St. Paul's Episcopal Church.

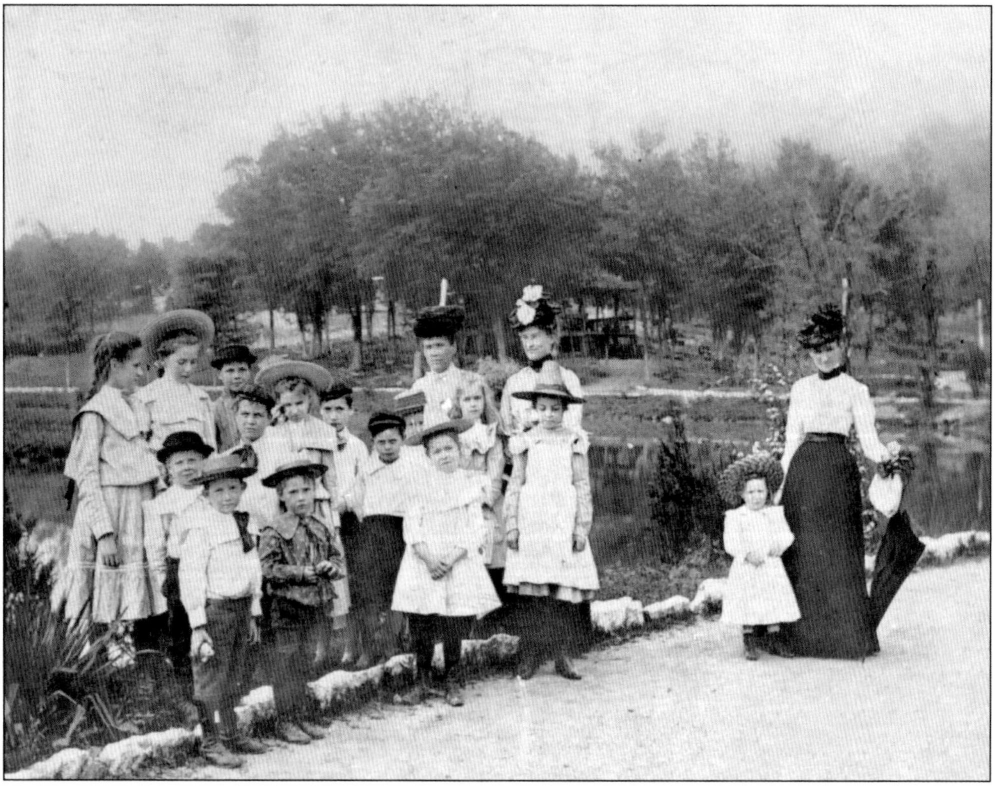

Insurance executive Hugh Huffaker's (1860–1933) true legacy was the advancement of education. Beginning his career as a teacher, he was elected school superintendent and commissioner of education. Serving on the Tennessee Board of Education, he helped to improve the quality of rural schools. Convincing the city commission to allow African American children to advance past the sixth grade, he was the first to employ African American teachers in public schools.

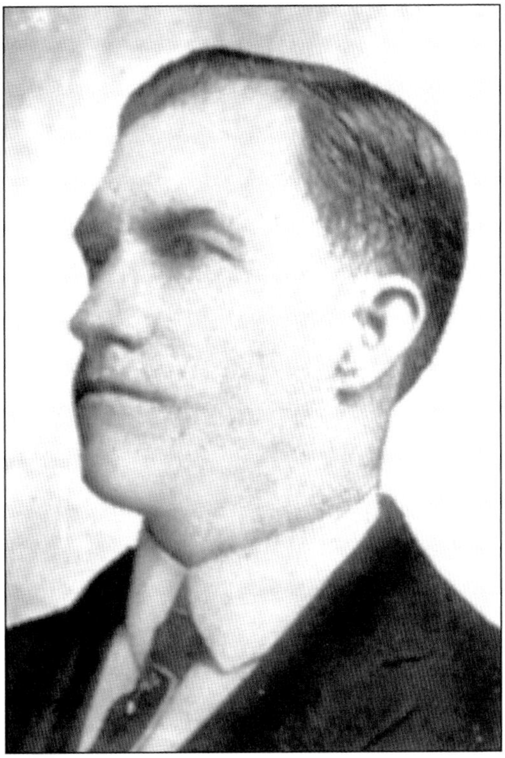

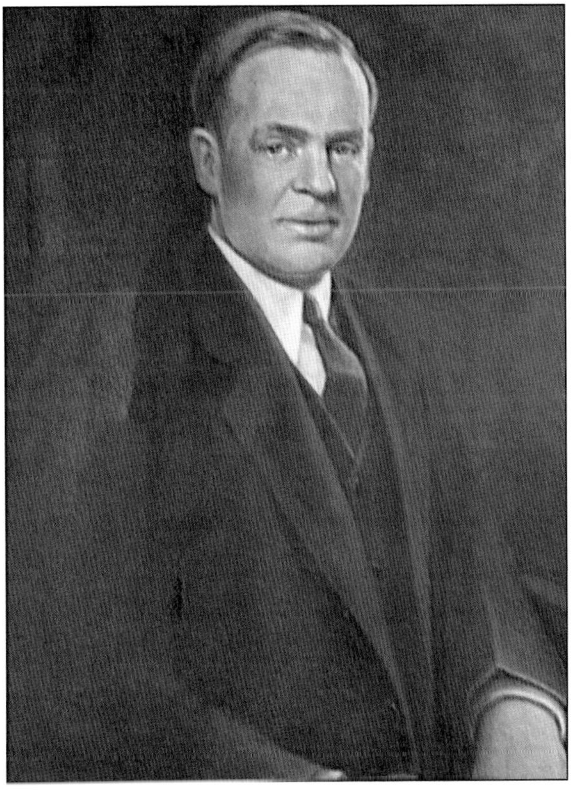

A lifelong educator, Alexander Guerry (1890–1948) served for nine years as the president of the University of Chattanooga, where he is credited with continuing to build the university during the Great Depression. He asserted that an educated man "knows there are such things as beauty and truth, not because someone has declared this to be so, but because he has read the story time and again—in history, in literature, in philosophy." (Photograph courtesy of the University of Tennessee Chattanooga.)

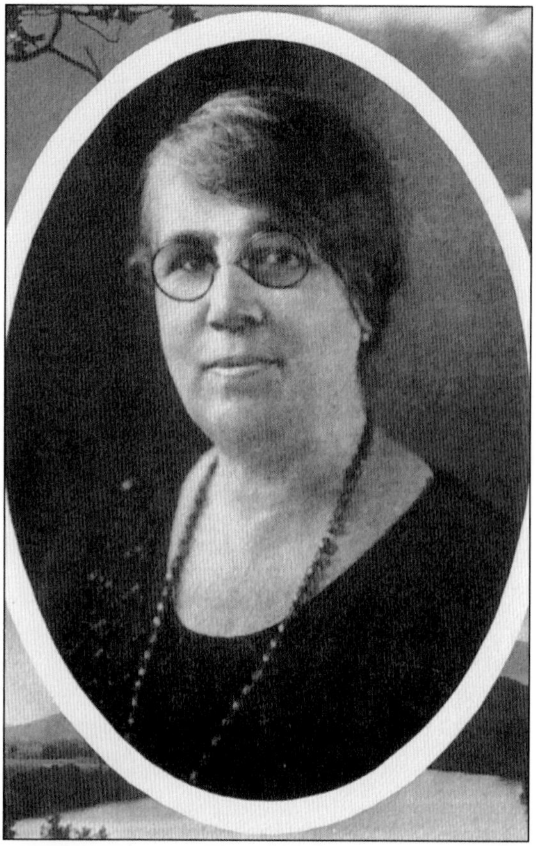

A teacher and head of the English department at Chattanooga High School for more than 30 years, Lucy Holtzclaw McDonald (1863–1935) supported aspiring writers throughout her career. After her retirement, she continued her support for the literary efforts of Chattanooga high school students. When she died of injuries after being struck by a car, former students, a number of Chattanooga's leading citizens, and members of the writer's club gathered to pay their last respects.

Located at the corner of High and Fifth Streets, Diana (1836–1932) and Rosalie (1842–1919) Duval's French and English School educated primary school students for 30 years. Students used both languages in the recitation of their studies. According to a *Chattanooga Times* article printed before the death of Diana, "students were taught to respect the property rights of others and deeds were called by their plain names, stealing was 'stealing' and lying was 'lying.' "

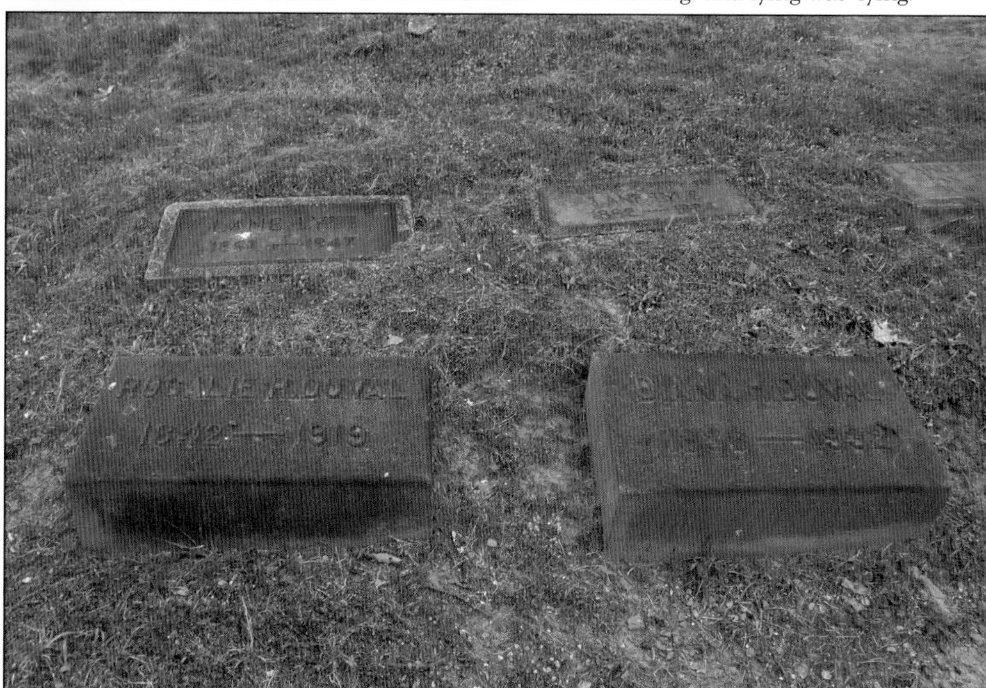

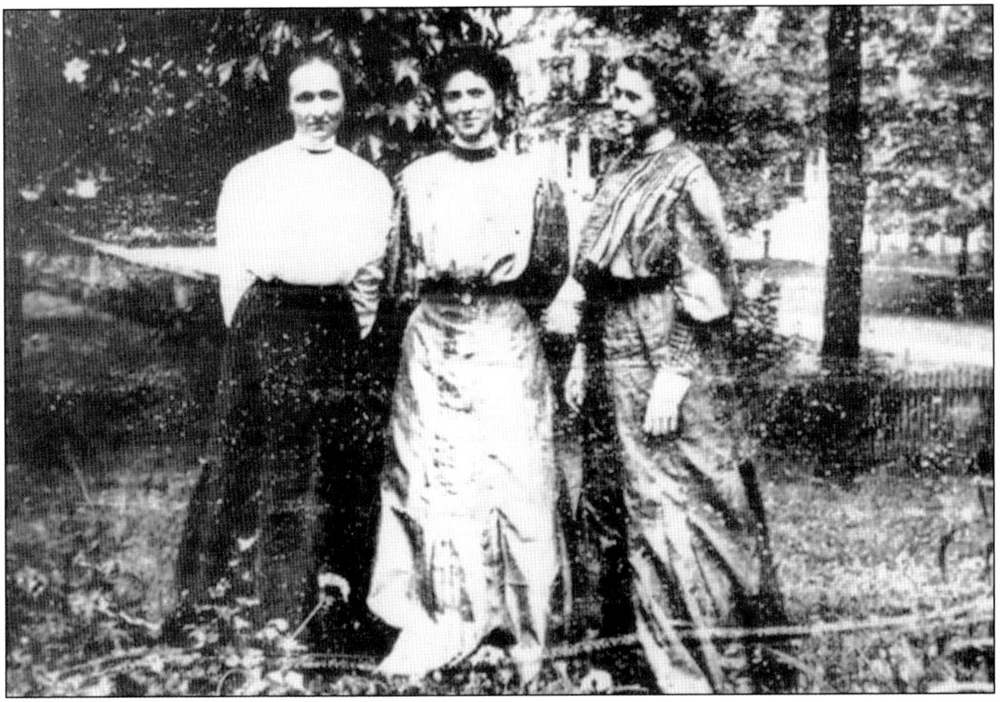

Grace McCallie (1865–1918) established the Girls Preparatory School with fellow teachers Eula Jarnigan (1877–1962) and Tommie Duffy (1874–1947) in 1906. Pictured here from left to right, Grace, Eula, and Tommie opened the school in Grace's Oak Street home. The women discovered that Chattanooga citizens were scandalized that three single women were sharing a home and included athletics in the school's curriculum. (Photograph courtesy of Girls Preparatory School.)

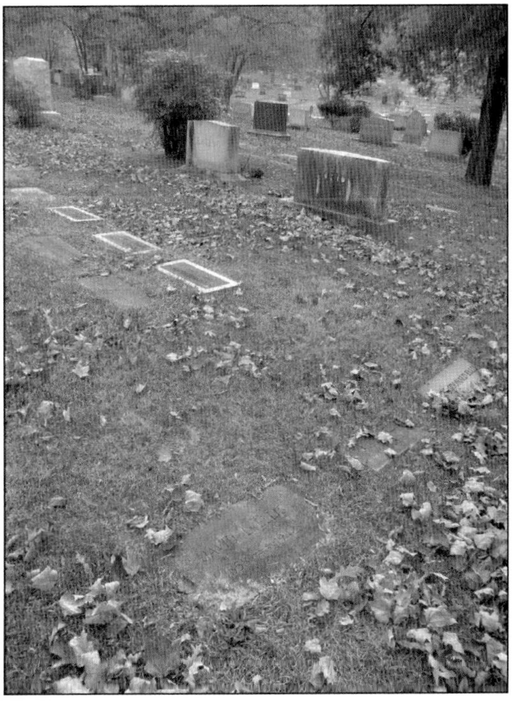

A graduate of Peabody College, David Ellis (1858–1942) was the principal of Mission School and later East Lake Grammar School from 1912 until his retirement in 1934. Active in civic affairs, he was chairman of the city's Navy Day Commemoration for 10 years. He was an elder at the Central Presbyterian Church, the father of four, and the grandfather of six.

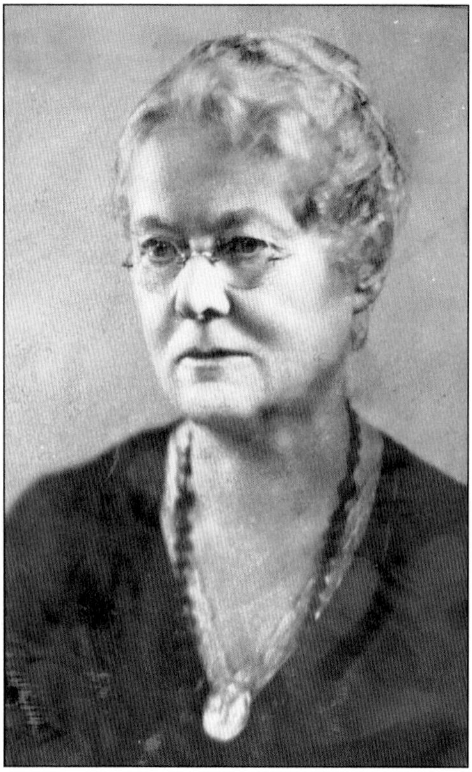

Coming to Chattanooga from Ohio at the age of 16, Annetta Trimble (1863–1948) taught mathematics at Chattanooga City High School for 50 of her 62 years with the school system. Serving also as registrar, she single-handedly kept all of the school records, including information on alumni. Beloved and respected, many students called upon her for advice and counsel long after graduation.

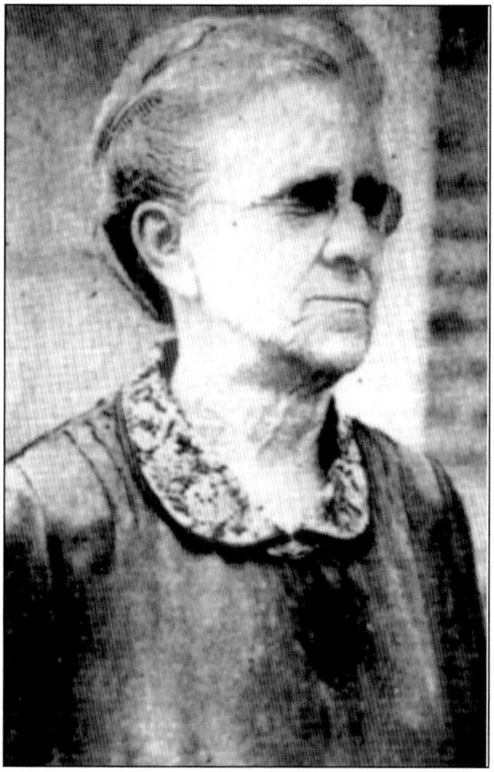

In 1896, Clara Carpenter (1860–1949) was named principal of the school on Douglas and Fifth Streets that eventually bore her name. The Clara Carpenter Elementary School was nationally recognized for its audio-visual program and served as a demonstration school for the University of Chattanooga. Carpenter and Annetta Trimble were the first women to receive the Kiwanis Award for Outstanding Civic Service. Carpenter retired after 58 years of teaching.

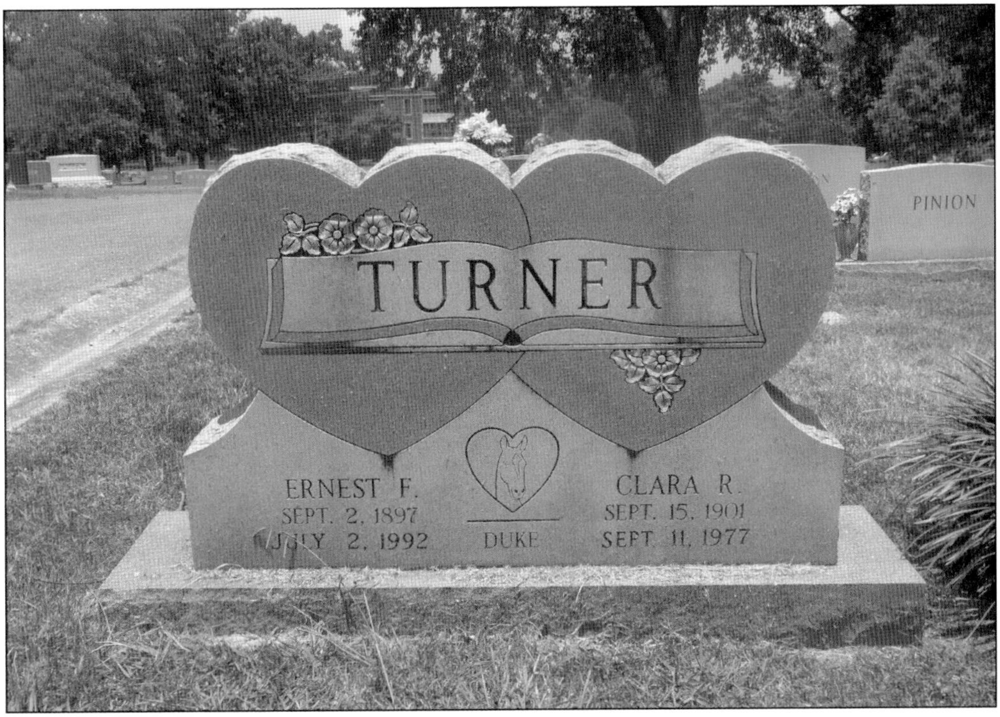

A teacher at East Lake Junior High School, Clara Roberts (1901–1977) married Ernest Turner (1897–1992) late in life. They owned "Duke, the Wonder Horse." Ernest taught Duke more than 20 tricks, which he performed for school groups and other organizations. He boarded Duke in Fort Oglethorpe, where one night the barn burned, killing Duke and 16 other horses. Duke's ashes are buried here with Ernest and Clara.

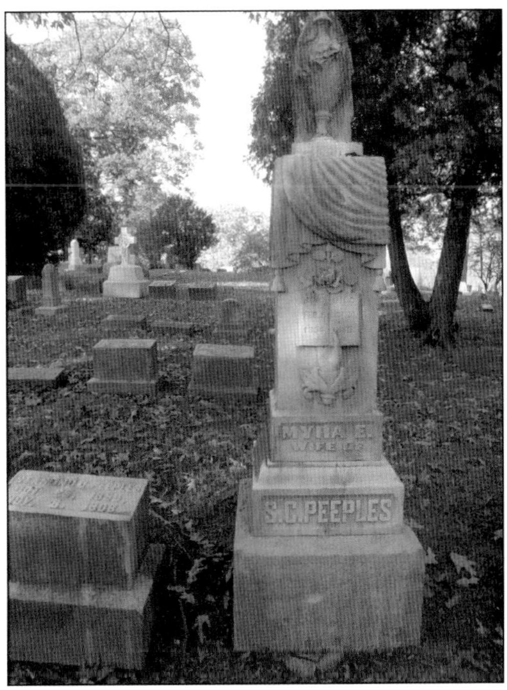

When Annette Peeples Dickey (1873–1953) joined the county school system, only one school had a music director. When she retired 25 years later as the music supervisor, every school in the county had a music program. She arranged and directed an annual choral event with hundreds of students participating. She learned 25 folk dances, which she taught to students, combining lessons in history, geography, and the arts.

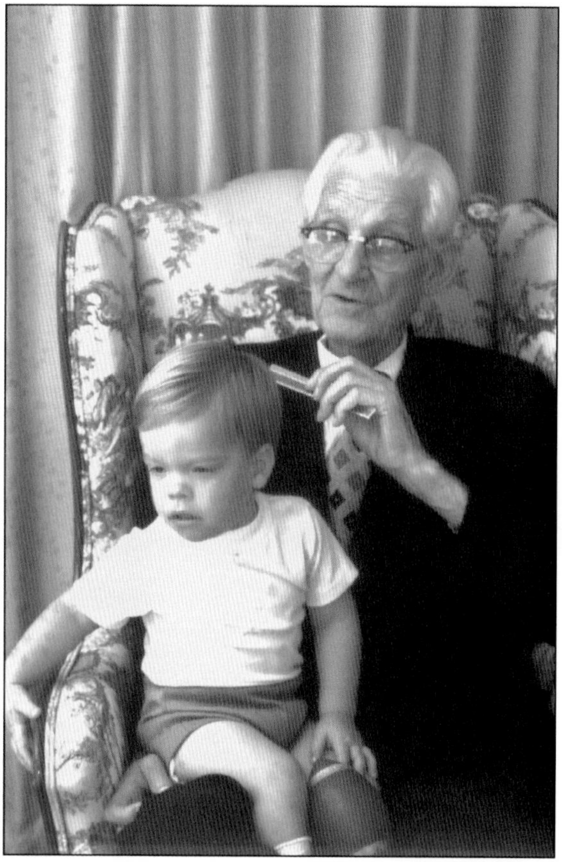

Opening the Chattanooga Barber College in 1924 at 1263 Market Street, W. T. Evans (1884–1980) trained many of the area barbers, including his son-in-law Buford Coulter. Customers received a free haircut from the student barbers, but were touched up by Evans before they left. With the onset of World War II, he closed the school due to a lack of students and opened a barbershop. He operated the shop until his retirement at 76. He is pictured here at age 95 with his great-great-grandson, Ryan Coulter.

Rising to the rank of colonel during World War II, Creed Bates (1894–1975), front row center, also served during World War I. The principal of City High School for 37 years, Bates was absolutely dedicated to making the school the best it could be and many students were successful as a result. He was also a civic leader, Sunday school superintendent, and maker of outstanding apple cider. (Photograph courtesy of Jeff Webb.)

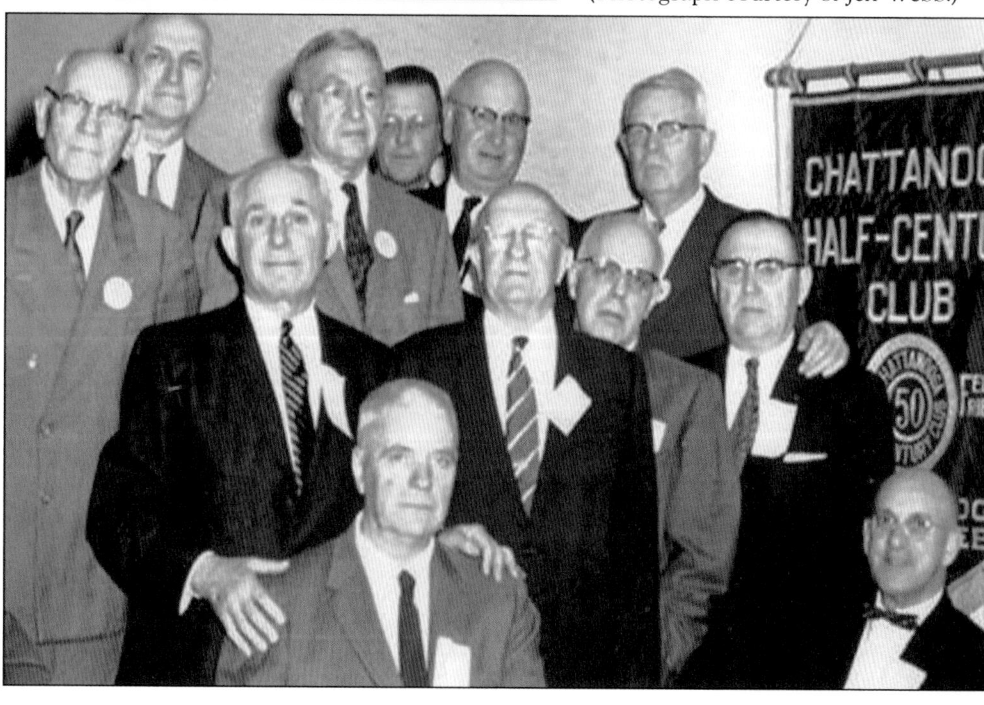

A graduate of Columbia University, Lena Barton Kain (1883–1979) began her career teaching third grade. She supervised the music program in the Johnson City schools and was the first superintendent of schools in Kingsport. Upon her marriage to John Kain III, she became the principal of Park Place Grammar School. Lena also helped found the Riverview Bird Sanctuary. She is shown here with her son, John Kain IV. (Photograph courtesy of Maria Kain Matthews.)

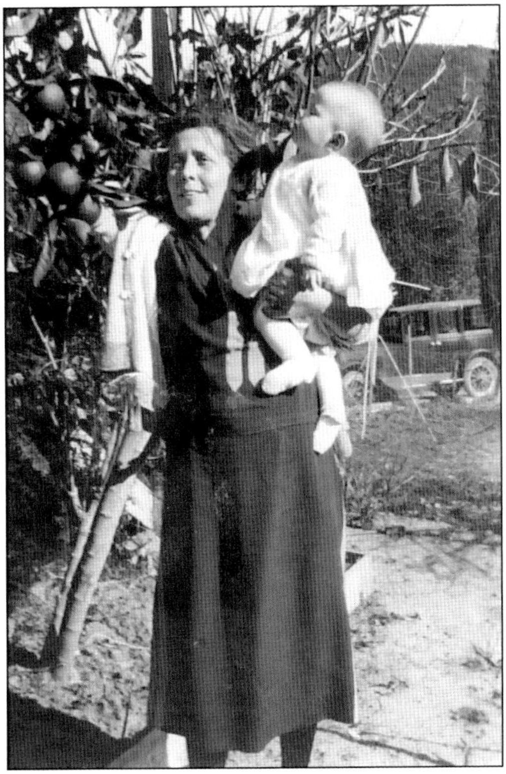

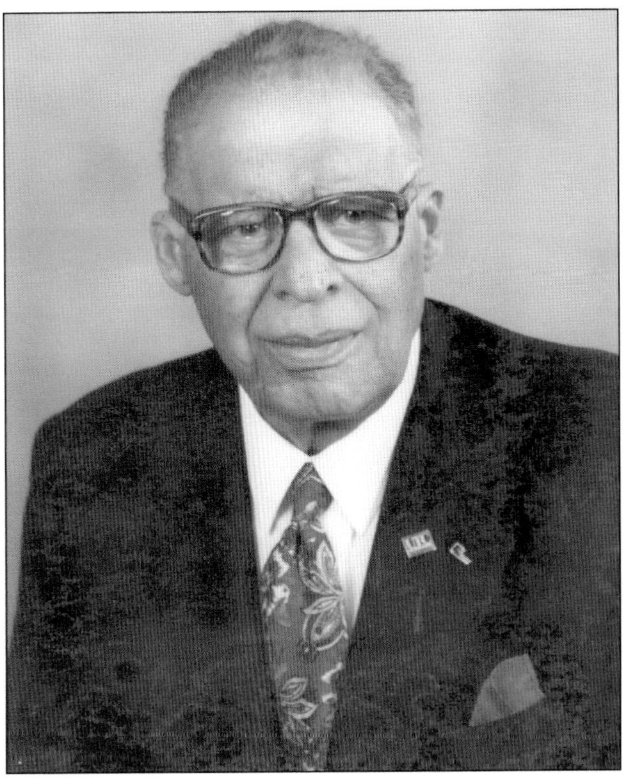

A veteran of 45 years with the Chattanooga City school system, Theodore Kennedy (1905–1978) taught at Howard High School, Orchard Knob Junior High, and Park Place School. Active in civic affairs and advancing the cause of education in the city, he was a president of the Chattanooga Education Association and was the first African American to be elected justice of the peace and foreman of a grand jury. (Photograph courtesy of the Bessie Smith Cultural Center.)

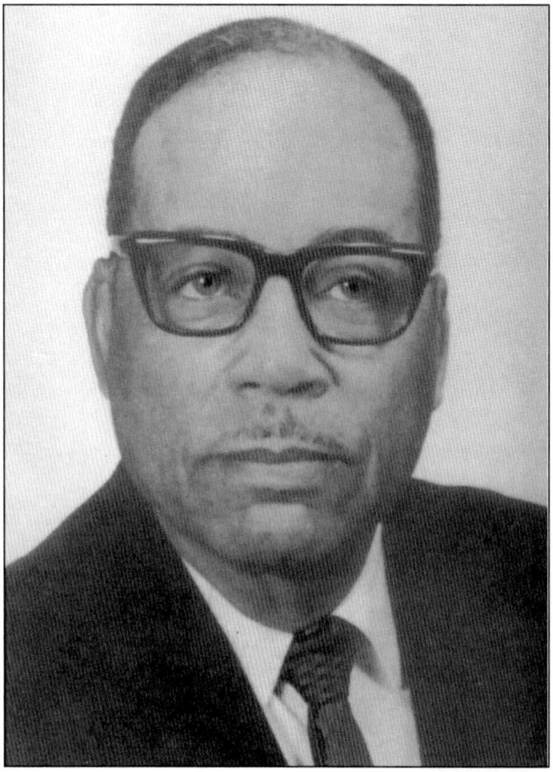

Claude C. Bond (1911–2000) became principal of Howard High School in 1956. Helping to lead the school system through the turbulent years of desegregation, he served on the school board and the Tennessee Board of Regents. The humanities building on the Chattanooga State Community College campus is named for him as well as a minority professorship in education at the University of Tennessee-Chattanooga. (Photograph courtesy of the Bessie Smith Cultural Center.)

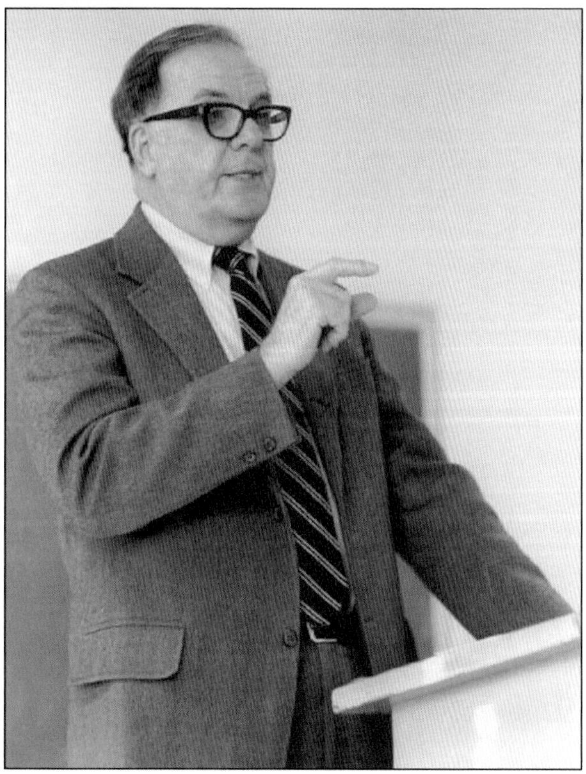

George Conner (1921–2002) is described in his obituary as a "remarkable teacher," "faithful friend," and "mentor of immense influence," but also as a "curmudgeon and notorious stickler for correct grammar." As a professor and head of the English department at the University of Chattanooga, he served the university for 26 years. He was a Guerry Professor, the university's highest faculty honor. The George Conner Professorship in American Literature was established in his honor. (Photograph courtesy of the University of Tennessee-Chattanooga.)

Jacola Goodwin (?–1995) taught at West Main Street, Clara Carpenter, and James Henry Elementary Schools. An advocate of teaching African American history in public schools, she was active in many areas of the community. She was the co-founder of the Chattanooga African American Museum, now the Bessie Smith Cultural Center. (Photograph courtesy of the Bessie Smith Cultural Center.)

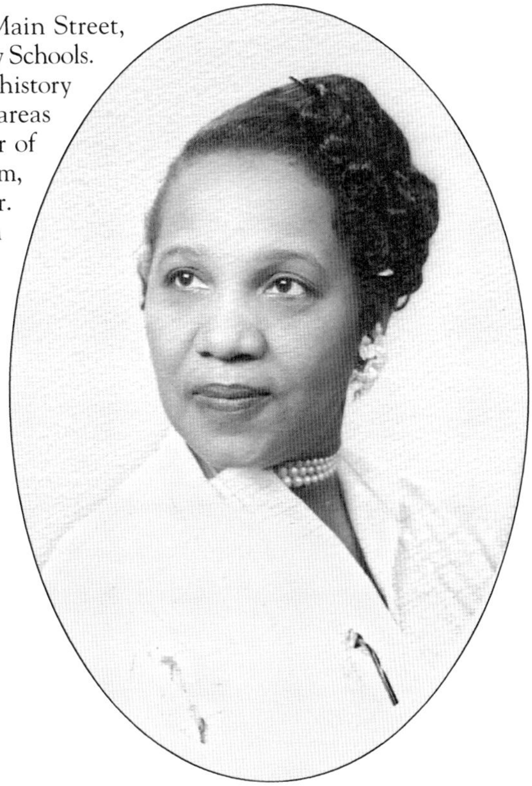

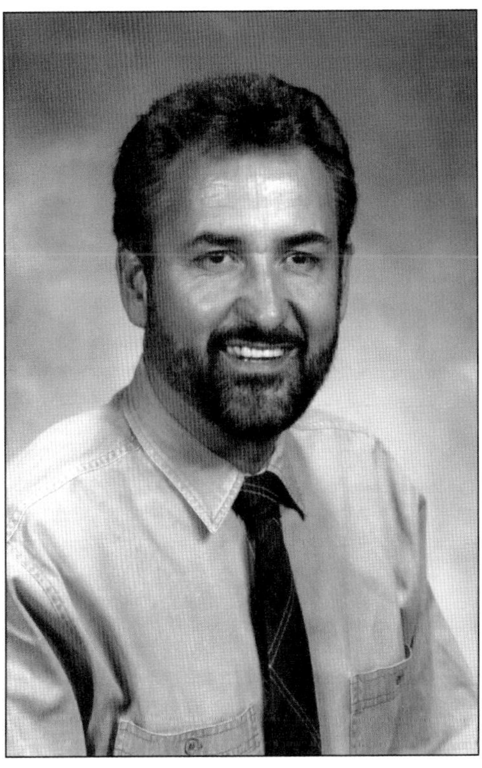

Determined to go to college, David Crawford (1941–2006) hitchhiked from his home in Scottsboro, Alabama, to Auburn with $100 in his pocket. He graduated with a master's degree in education and returned to Chattanooga, where he married his high school sweetheart and taught at Lookout Valley High and Junior High for 33 years. He was named Chattanooga Teacher of the Year and Tennessee History Teacher of the Year, and received the Tennessee Outstanding and Exemplary Teaching Award. (Photograph courtesy of Jeanne Crawford.)

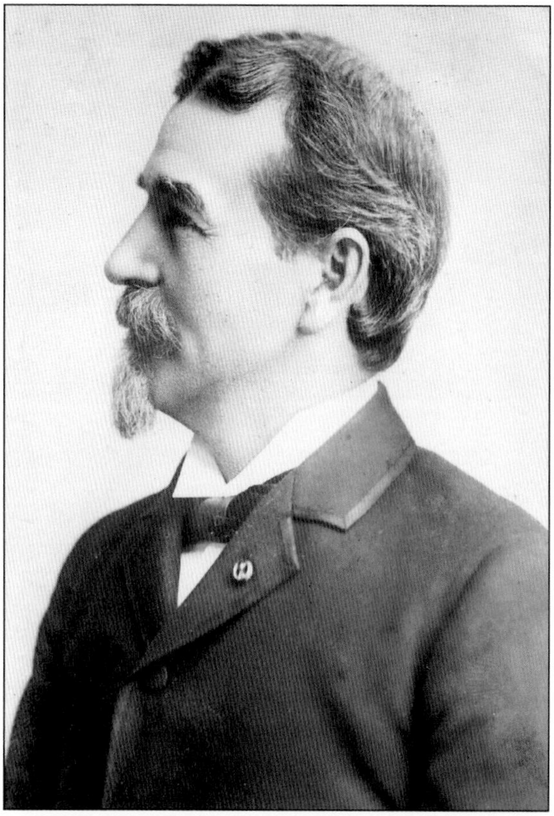

Capt. Hiram Chamberlain (1835–1916) served as chief quartermaster in the Union Army. Ohio-born, he moved to the Chattanooga area in 1867 and was associated with John Wilder in the Roane Iron Company and organized the Citico Furnace Company. He was president of the School Board of Chattanooga and the Board of Trustees of the University of Chattanooga. The university's Chamberlain Field was named for him.

Little is known about Hattie Ackerman (1840–1878). Born in Michigan, by the mid-1870s she was teaching at Chattanooga High School. In the spring and summer of 1878, yellow fever spread rapidly across the south. Chattanooga recorded its first death in August and many people fled the city in search of healthier areas. Ackerman was among those who volunteered to remain and care for the sick. She succumbed to the disease on October 13. Originally buried in Citizen's Cemetery, she was moved to Forest Hills Cemetery in 1928.

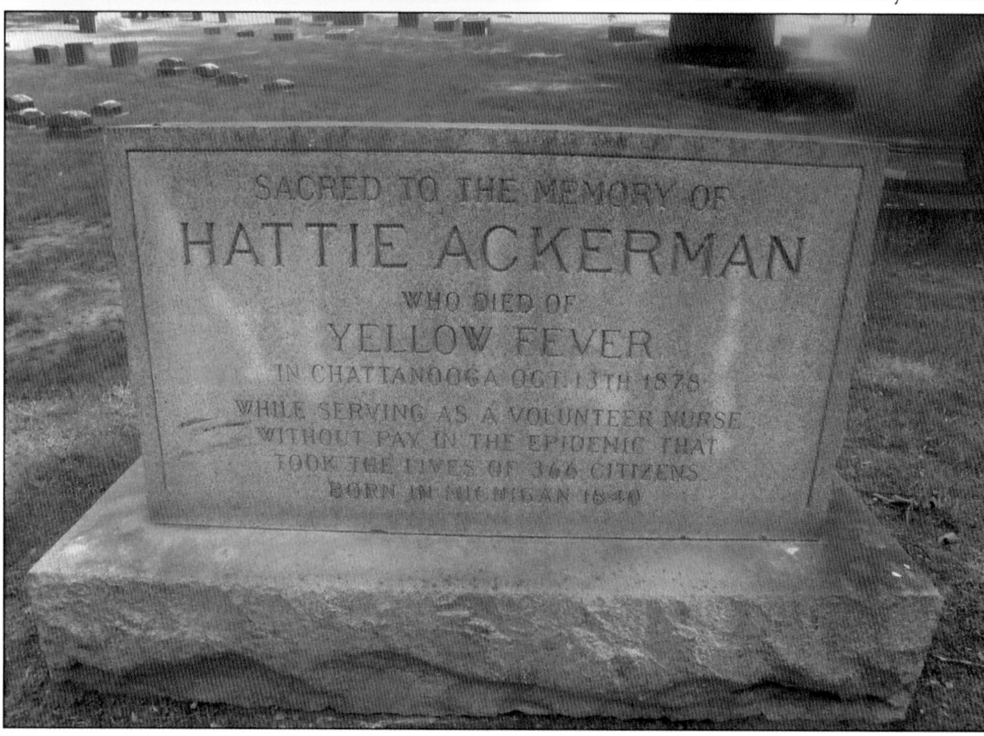

Seven

Medicine

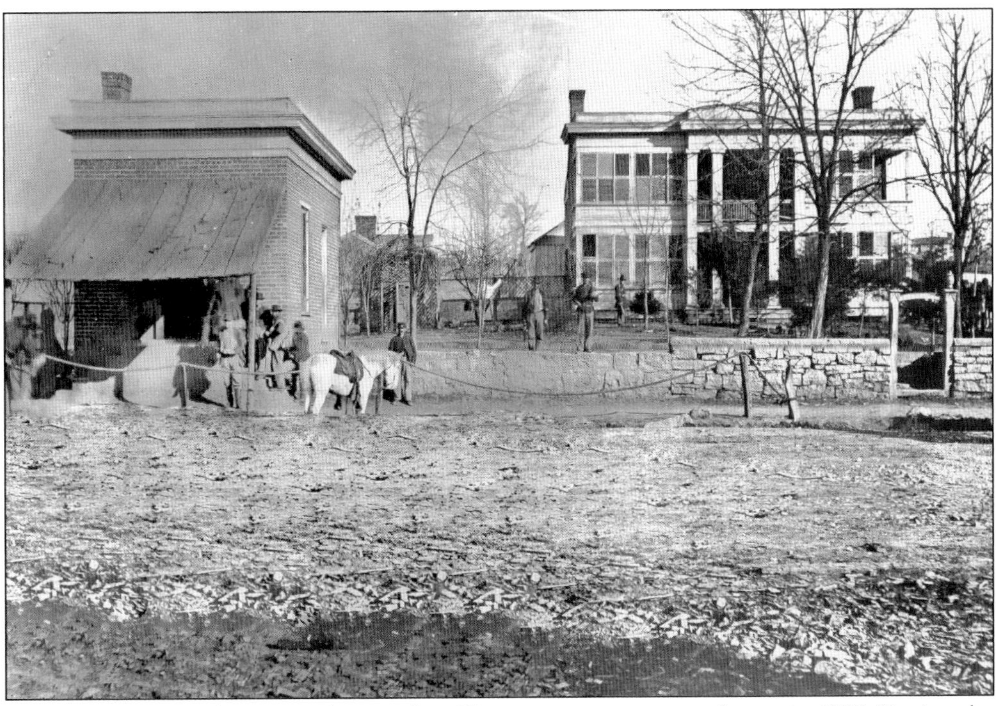

Dr. Philander Sims (1828–1920) arrived in Chattanooga as a young doctor in 1856. During the Civil War, he tended the wounded from both sides. He also treated the sick during the cholera and yellow fever epidemics of the 1870s, even when others shunned them. He was well known for his work in prison reform, for the care of those with contagious disease, and for the prevention of epidemics. This photograph shows his home and office.

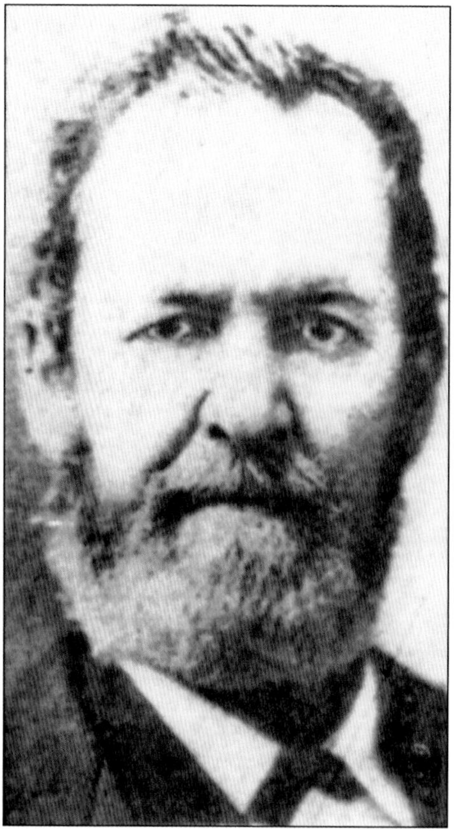

Dr. Joseph Gillespie (1821–1896) came to Ross's Landing after completing his medical training at the Louisville Medical College. In 1848, he married Penelope Whiteside, daughter of James Whiteside and his first wife, Thankful. Gillespie served as mayor of Chattanooga in 1844 and 1845. An ardent supporter of the Confederacy, he was arrested by Union troops for his outspoken views, but was released to treat the wounded from the many battles in and around Chattanooga.

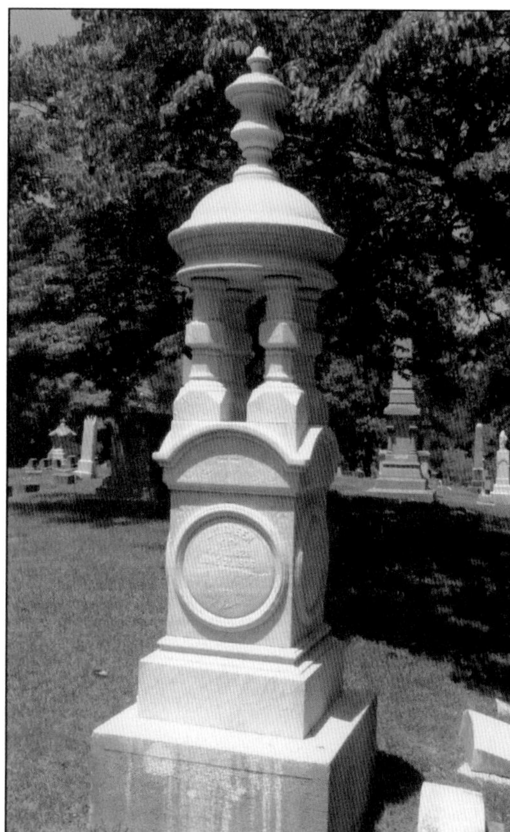

Originally from Kentucky, Dr. Lapsley Yantis Green (1829–1906) and Caroline Walker (1831–1903) settled in Chattanooga shortly after their marriage. When the Civil War broke out, Dr. Green joined the Confederate Army, rising to the rank of regimental surgeon in the 19th Tennessee Infantry Regiment. Caroline stayed in the city and is listed as one of the volunteer nurses who tended the sick and wounded throughout the war.

When Elizabeth Anderson McFarland (1829–1863) came to the John Ross home as a bride, her husband, Thomas, was a successful merchant and landholder. During the Civil War, her home was used as a hospital for both Union and Confederate wounded. She died of camp fever, contracted while nursing the sick and wounded. In 1911, Elizabeth and Thomas were removed from their family cemetery and reinterred at Forest Hills Cemetery.

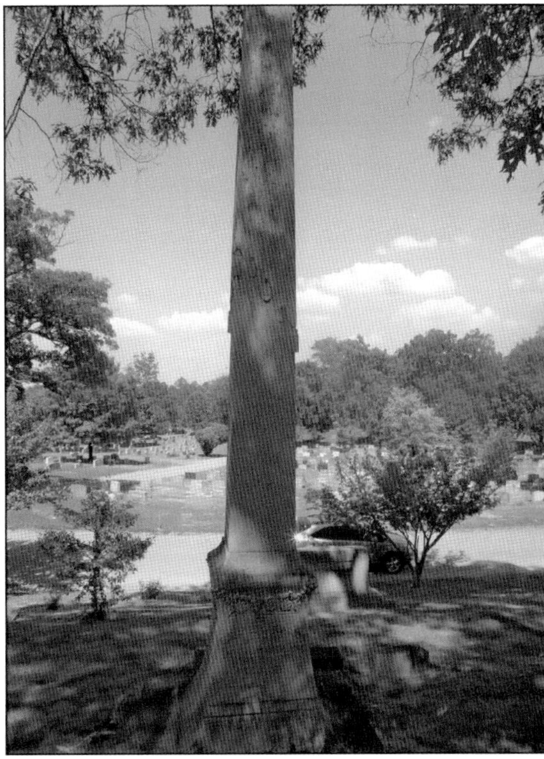

An 1873 graduate of Belleview Hospital Medical College in New York, George Baxter, M. D. (1850–1908), established his surgical practice in Chattanooga in 1875. He contracted yellow fever during the epidemic of 1878, but remained in the city to tend the sick. When Erlanger Hospital opened in 1899, Baxter was named chief of staff.

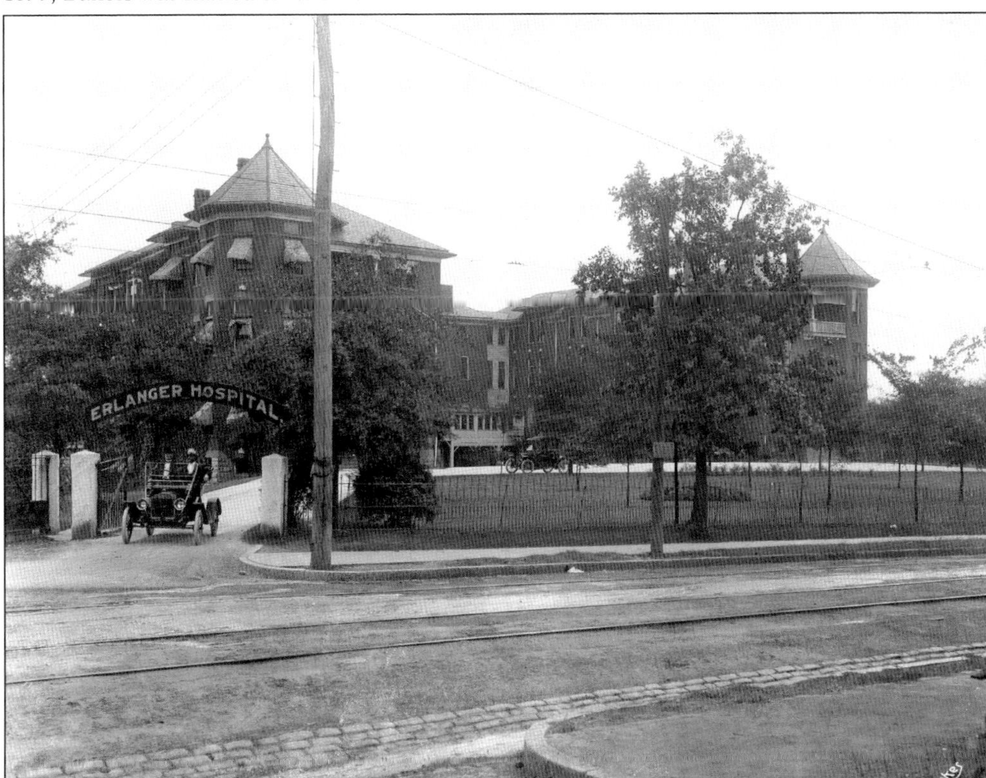

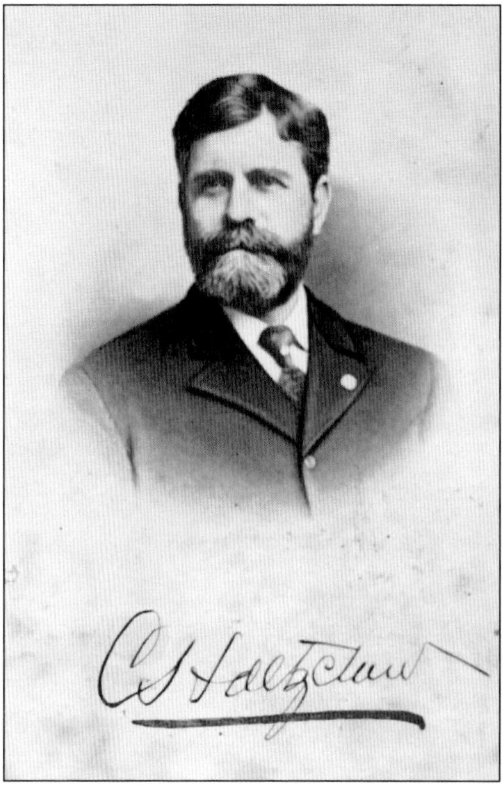

Dr. Cooper Holtzclaw (1861–1929), a graduate of the Atlanta Medical College, began his medical practice in Dalton. In 1884, he opened a practice in Chattanooga. Over the next 40-plus years, he served as chief surgeon of the Hamilton County Infirmary, played a prominent role in the founding of Baroness Erlanger Hospital, and served on the faculty of the Chattanooga Medical College.

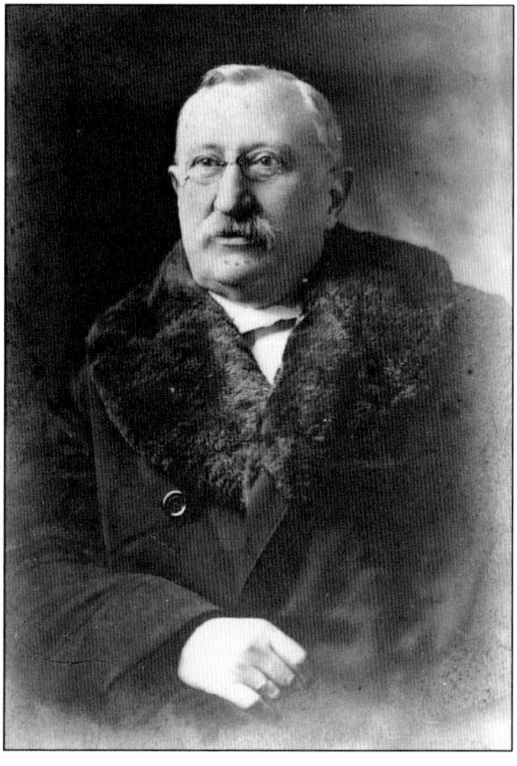

Born and educated in Germany, Dr. Henry Berlin (1852–1916) came to Chattanooga in the 1870s. A faculty member of the Chattanooga Medical School, he was on the first medical staff of Erlanger Hospital. In 1914, while he was on a trip with other local physicians, war was declared and the party was routed to England. Berlin's friends were forced to smuggle him onto a return ship as a stowaway to prevent him from being interned.

Born in Germany, Sister Lucy Wissmann (1869–1966), Chattanooga's first trained nurse, arrived in Chattanooga in 1895. She was Dr. Henry Berlin's surgical nurse for 14 years. After his death, she became a much sought-after private duty maternity and baby nurse. She cared for 336 children. Pictures of "her babies" adorned the walls of her Barton Avenue home until her death. (Photograph courtesy of Erlanger Medical Center.)

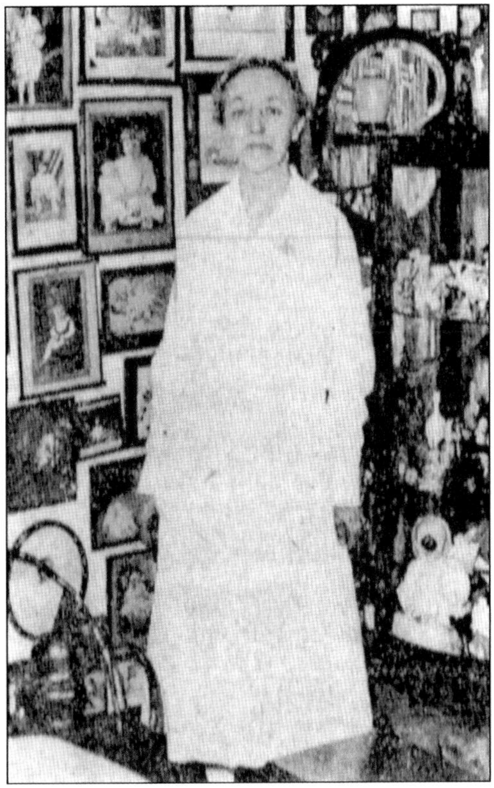

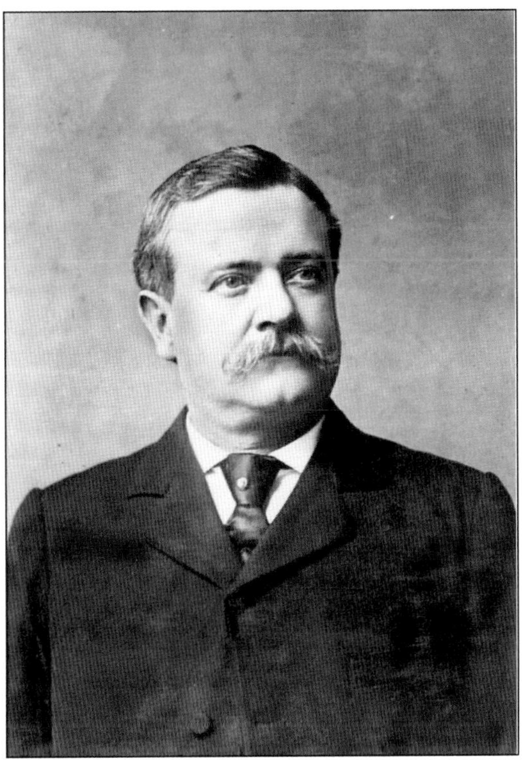

Ohioan Dr. John Rathmell (1852–1915), a graduate of Ohio Wesleyan University, came to Chattanooga to practice medicine about 1884. He was instrumental in organizing the Chattanooga University College of Medicine and served as the dean of the college until its closure.

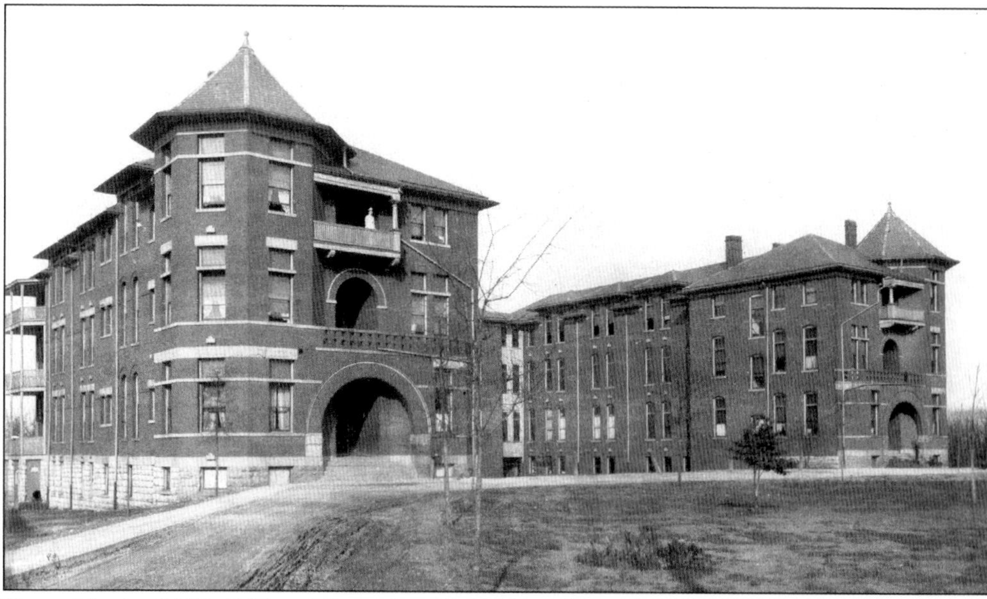

Sisters Martha (1887–1943) and Emma Igou (?–1918) graduated from the Erlanger School of Nursing in 1911. Emma died in the flu epidemic of 1918, while Martha continued a 50-year nursing career. From about 1920 until shortly before her death, she held supervisory positions at the hospital. At that time, many nursing supervisors lived in a home adjacent to the hospital. They routinely worked 12-hour shifts, five days a week.

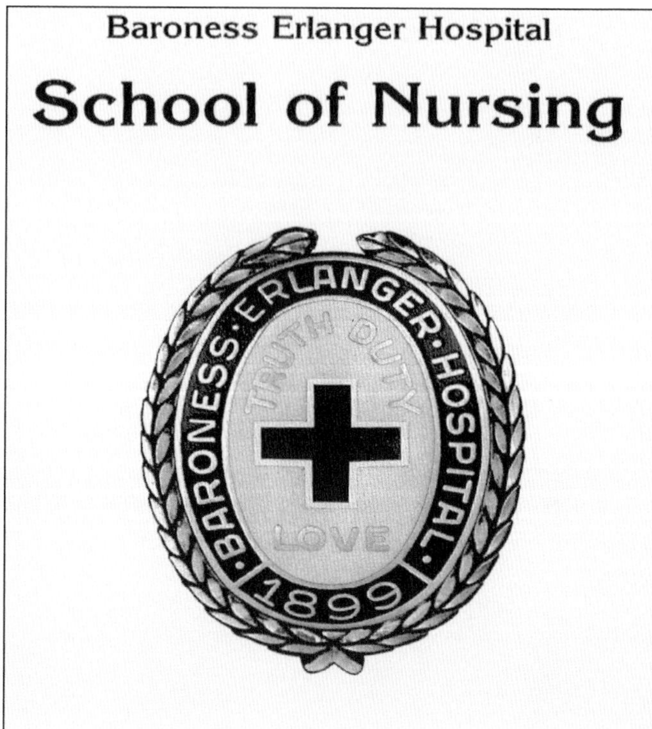

Helen Steele (1891–1961) was the Erlanger Hospital's director of nursing from 1946 through 1949. She had returned to hospital duty during World War II, when the hospital saw more than 100 nurses leave to join the armed services and the Red Cross. She remained to help guide the hospital through the busiest years of the post-war baby boom and the creation, in 1947, of Carver Hospital, a facility for African Americans. (Photograph courtesy of Erlanger Medical Center.)

Elizabeth Parker Newman (1905–1981) was the Director of Nursing Education at the Erlanger School of Nursing from 1938 until 1950. At that time, nursing education was open exclusively to single women and included a rigorous three-year program, mandatory residence in the nursing dormitory on the hospital campus, and at least five hours per day of duty in the hospital.

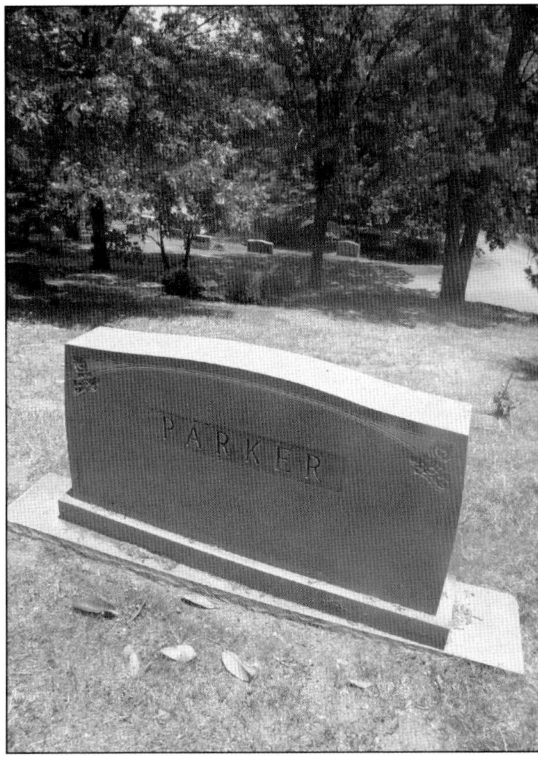

Graduating from the Erlanger School of Nursing in 1907, by 1914 Harriet Pearson was the hospital superintendent, a post she held for the next 22 years, until the position was given to physicians. Seeing the hospital though the expansions of the 1920s and the Depression of the 1930s, her obituary describes her as "strict in everything," especially the education of the nurses and the managing of young interns. This photograph shows Erlanger Hospital in the early 1920s.

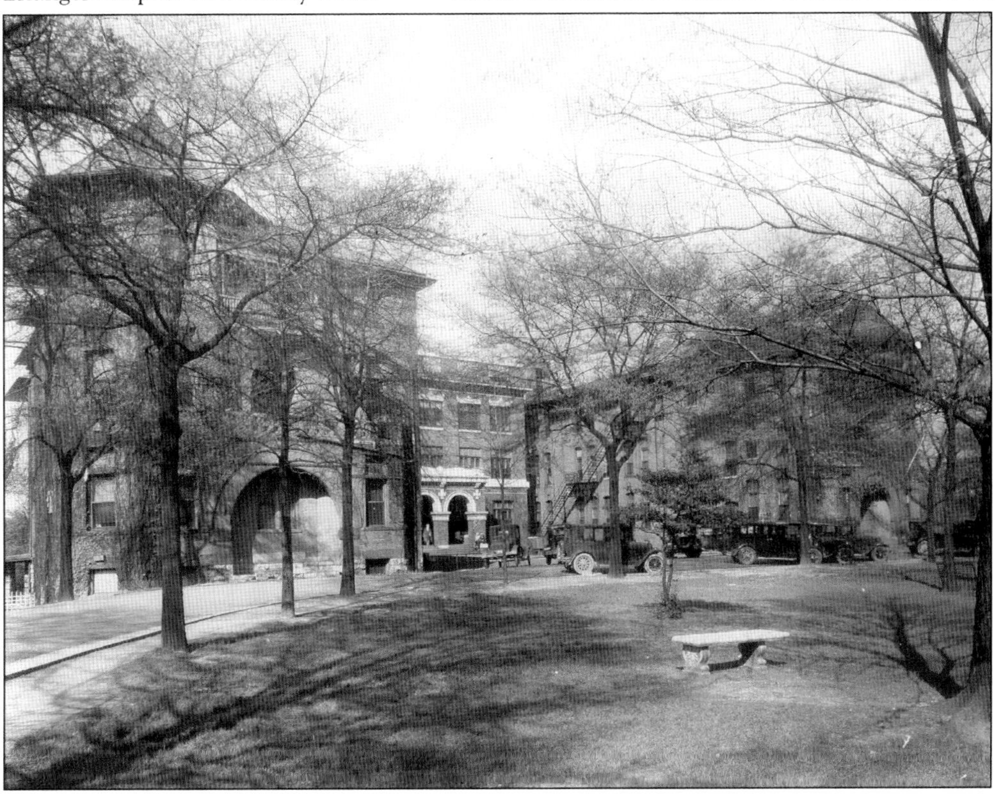

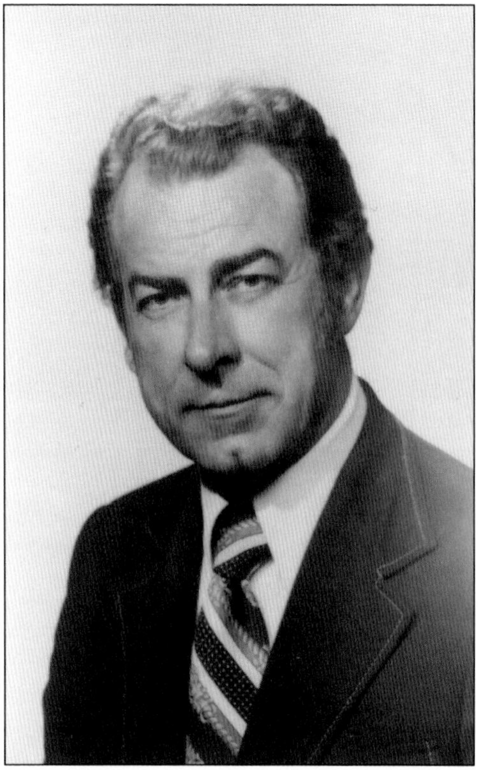

Serving as a physician in both the U.S. Navy and Army, Dr. Maurice Rawlings (1922–2010) also attended Pres. Dwight Eisenhower and the Joint Chiefs of Staff. A cardiologist and clinical professor at the University of Tennessee, he was an internationally recognized consultant and author. Several of his books, including *Beyond Death's Door*, were based on interviews concerning the experiences of clinically dead patients after their resuscitation. (Photograph courtesy of Patty Rawlings Proudy.)

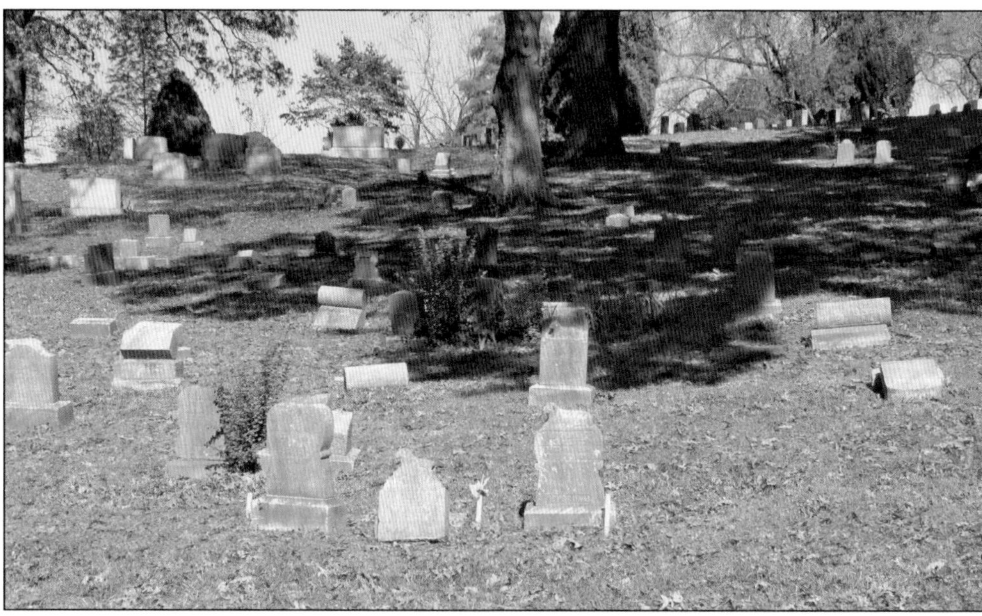

Gertrude Graham, M.D. (?–1912), died during an operation at Erlanger Hospital. A practicing physician in Chattanooga, she secretly married Hugh Timothy 10 months before her death. Timothy was studying medicine in Atlanta and the couple was not living together. The marriage was not announced until her death. Her grave at the rear of Forest Hills Cemetery is unmarked.

Eight

The Arts, Entertainment, and Athletics

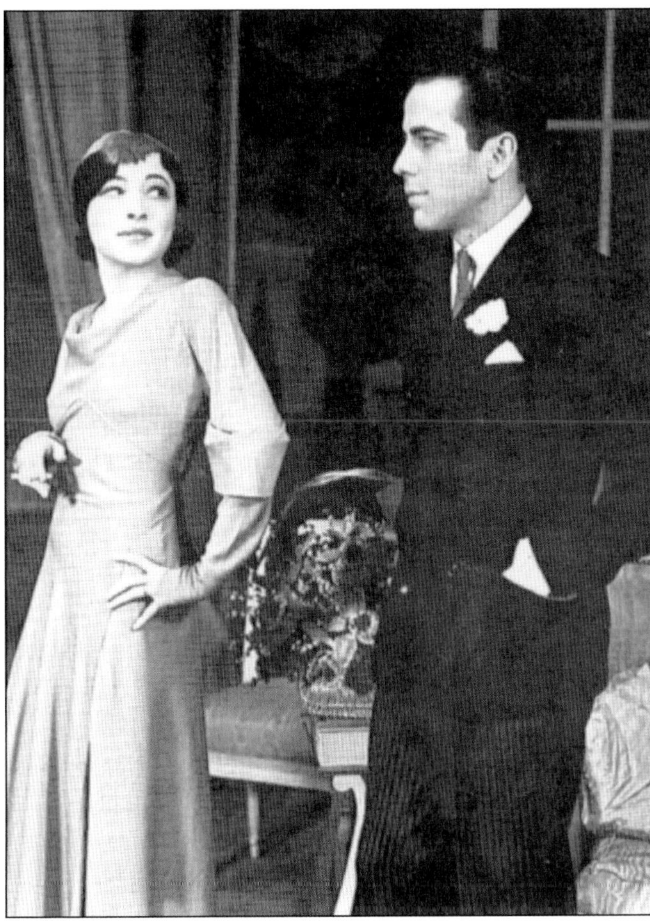

Dorothy Patten (1905–1975) wanted to be an actress from early childhood. The only child of Zeboim Charles Patten and Helen Lyerly, she made her Broadway debut in 1930 in *Stepdaughters of War*. Shown here with Humphrey Bogart in the 1933 production of *The Mask and the Face*, she appeared in 30 Broadway productions, as well as several movies and television shows. (Photograph courtesy of the Forest Hills Cemetery.)

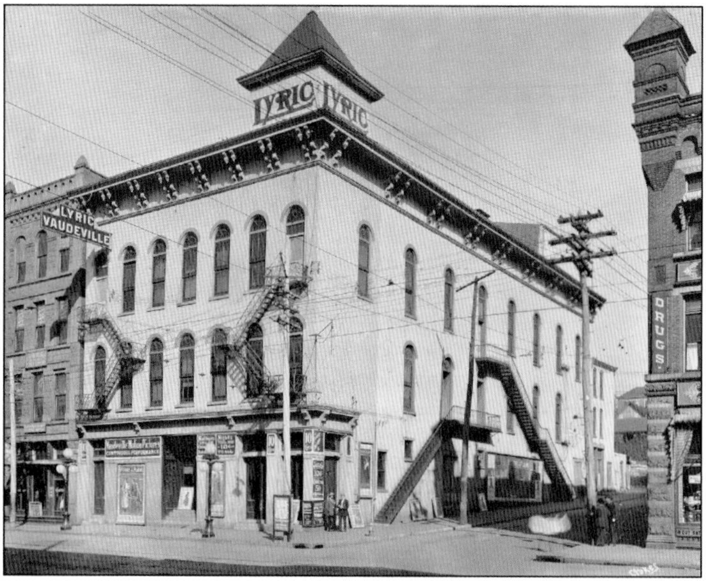

When the Tivoli Theater opened in 1921, one of the highlights was the debut of the Tivoli Symphony Orchestra, which accompanied silent movies. This debut was one of the highlights of Louis Pahmeyer's (1824–1900) career as a professional musician. He played the flute with the Tivoli Orchestra, as well as the Lyric Theater and Saffer's Orchestras. He also played the piccolo with Spence's Military Band.

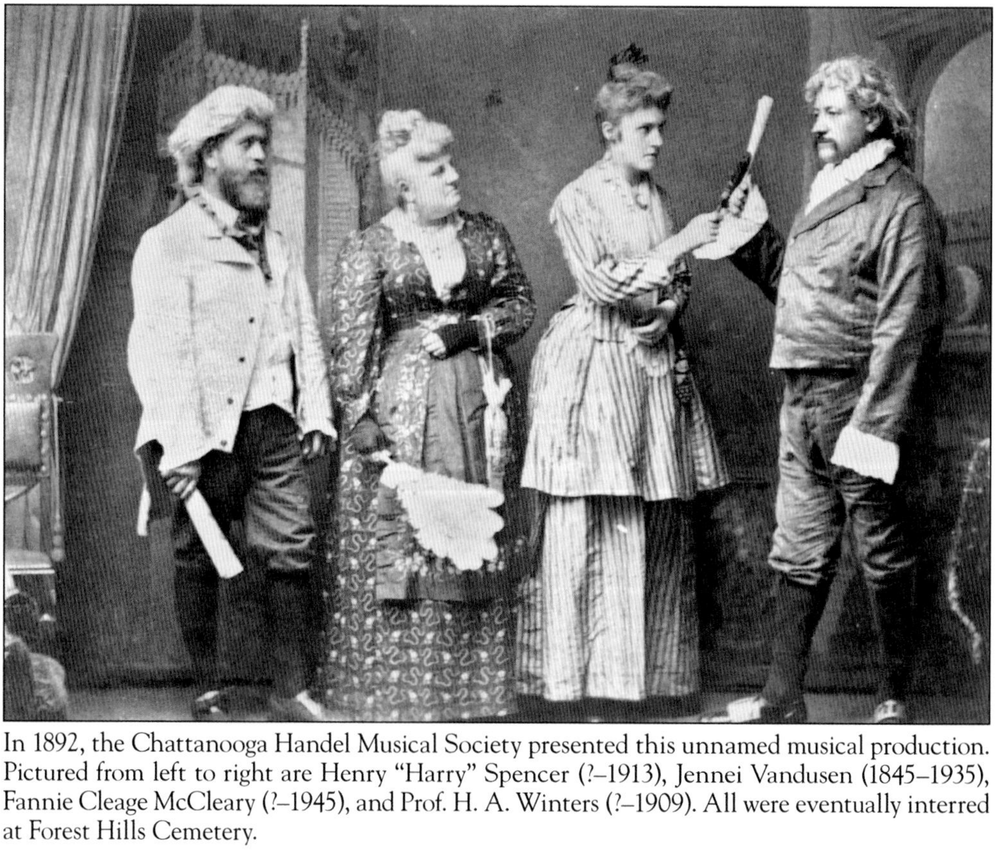

In 1892, the Chattanooga Handel Musical Society presented this unnamed musical production. Pictured from left to right are Henry "Harry" Spencer (?–1913), Jennei Vandusen (1845–1935), Fannie Cleage McCleary (?–1945), and Prof. H. A. Winters (?–1909). All were eventually interred at Forest Hills Cemetery.

Arthur Stivers (1855–1929) was a manger at Loomis and Company, a lumberyard and furniture business on West Eighth Street. He was also an amateur photographer. Stivers's photograph scrapbooks, including early pictures of many area landmarks, were eventually donated to the Chattanooga-Hamilton County Library.

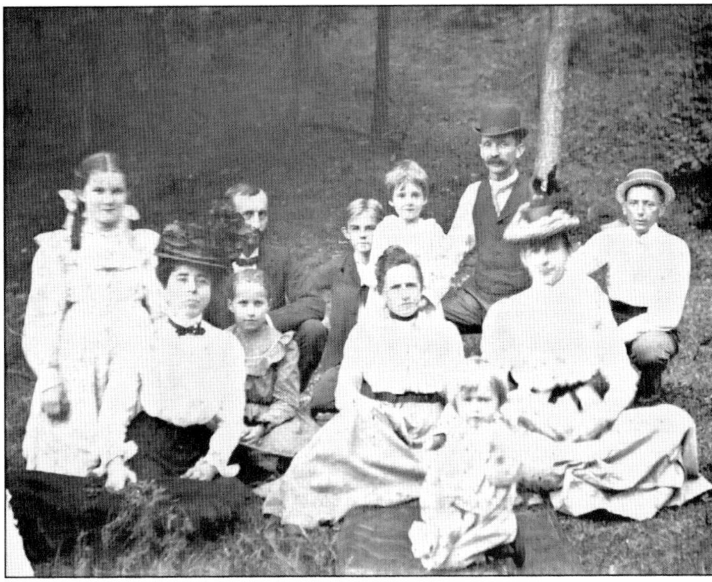

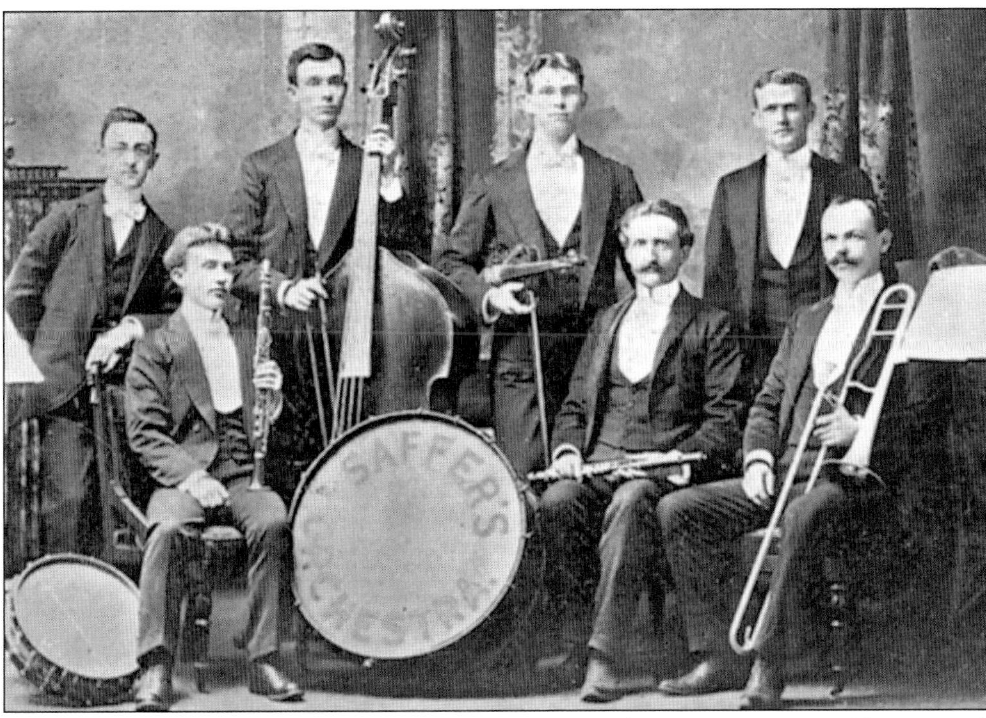

Saffer's Orchestra is pictured here around 1900 at the Lookout Mountain Inn. Chattanooga's leading orchestra from 1900 until 1915, members included, from left to right, Charles Parks, drums; Thomas Thorbahn, clarinet; Frank Saffer, bass violin; George Saffer, violin; Louis Phameyer (1876–1900), flute; George Gault (1875–1913), piano; and William Stuart, trombone.

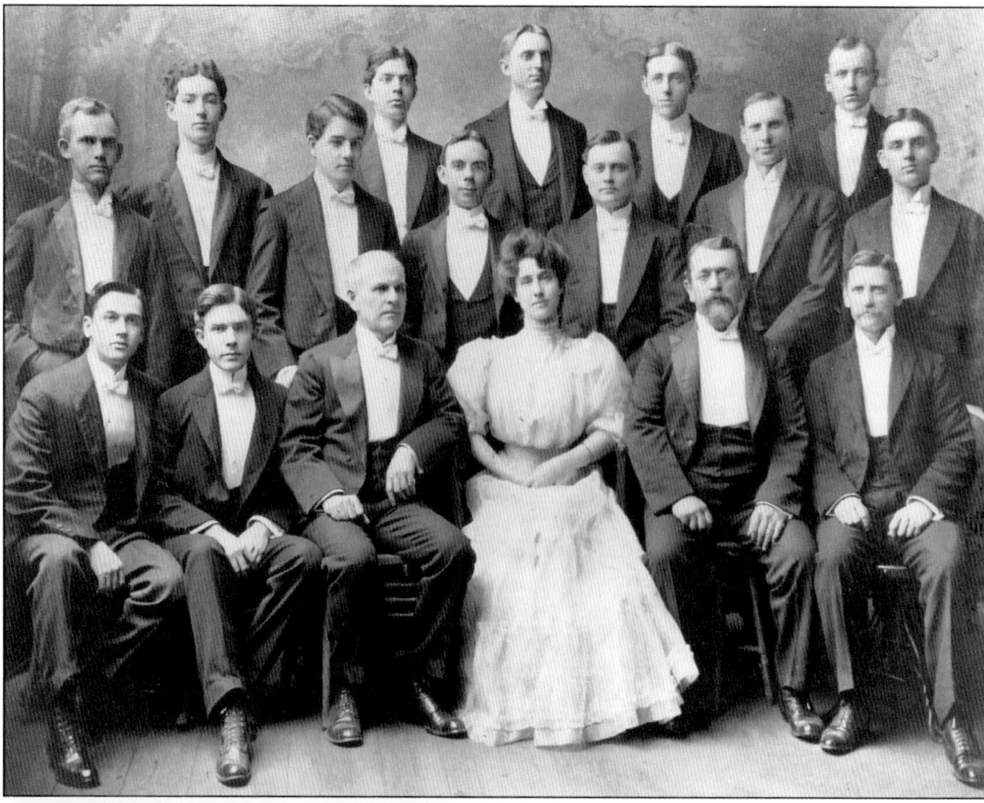

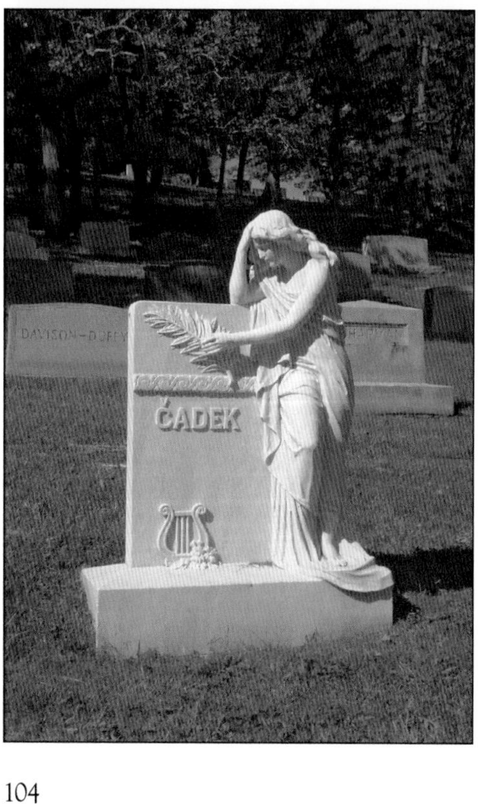

In 1907, the Chattanooga Glee Club sat for this picture. Members included, from left to right, (first row) Guy Landis, Glenn Young, William Stephens (?–1912), Jennie Moore (accompanist), Herbert Spencer (?–1956), and Richard George (1863–1955); (second row) Lon Warner (1872–1942), Walter Heasty, Dick Park (1872–1942), W. L. Catlin Jr. (?–1932) R. F. Callaway, Henry Becker (1879–1940), and Ishmail Payne; (third row) A. Bryson Webb (died at age 36), unidentified, Robert Porter (?–1961), and Joe Arledge (?–1949).

Born in Prague, violinist Joseph Cadek (1868–1927) immigrated to the United States in 1892 to join the Boston Symphony and played with them at the Lookout Mountain Inn during the summer of 1893. Stating that the area reminded him of his home in Europe, he returned to Chattanooga, eventually opening the Southern Conservatory of Music and later Cadek Conservatory. Following his death, the conservatory was merged with the then-University of Chattanooga.

Hinton Alexander (1850–1925) attended Fisk University and was a member of the Fisk University Jubilee Singers. He returned to Chattanooga from Nashville and was a mail carrier from 1883 through 1921.

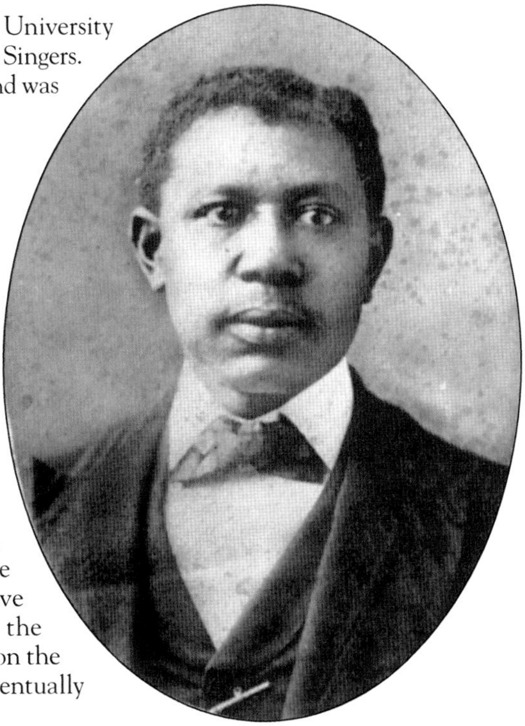

George Thomas Hunter (1886–1950) came to Chattanooga to work at his uncle Benjamin Thomas's Coca-Cola Bottling Company. Beginning with a clerical position, he rose to company president. In 1917, he took leave from the company to serve as a captain in the U.S. Army. A bachelor, he built the mansion on the bluff overlooking the Tennessee River that eventually became the Hunter Museum of Art.

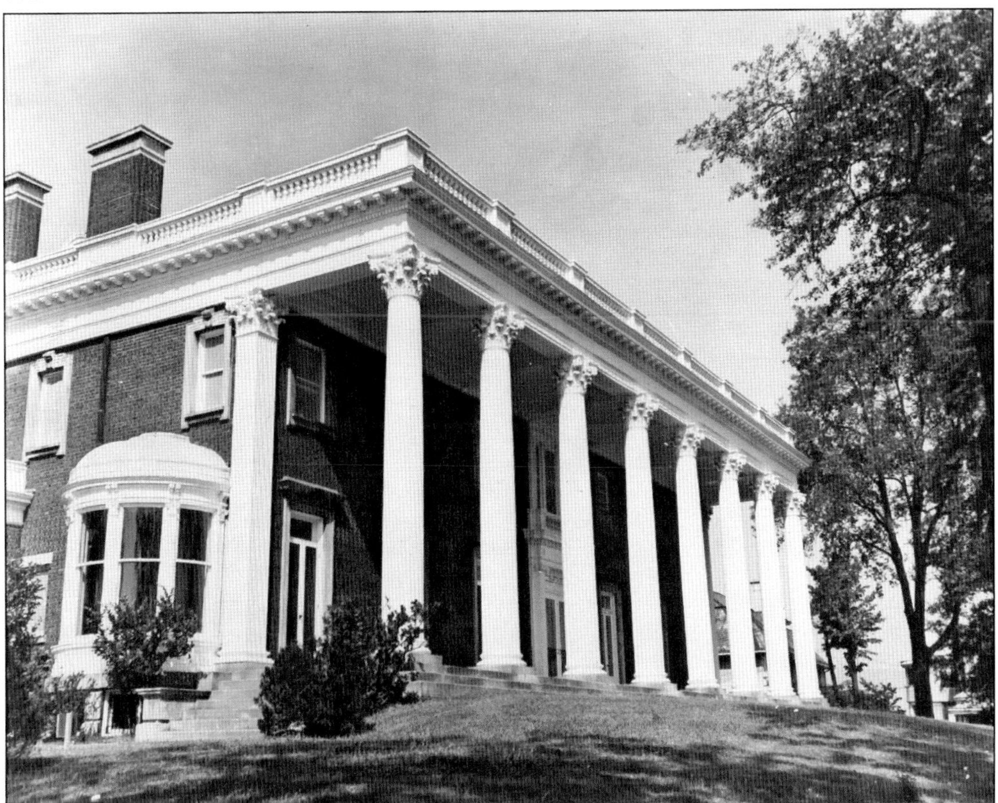

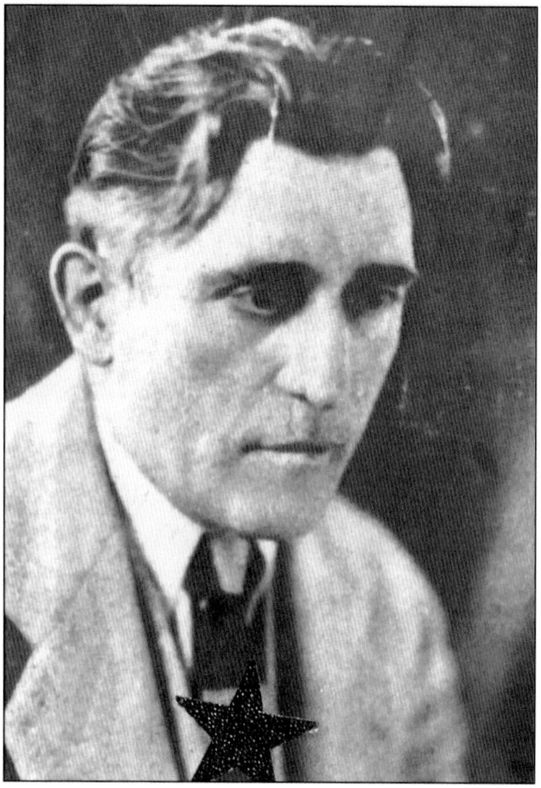

According to a 1920 review in the *Lookout*, "to hear Oscar Seagle sing is to enter deeply in the romance, the passion and the joy of living that distinguishes the Southland." A baritone, Seagle (1878–1945) studied in France and later opened a school in Paris. With the advent of World War I, he returned to America and performed and taught vocal music across the United States. He returned home to Chattanooga on several occasions to give concerts, including a 1920 concert with evangelist Billy Sunday.

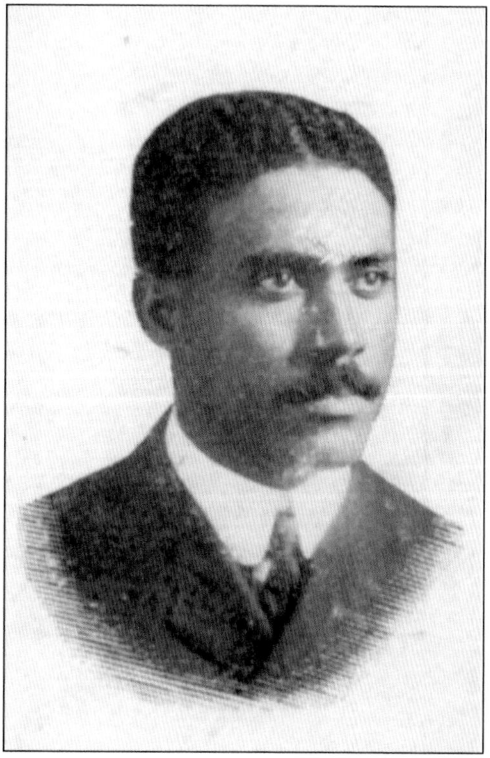

J. Bliss White (1848–1927) was a lawyer and an orator, but his most-lasting contribution was as an author. In 1904, he wrote the *Biography and Achievements of the Colored Citizens of Chattanooga.* Without this excellent resource much of the history of African Americans in Chattanooga would have been lost forever.

Newspaperman, poet, and musician Lorenzo "Lon" Warner (1865–1927) wrote this poem while living in St. Elmo. Born in Ohio, he came to Chattanooga in 1885. Warner worked for the *Chattanooga Times* for a number of years before moving to work in Knoxville and later Miami, Florida. His obituary states that his "heart-home" however, was always Chattanooga.

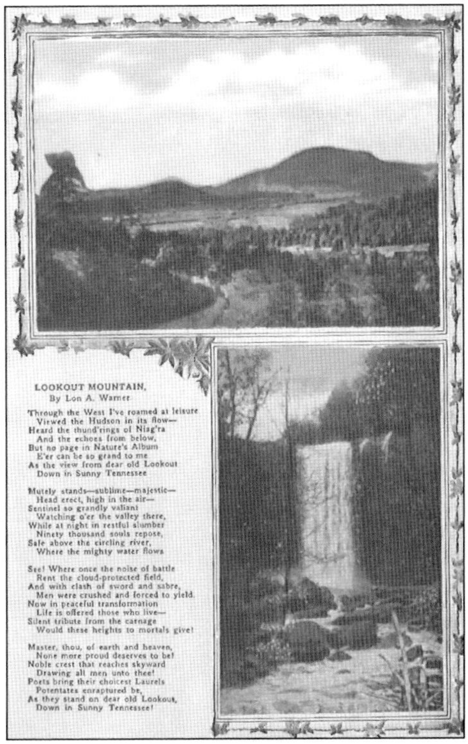

LOOKOUT MOUNTAIN,
By Lon A. Warner

Through the West I've roamed at leisure
Viewed the Hudson in its flow—
Heard the thund'rings of Niag'ra
And the echoes from below,
But no page in Nature's Album
E'er can be so grand to me
As the view from dear old Lookout
Down in Sunny Tennessee

Mutely stands—sublime—majestic—
Head erect, high in the air—
Sentinel so grandly valiant
Watching o'er the valley there,
While at night in restful slumber
Ninety thousand souls repose,
Safe above the circling river,
Where the mighty water flows

See! Where once the noise of battle
Rent the cloud-protected field,
And with clash of sword and sabre,
Men were crushed and forced to yield.
Now in peaceful transformation
Life is offered those who live—
Silent tribute from the carnage
Would these heights to mortals give!

Master, thou, of earth and heaven,
None more proud deserves to be!
Noble crest that reaches skyward
Drawing all men unto thee!
Poets bring their choicest Laurels
Potentates enraptured be,
As they stand on dear old Lookout,
Down in Sunny Tennessee!

Called the "Tennessee Nightingale" by the time her parents moved to Chattanooga in 1932, Grace Moore (1901–1947) had already established herself as a Broadway and movie operatic soprano and actress. Seen here in 1937 with Cary Grant and other members of the cast of *When You Are In Love*, she was nominated for an Oscar for Best Actress for her role in *One Night of Love*. (Photograph courtesy of Forest Hills Cemetery.)

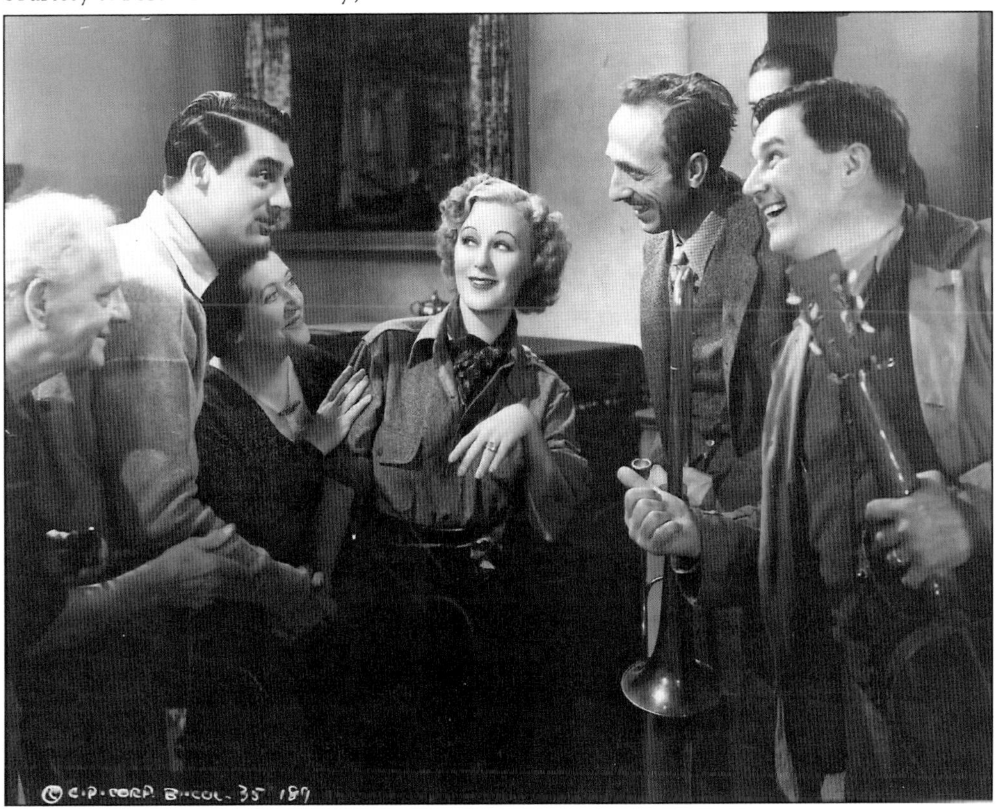

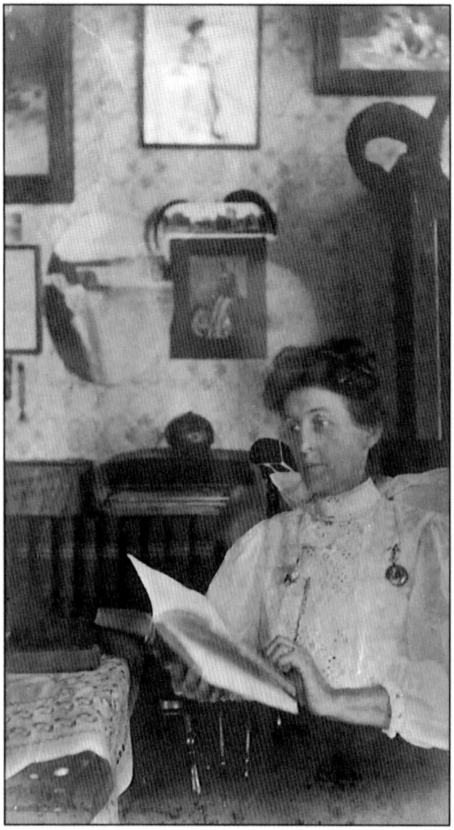

According to the *Chattanooga Times*, Cora Sanders Mighton (1865–1948) was a "spunky red-head." She attended the University of Chicago prior to her marriage to builder James Mighton. An artist, she painted many oil and watercolor landscapes and still-lifes. A mother of two, she traveled across the United States while her husband worked as a contractor on various construction projects. The couple were in San Francisco in 1906 when the great earthquake struck. (Photograph courtesy of John Doyle.)

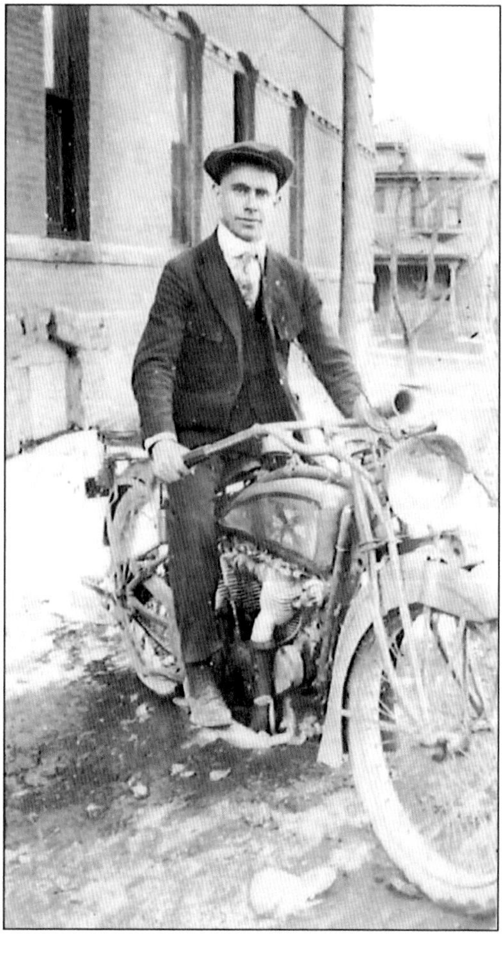

Following his sweetheart Ruby Losey to Tennessee from Indiana, Leo Lambert (1895–1950) began exploring the caves on Lookout Mountain. Feeling that these caves should be open to the public, he purchased 30 acres on the side of the mountain. Drilling down 260 feet, Lambert descended down the shaft and found astounding formations and a 145-foot waterfall. Lambert's discovery, which he named Ruby Falls, was opened to the public in 1930. (Photograph courtesy of Jeanne Crawford.)

Pinning her dress down the middle and wearing men's work boots, Ruby Lambert (1896–1951) followed her husband 420 feet down into the cave to the waterfall he discovered in December 1928. She later recalled that he said to her, "Do you see that falls, the one God gave us . . . we are going to call it Ruby Falls." Reuben Hunt designed the Cavern House from sketches provided by Leo and Ruby. The building continues to serve as the entrance to Ruby Falls. (Photograph courtesy of Jeanne Crawford.)

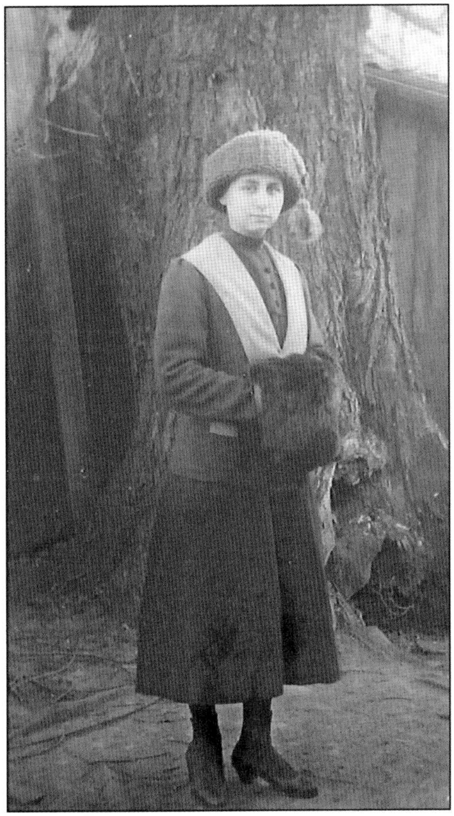

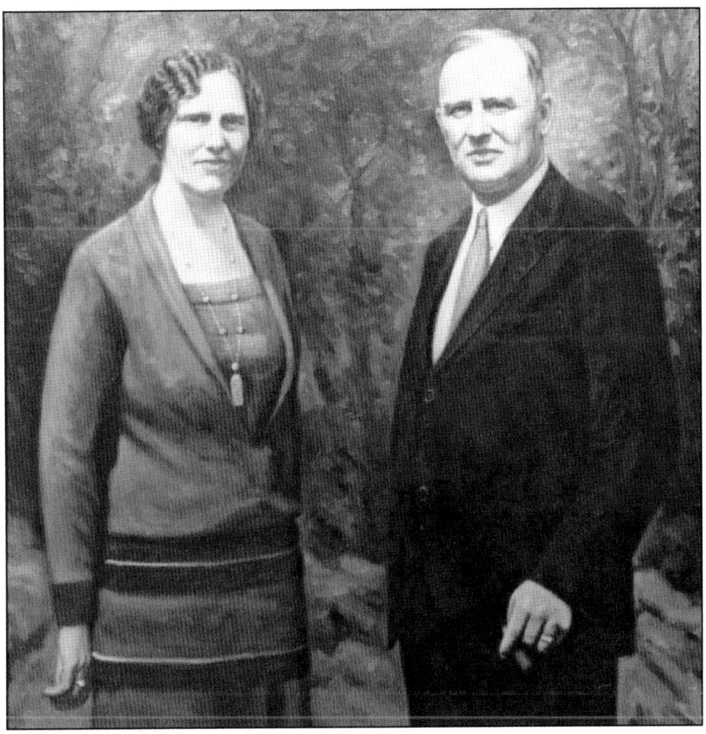

Garnet (1883–1954) and Frieda Untermohlen Carter (1880–1964) developed the Fairyland community on Lookout Mountain in 1924. A marriage of business sense and artistic imagination, Garnet invented "putt-putt golf," originally called "Tom Thumb Golf." At the same time, Frieda laid out the trails and gardens atop Lookout Mountain, which were to become Rock City Gardens. When they opened to the public in 1932, Garnet arranged to have "See Rock City" painted on approximately 900 barns across America.

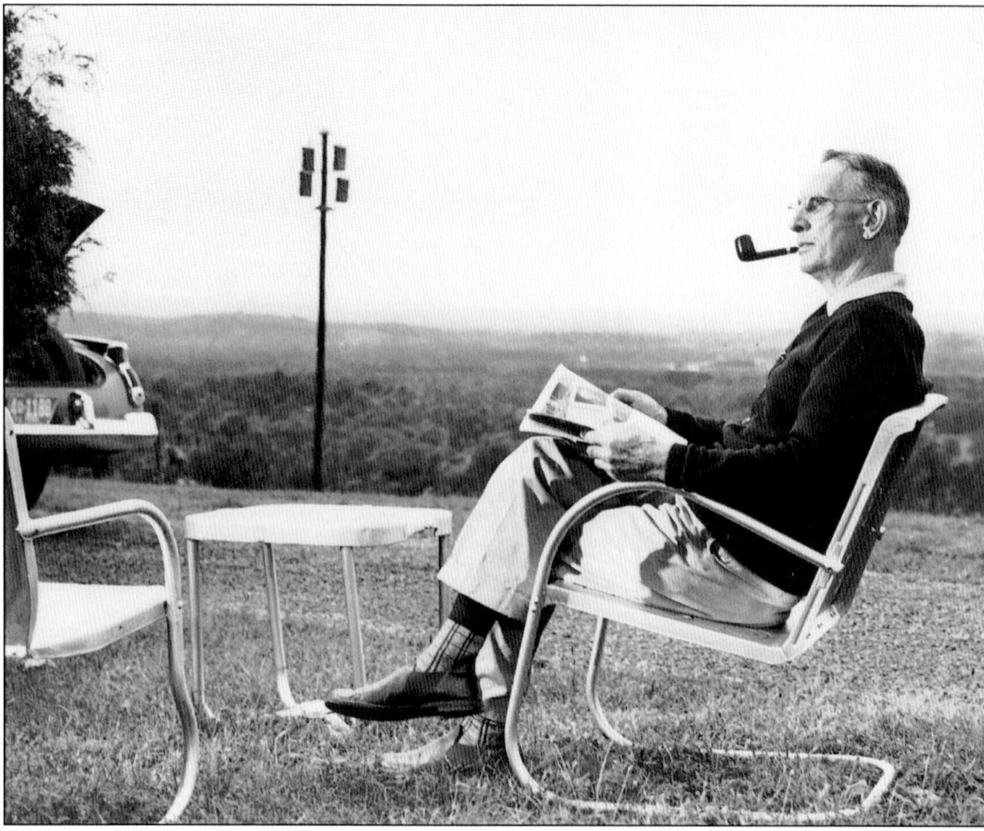

A native of Indiana, Claude Fuller (1877–1957) held 50 patents and designed brick-making plants. Retiring in 1933, he wrote five books on historic firearms. According to the *Chattanooga Times*, he had one of the "finest collections of (historic guns) in the United States," which he gave to the Chickamauga National Military Park. He also donated his collections of Confederate currency and bank notes and hundreds of Chattanooga-related soft drink, medicine, and liquor bottles to museums. At his death he donated his home and property to the Audubon Society.

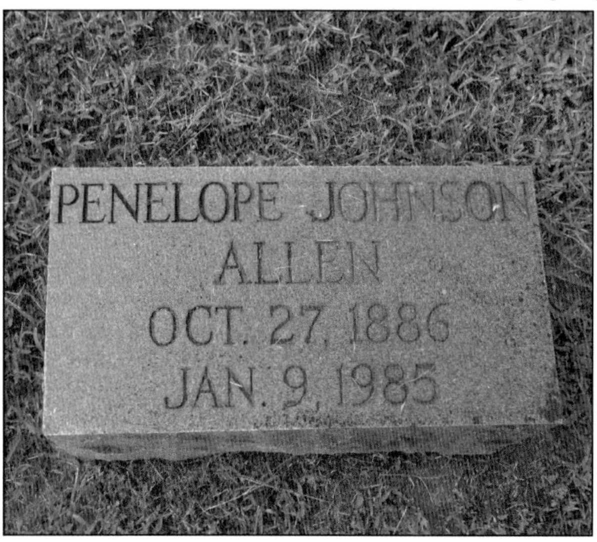

Penelope Johnson Allen (1886–1984) was a beauty queen, writer, historian, and munitions plant supervisor. Named "Queen of Love and Beauty" in 1904, she graduated from Chattanooga High School and later Western College in Oxford, Ohio. She went on to write for the *Chattanooga Times* and *Chattanooga News-Free Press* and authored books on Tennessee history. During World War I, she supervised an artillery shell plant in Virginia. In her later years, Allen encouraged other aspiring historians from her St. Elmo home.

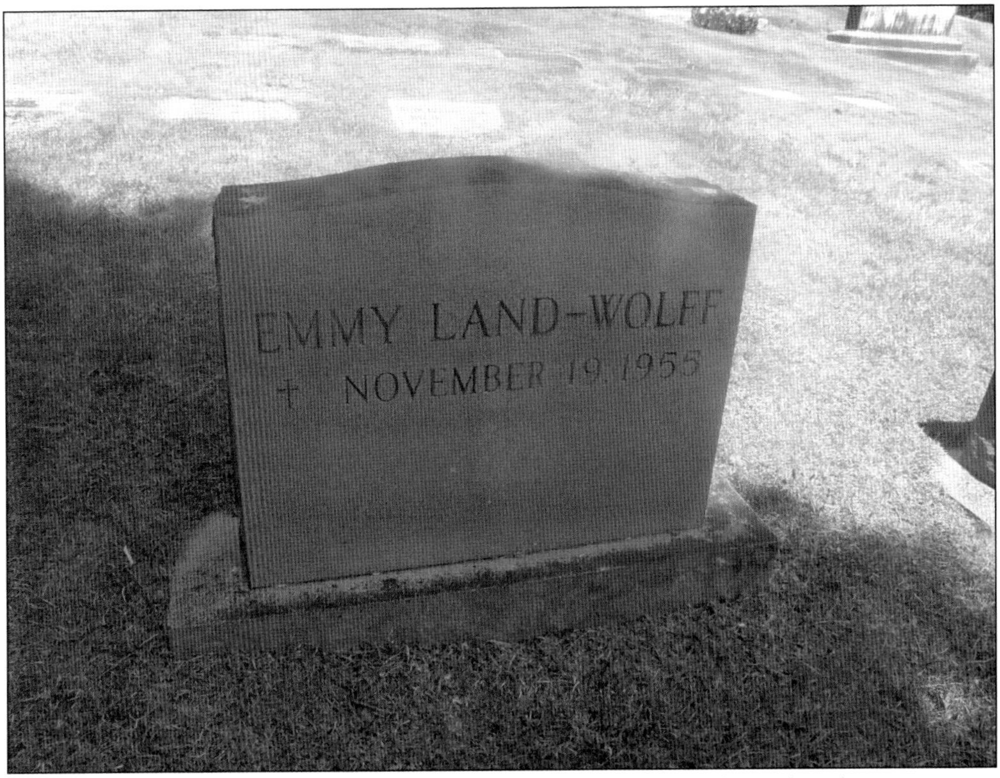

Making her operatic debut in 1912, Emmy Land Wolff (?–1955) performed in the major opera houses of Europe. She married Dr. Werner Wolff, the conductor of the Hamburg Opera, in 1923. Forced to flee Nazi Germany, in 1940 the couple came to the University of Chattanooga. In 1943, they helped found the Chattanooga Opera Association, with Emmy as the coach and stage director. Under her guidance, the company had a 25-opera repertoire.

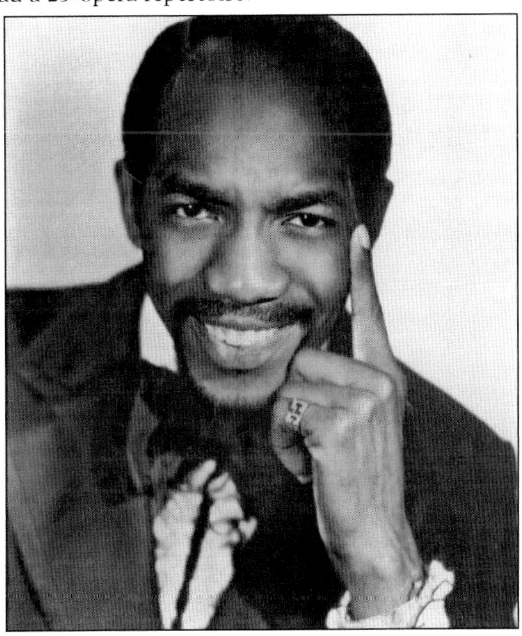

Cortez "Tez" Greer (1940–1976) had a "voice as deep as a well and as soft as butter." Greer, a graduate of Howard High School, first preformed for a national audience on the Ted Mack Original Amateur Hour. Touring with such entertainers as James Brown and Bill Cosby, he also performed regularly in Las Vegas. His only completed album, "Live at Scarlett O'Hara's," remains a tribute to this "all dynamite" entertainer. His life was cut short by carbon monoxide poisoning from a leaky gas furnace. (Photograph courtesy of Forest Hills Cemetery.)

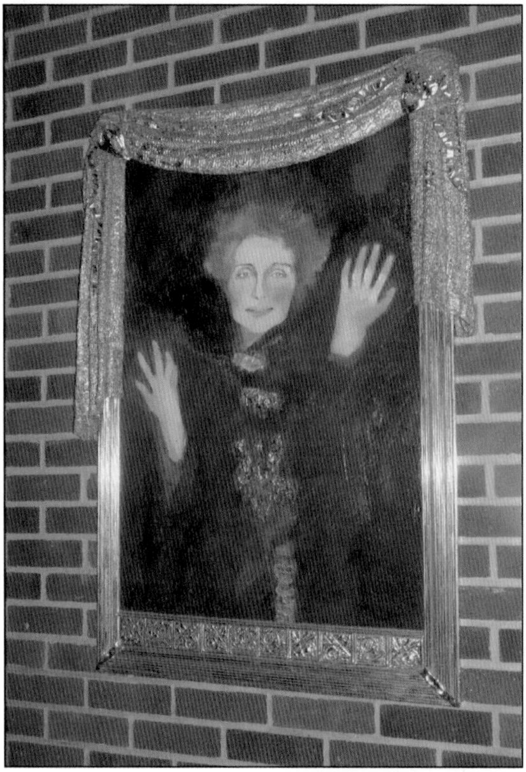

Dorothy Ward Hackett (1906–2001) was Chattanooga's "First Lady of Drama," according to the *Chattanooga Times*. On the faculty of the University of Chattanooga for 37 years, she taught theater and directed plays. She helped found the Chattanooga Opera Association, serving as stage director for 32 years. Hackett founded the Festival Players and wrote 33 children's plays. The University of Tennessee-Chattanooga Fine Arts Center, where this painting of her is displayed, is named in her honor. (Photograph courtesy of the University of Tennessee-Chattanooga.)

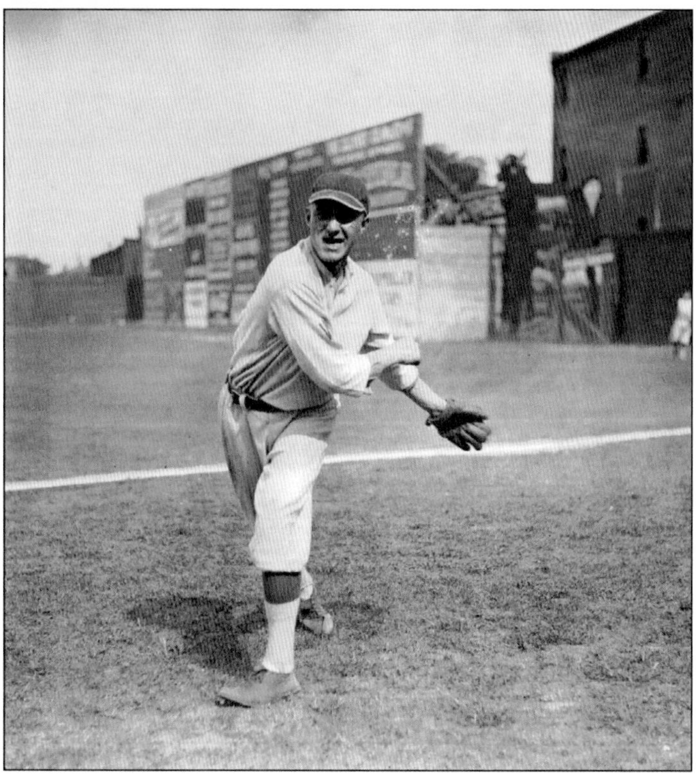

Joseph "Joe" Engel (1893–1969), seen here in 1913, pitched for the Washington Senators. In 1919, he was hired as a scout for the Senators and in 1929 he came to Chattanooga to manage the Lookouts. The fans loved his zany promotions, earning him the nickname "The Barnum of Baseball." Engel bought the Lookouts in 1936 with the help of 1,700 fans, and built the stadium, which still bears his name. This "King of the Minor Leagues" was inducted into the Baseball Hall of Fame in 1994. (Photograph courtesy of Forest Hills Cemetery.)

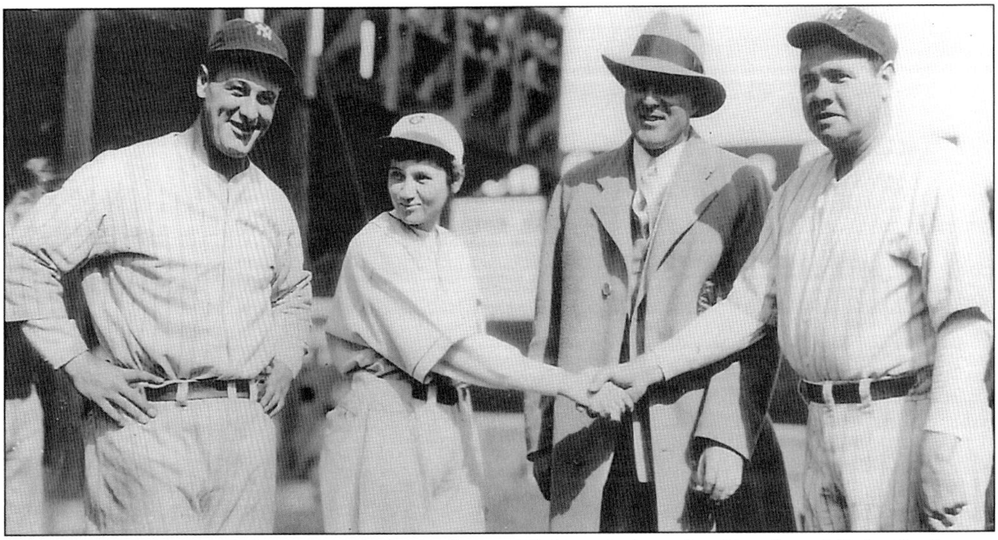

Virne "Jackie" Mitchell (1912–1987) shown here with Lou Gehrig, Joe Engel, and Babe Ruth, was only 17 years old when she was signed by Joe Engel to pitch for his Chattanooga Lookouts. On April 2, 1931, in an exhibition game witnessed by more than 4,000 Chattanooga fans, Mitchell struck out both Ruth and Gehrig. Shortly after the game, baseball commissioner Kenesaw Landis voided her contract, stating that the game of baseball was "too strenuous for women."

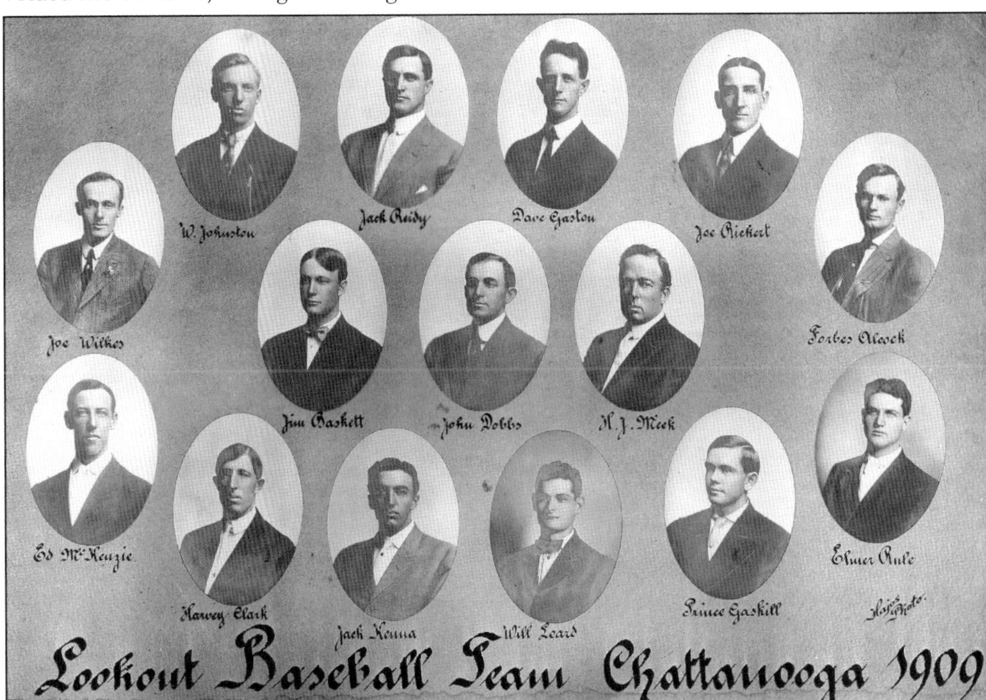

This photograph of the Chattanooga Lookouts in 1909 shows John Gordon "Johnny" Dobbs (1866–1934). Dobbs enjoyed a 40-year career in baseball. An outfielder, he played for the Cincinnati Reds, Chicago Cubs, and Brooklyn Dodgers. He coached and managed minor league clubs for 27 years. According to his obituary he was known as the "Sage of Ringgold," and was considered "one of the finest judges of baseball talent in the country."

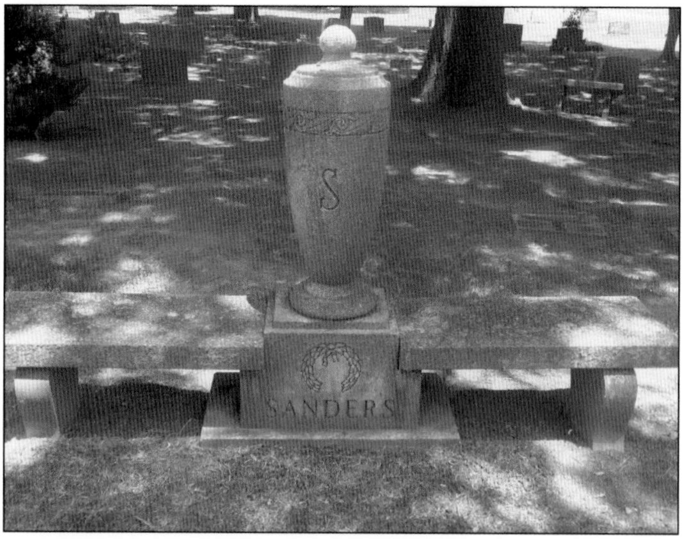

Warren Sanders (1877–1962) pitched 10 seasons in the minor leagues and two seasons, 1903 and 1904, in the majors for the St. Louis Cardinals. During the 1902 season, he pitched 308 innings for Nashville with a win-loss percentage of .647. Retiring from baseball in 1914, he moved to Chattanooga, went to work for the railroad, married, and reared a family. He was an active member of Senior Neighbors at the time of his death.

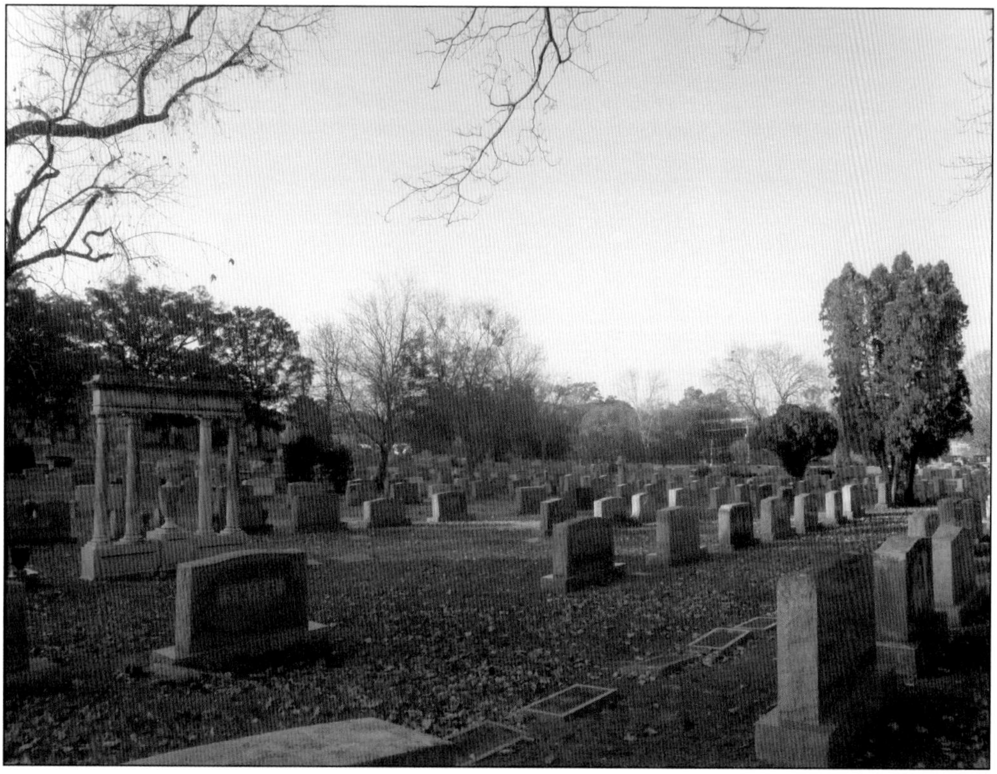

According to his obituary, James "Jimmy" Johnson (1890–1967) was "one of baseball's all-time great utility players." Johnson played in the major leagues for 13 years, 10 of them with the Brooklyn Dodgers. Playing a total of seven positions with the Dodgers, he was part of the 26-inning game in 1920 and played in two World Series. Born in Cleveland, Tennessee, he played against his own brother, Cleveland Indian "Doc" Johnson, in the 1920 Series. After his retirement from baseball, he was the park superintendent at Engel Stadium.

Beginning his professional baseball career in 1908 with the Kitty League in Jackson, Tennessee, outfielder and second baseman William David "Dave" Gaston (1879–1948) played and managed in the Cotton States, Ohio and Pennsylvania, South Atlantic, and Southern Leagues. Announcing his marriage to Emma Kansinger in 1908, the *Chattanooga News* described him as "quiet and gentlemanly on the field and sure to become a great favorite with the rooters here." (Photograph courtesy of Terry Blunt.)

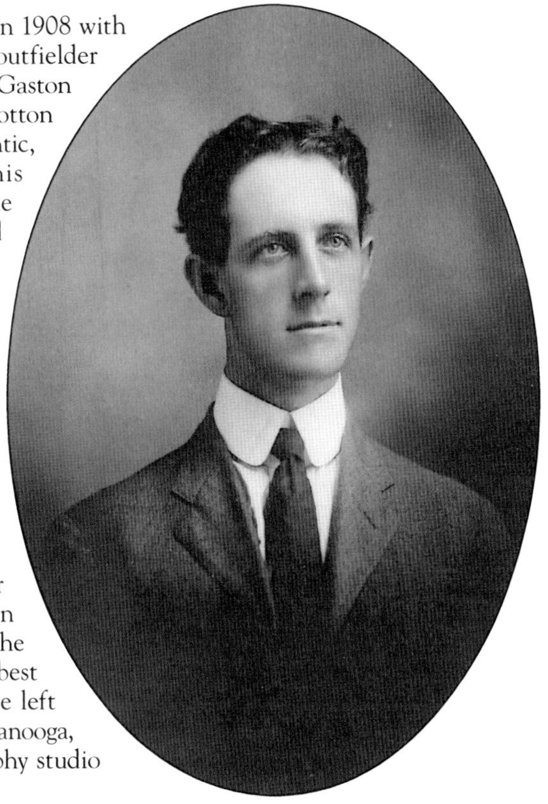

Major league pitcher, George "Slats" McConnell (1877–1964) was born in Shelbyville, Tennessee. He began his career with the New York Highlanders/Yankees in 1909. Traded to the Chicago Cubs in 1913, he completed his career in 1916. McConnell's best year was 1915 when he won 25 games. He left baseball after the 1916 season, moved to Chattanooga, married, had a family, and ran a photography studio until his death.

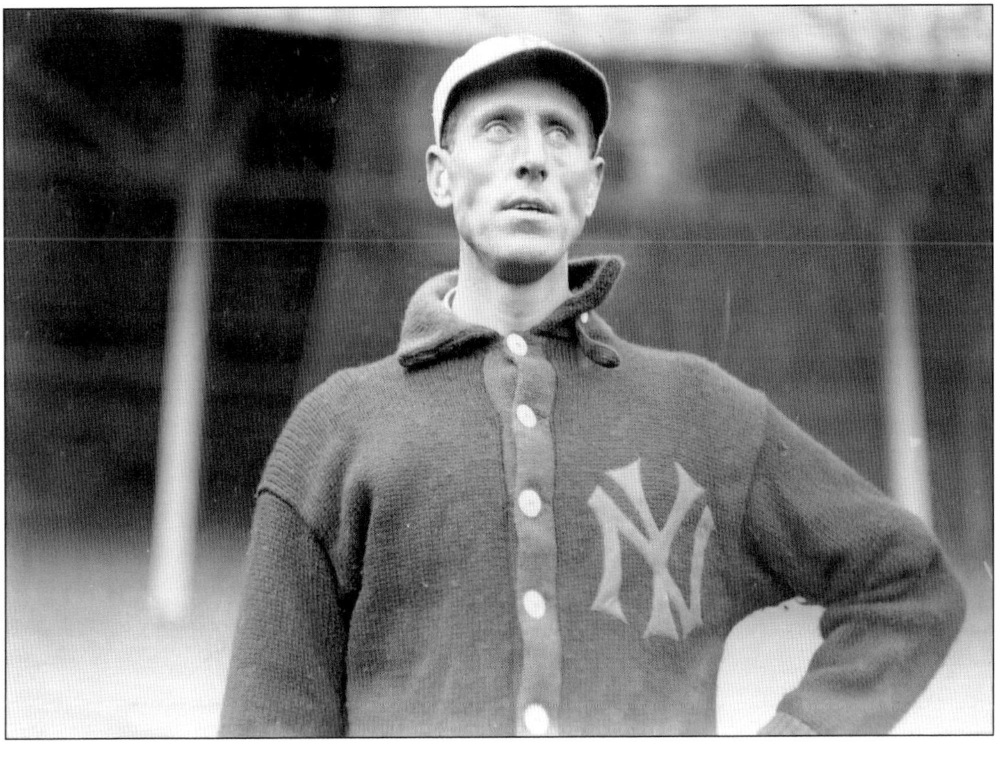

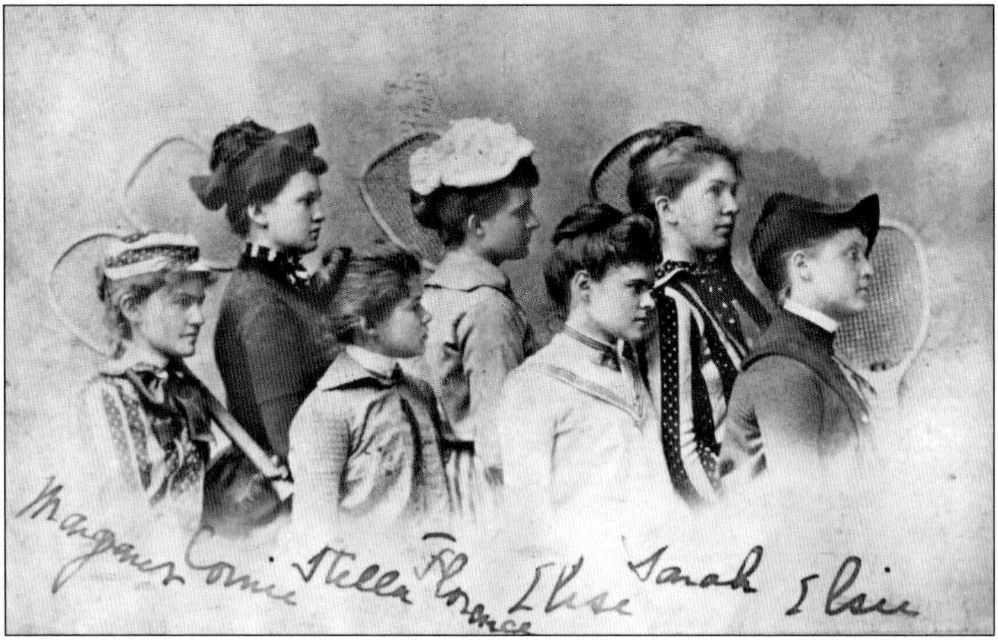

Pictured here about 1888, the young women of Chattanooga First Tennis Club played on L. J. Sharp's lawn. They included, from left to right, Margaret Key (1866–1955), Cornelia Carlie Reid (1866–1938), Stella Hutcheson Dabney, Florence Eckert, Elise Hutchenson Chapin (1868–1929), Sarah Key Patten (1865–1958), and Elise Finlay Payne.

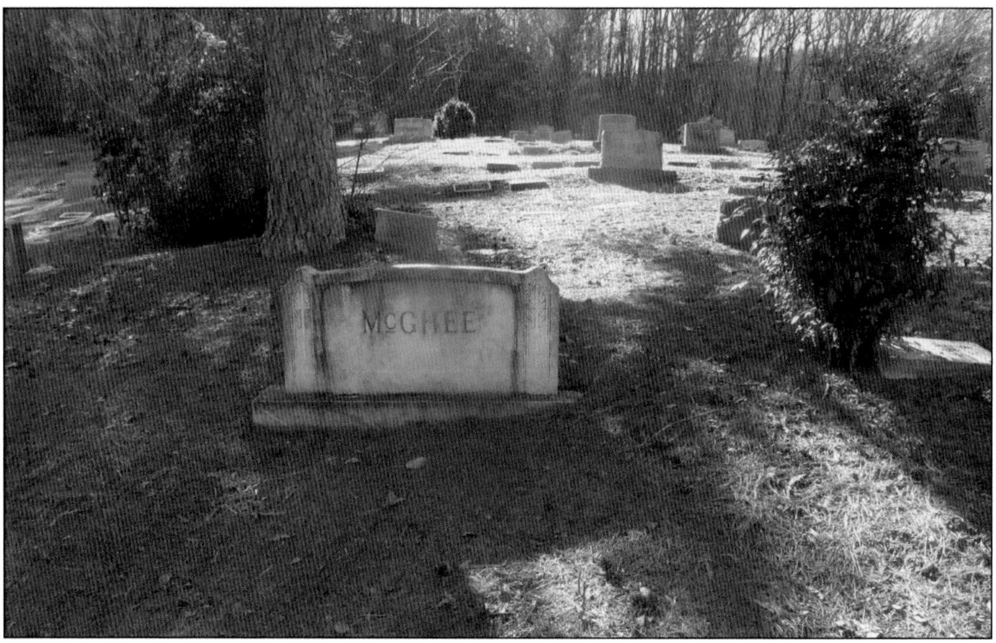

Wylma McGhee Reid (1928–2008) was Chattanooga's first national tennis champion at age 18. Lacking formal lessons, she began competing at age nine, winning several city tournaments. A graduate of Howard High School, Reid went to Atlanta's Clark College. As a junior she won the Tennessee State Negro Women's Championship and the Annual National Negro Tournament. She worked for 20 years at the National Institute of Health in Washington, D.C.

Nine

The Military

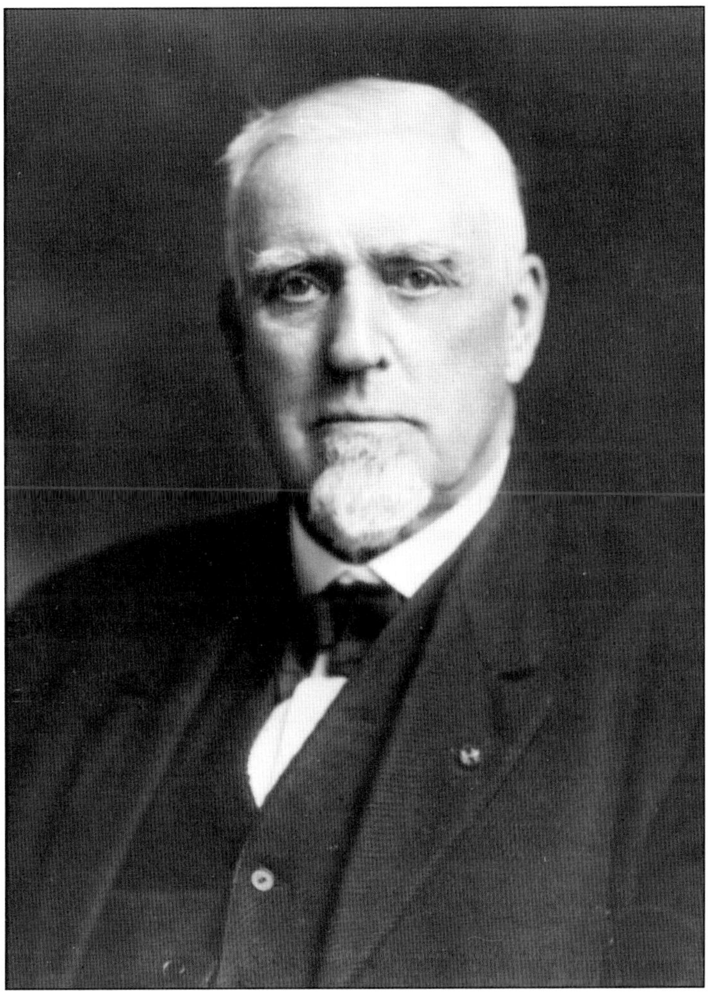

Gen. John Wilder (1830–1917) first became acquainted with Chattanooga when his unit, the 17th Indiana Infantry Regiment, bombarded the city in 1863. In 1866, he returned to Chattanooga to found the Roane Iron Works. He was also instrumental in developing the railroad system in east Tennessee. Along with other Civil War veterans, he helped develop the Chickamauga Battlefield as a memorial park. Wilder Tower, located in the Chickamauga Military Park, is named in his honor.

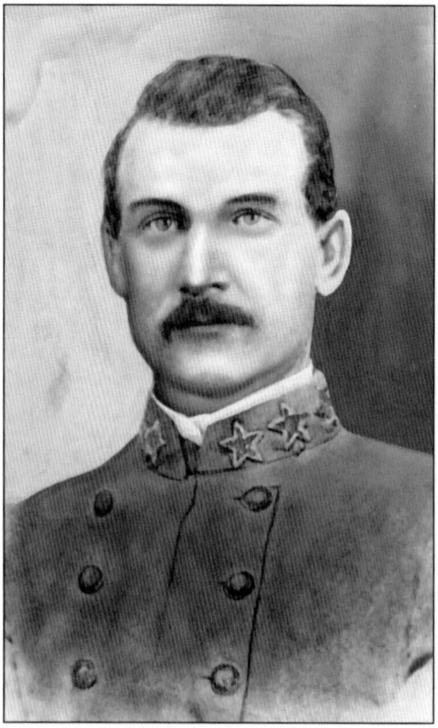

Francis Marion Walker (1827–1864) practiced law in Chattanooga prior to the Civil War. Ambitious and intelligent, he became an alderman and district attorney general. Although an ardent Unionist, he joined the Confederate Army following Tennessee's secession. Serving with the 19th Tennessee Infantry Regiment, he was killed at the Battle of Atlanta, one day after his promotion to brigadier general.

Robert Kirk Walker (1925–2008, center) served as an officer in the U.S. Navy during World War II. He was recalled to active duty during the Korean Conflict and served two years. A lawyer, he was active in civic affairs and served as mayor of Chattanooga from 1971 through 1975. During his time in office, the city nearly doubled in size due to annexation, Miller Park was founded, and the Chattanooga Area Regional Transportation Authority (CARTA) was established.

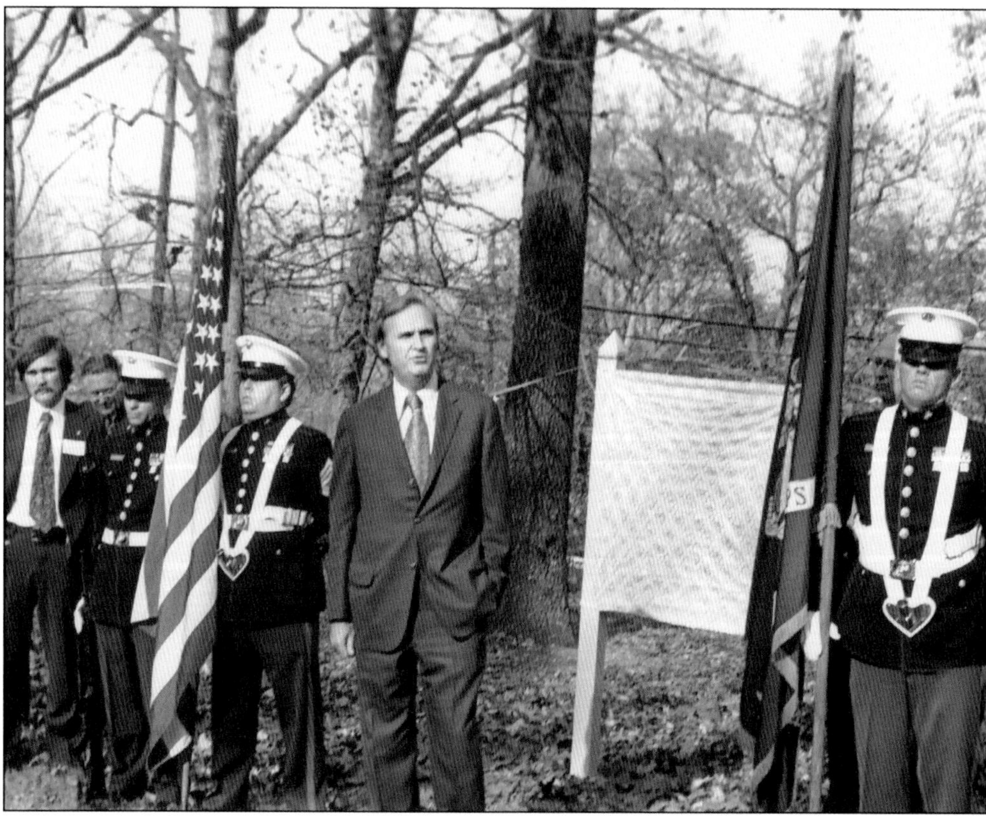

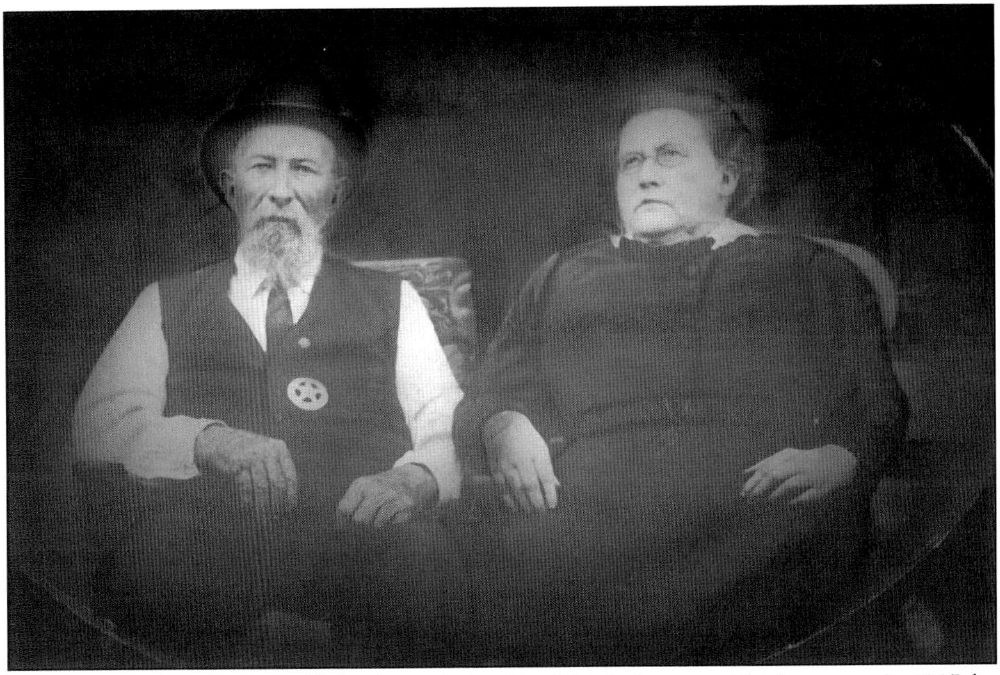

Henry Clay Miller (1840–1917) fought with the 81st Ohio Infantry at Chickamauga. In 1907, he moved with his wife, Rebecca Jane, and their family to St. Elmo from Ohio where he owned a general store. The couple operated a general store in St. Elmo for many years. Henry was a Forest Hills Cemetery guard from 1913 to 1917. He is wearing his guard badge in this picture.

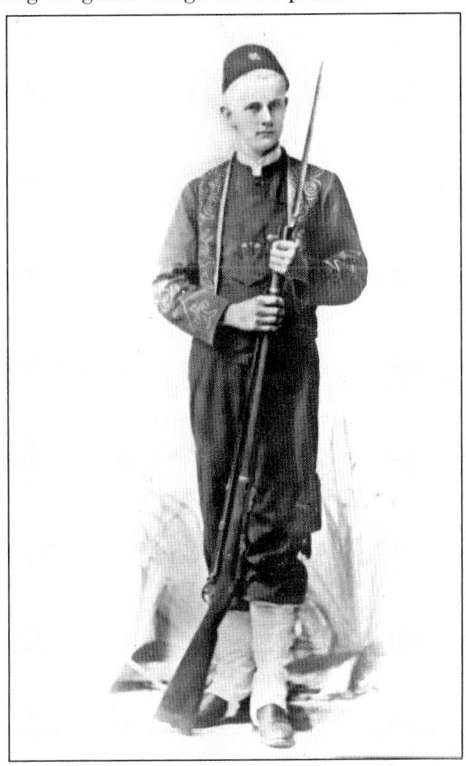

Walter Spencer (1872–1942), pictured here in 1889, was a member of the Morlein Zouves, Tennessee State Guard. He served during the 1891–1893 conflict with striking coal miners at Coal Creek, Tennessee. Later he operated Spencer's Newsstand at 15 East Ninth Street.

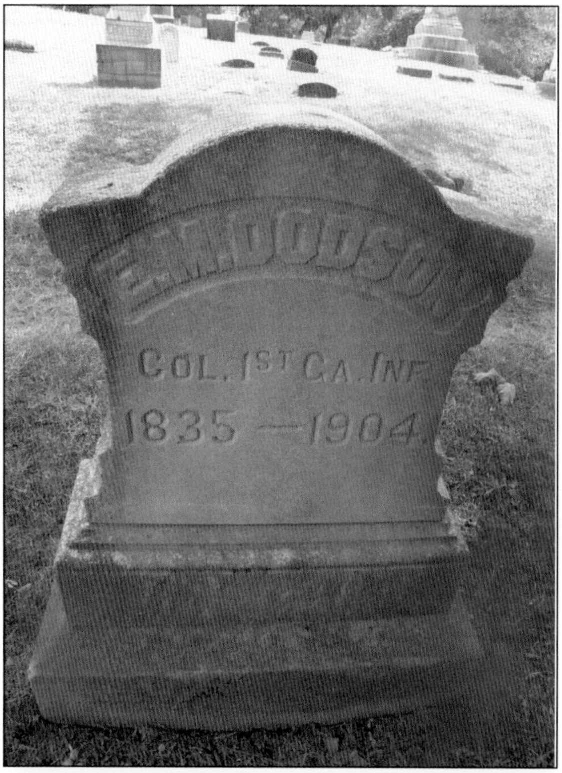

Wounded during the battle of Missionary Ridge, Maj. Elijah Dodson (1835–1904) lived to fight at the Battle of Kennesaw where he was permanently disabled. Moving to Chattanooga in 1871, he helped develop Sherman Heights. Dodson Avenue is named for him. He was active in the development of the Chickamauga and Chattanooga National Military Park.

Born in Hickory Valley, Lewis Shepherd Jr. (1845–1917), was a student at Von Aldehoff's Academy on Lookout Mountain when the Civil War broke out. Enlisting in the 5th Tennessee Cavalry, he served in Tennessee and Kentucky and fought at Chickamauga under Confederate generals Forrest and Wheeler. Captured, he was paroled and joined the 16th Tennessee Volunteer Infantry Regiment.

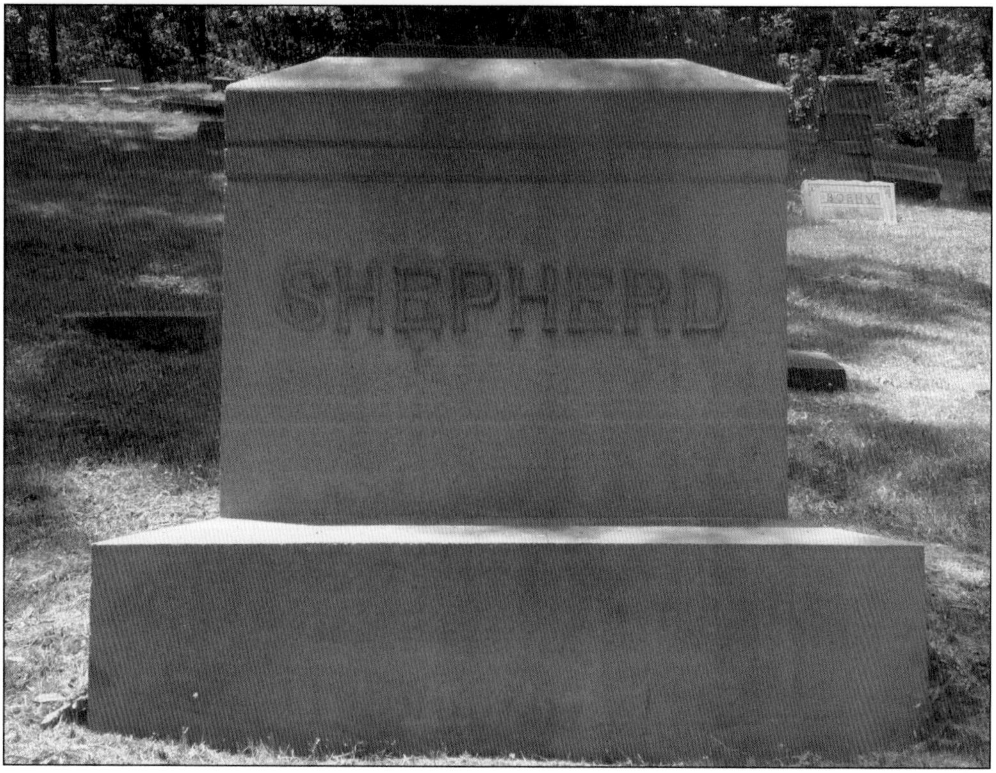

The son of U.S. senator Spencer Jarnagin, Gustavus "Gus" Jarnagin (1884–1914) had an appointment to the U.S. Naval Academy, but resigned to enlist in the Confederate Army. Coming to Chattanooga shortly after the war, he eventually opened a grocery store. In 1893, he married his former boss's daughter, Irene Rouhs.

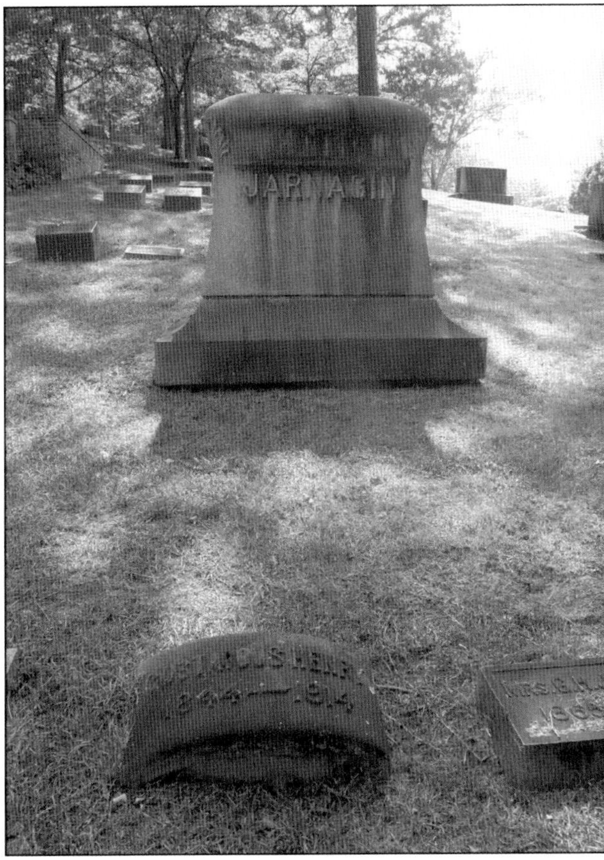

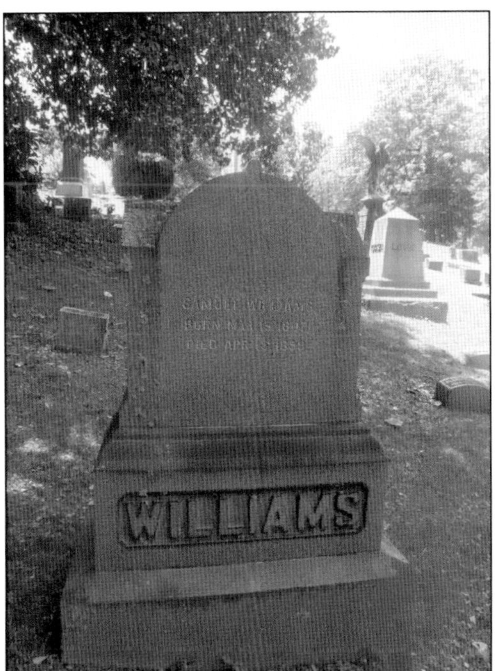

Samuel Williams (1807–1898) opposed secession, but was sympathetic to the Confederacy. He apprehended James Andrews, the leader of Andrews Raiders who escaped from jail in Chattanooga following his attempt to sabotage the rail lines south of Chattanooga. When Federal forces occupied Chattanooga, Williams was forced to hide out, sneaking home occasionally to visit his wife. His wealth and land holdings substantially reduced, he was eventually pardoned by Pres. Andrew Johnson.

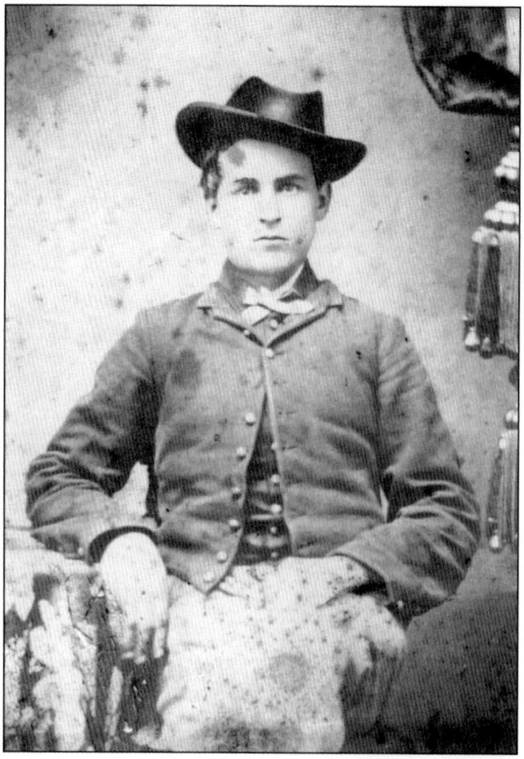

Samuel "Sam" Duncan (1845–1915) joined the Pennsylvania Calvary at the beginning of the Civil War. Fighting through Tennessee and Georgia, he was mustered out in Macon in 1865. Rather than return home, he remained in the south and married Estelle Hodges of Rome, Georgia. Sam eventually went to work for the Chattanooga Electric Railway. Active in the Grand Army of the Republic, he was elected as an alderman. Duncan Avenue is named for him. (Photograph courtesy of Roy McKinney.)

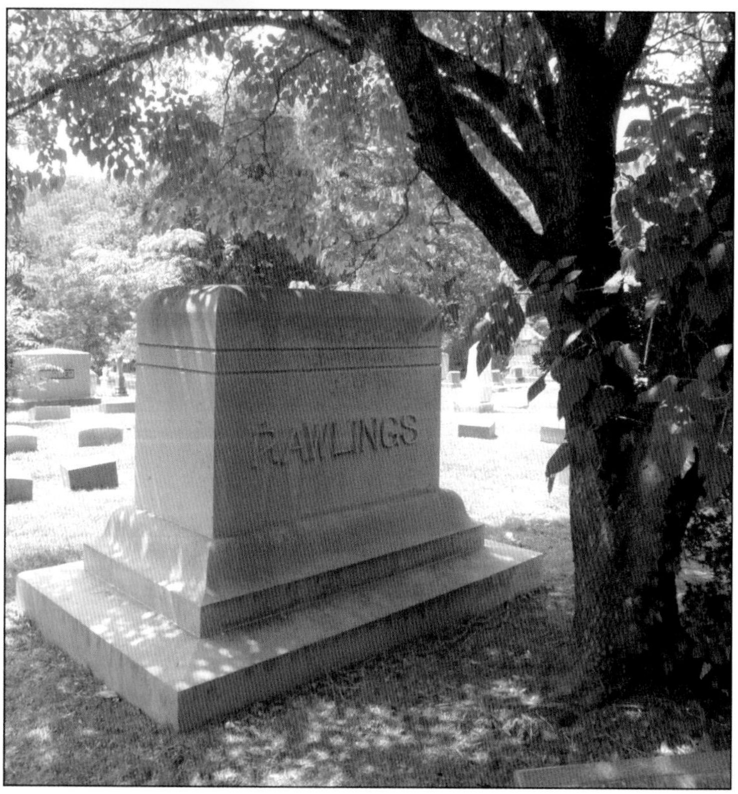

Second Lt. John Rawlings (1840–1923) served in Augusta with the medical department of the Confederate Army. A pharmacist, he opened a store in St. Elmo. His home, located where the parking lot for the Incline Railway is today, was the site for the garden party held by A. M. Johnson to dedicate, "St. Elmo" as the name for his new community.

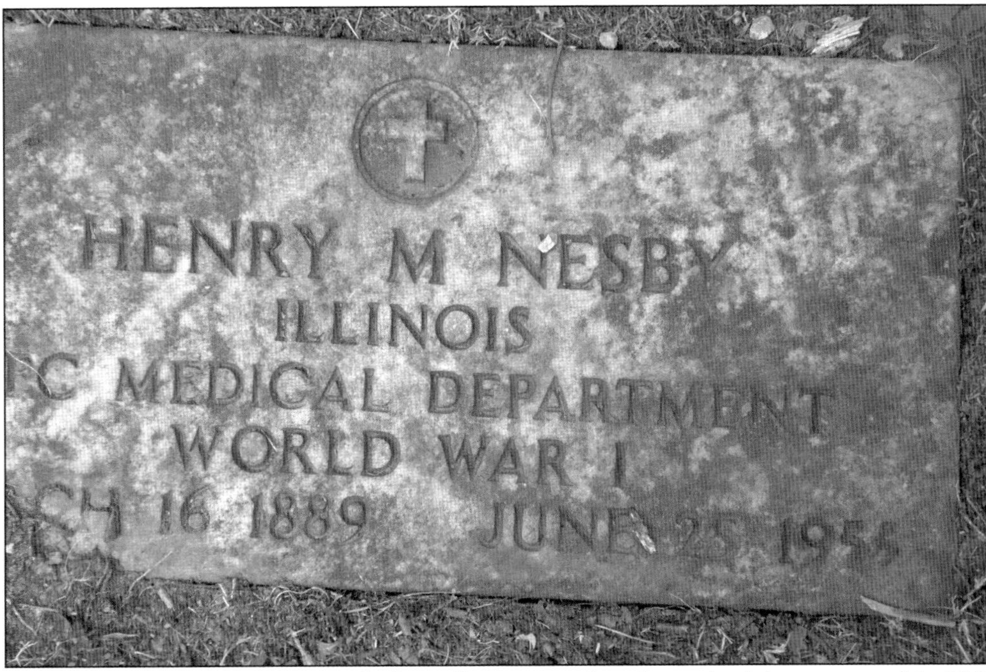

Henry Nesby (1889–1930), originally from Illinois, served in the medical department of the U.S. Army during World War I.

German born Casper Saffer (1836–1901) was working as a barrel maker in Cincinnati when he joined the 4th Ohio Calvary. Captured in 1864 around Atlanta, he was sent to the infamous Andersonville Prison. Coming to Chattanooga after the war, he eventually opened a salon on Eighth Street. When he died, his obituary stated: "Few men in business . . . enjoyed to a higher degree the respect and esteem of the people of the city. He was a kindly, good-hearted man . . . and the announcement of his death will create universal regret throughout the city."

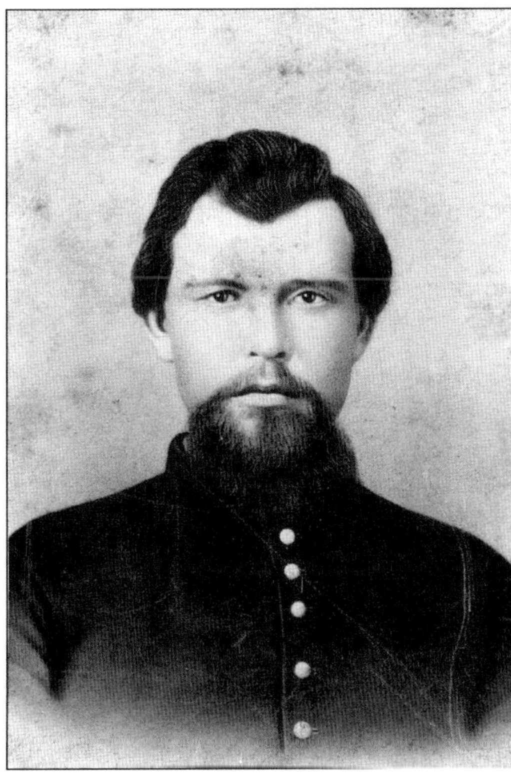

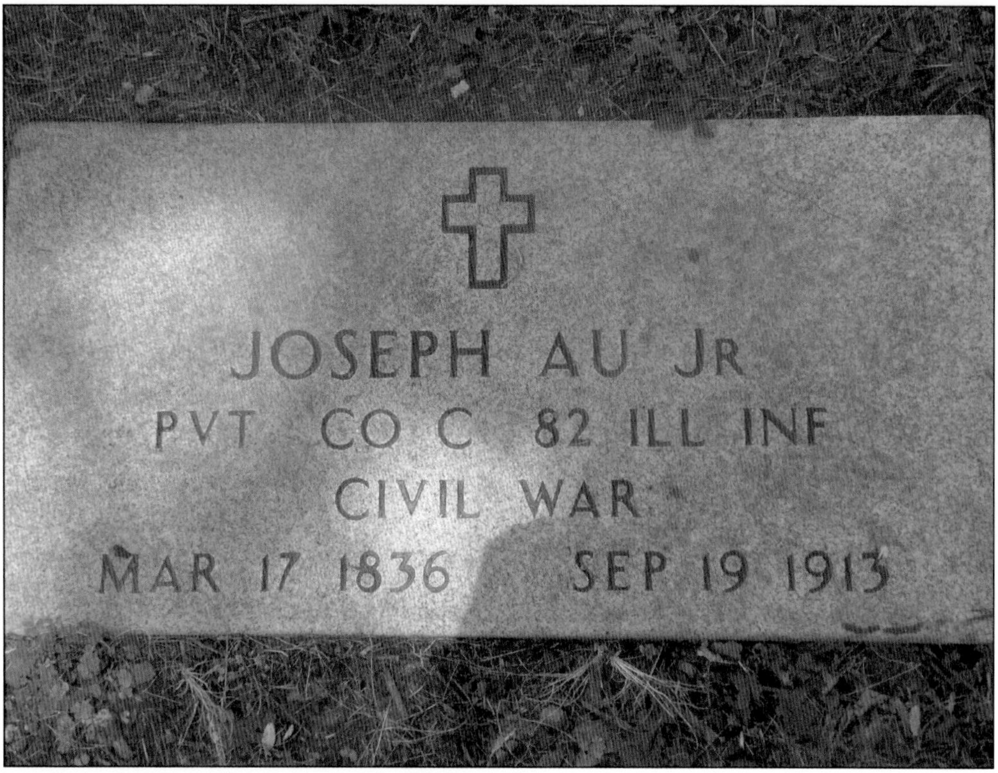

Joseph Au (1836–1913) was a private in the 82nd Illinois Volunteer Infantry during the Civil War. He was one of the many former Union soldiers who moved to Chattanooga after the war.

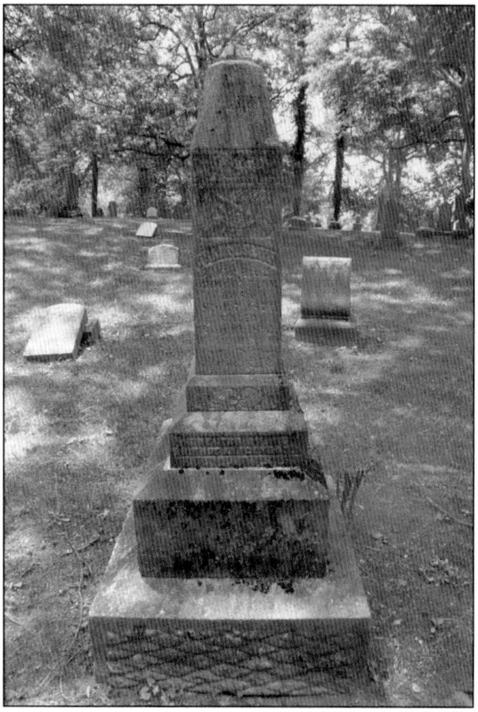

Pvt. Frank Smith (1871–1892) of the Provisional Battalion, Army of the Tennessee was killed during attempts to quell labor riots in Coal Creek, Tennessee. He was remembered during services at Forest Hills Cemetery in 1892. During the services, Dr. S. T. Westfall offered prayer, Oscar Seagle sang a solo, and mayor J. B. Frazier gave an address. According to the *Chattanooga Times*, Smith "fell at his post of duty, with his face toward the enemy, during the hottest part of the fight."

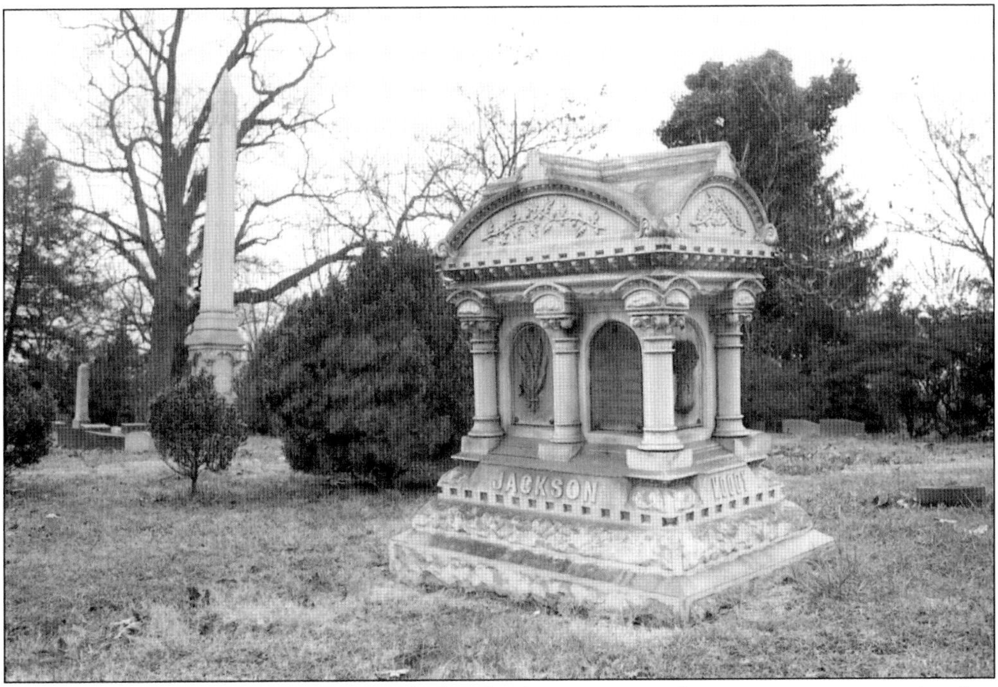

Jesse Moody's (1869–1902) grave is marked with what appears to be an ornate stone marker, but it is actually metal molded to resemble stone. Moody died as a result of exposure and a fever that he contracted in the Philippines during the Spanish-American War. According to his obituary, he served with "distinction and bravery in the Cuban campaign."

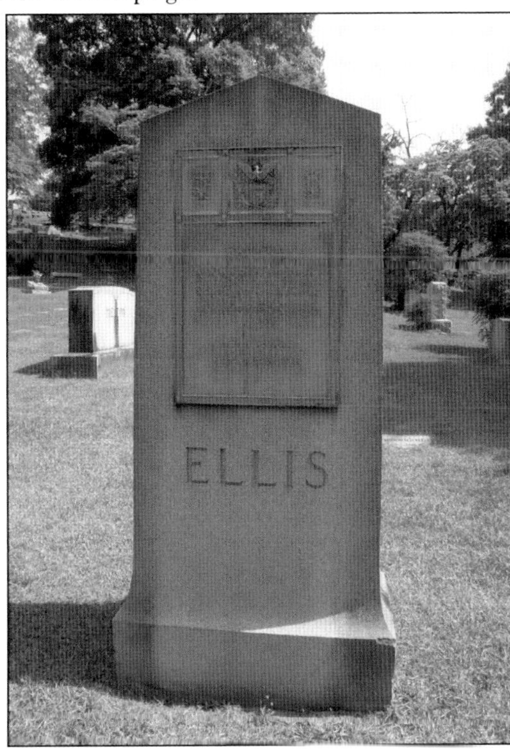

Sgt. Frank Ellis (1893–1918) of C Company of the 52nd Engineer Combat Battalion (Heavy) of the American Expeditionary Forces, died while fighting in Flanders during World War I.

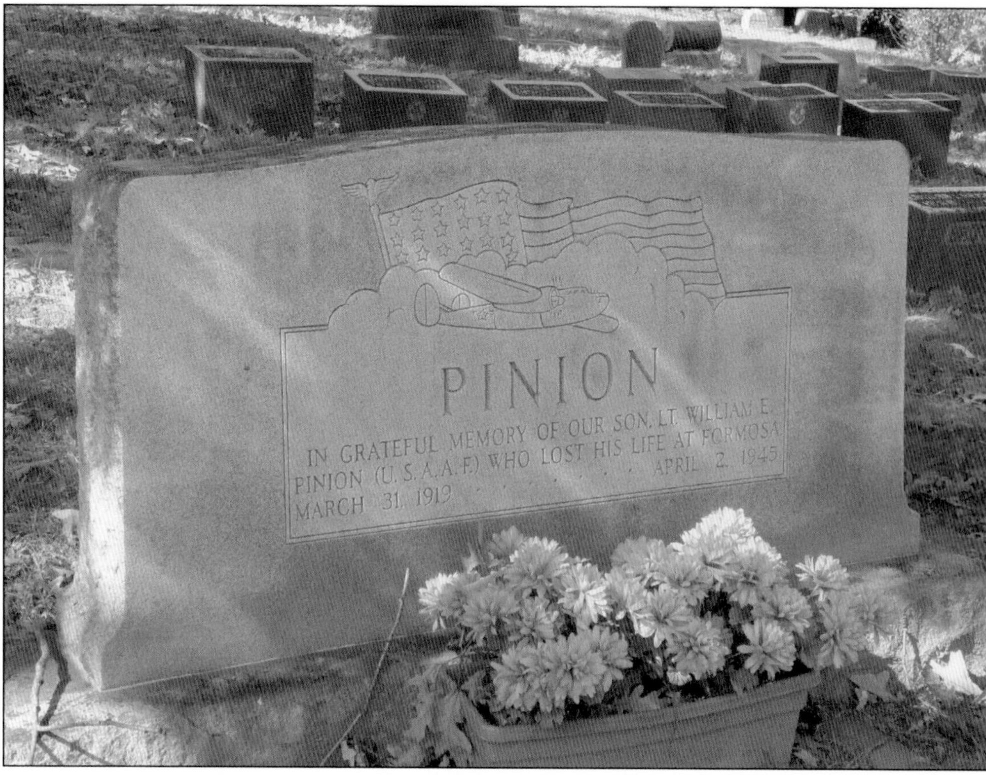

U.S. Air Force Lt. William Pinion (1919–1945) died when his plane went down over Formosa (commonly known as Taiwan) during World War II. This stone was placed at Forest Hills Cemetery by his parents in his memory.

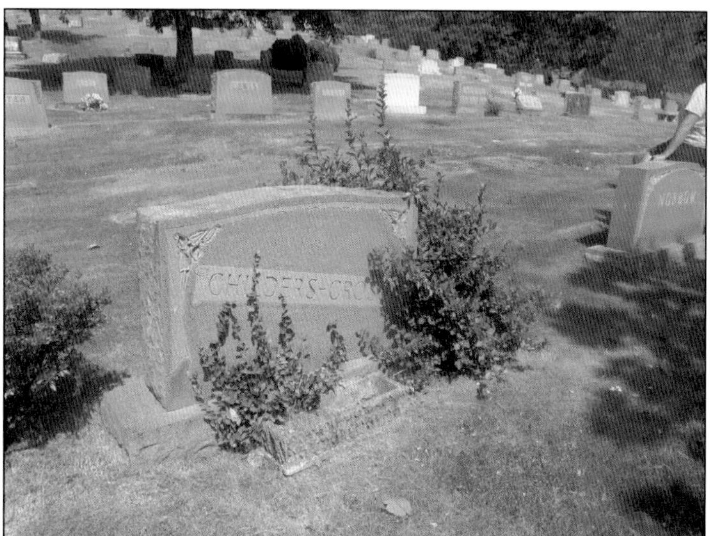

A test pilot with the U.S. Air Force, Maj. Carl Cross (1927–1966) died in a midair collision over Edwards Air Force Base. He was the copilot of the XB70 research bomber. He previously received four Air Medals for flying frontline support missions in Korea and later in South Vietnam. Cross also received two Commendation Medals.

Bibliography

Armstrong, Zella. *The History of Hamilton County and Chattanooga, Tennessee Volumes I and II.* Lookout Mountain, Tennessee: Lookout Mountain Publishing Company, 1931.

Arnold, Dean. *Old Money New South.* Chattanooga, Tennessee: Chattanooga Historical Association, 2006.

Black History Series: Chattanooga. Charleston, South Carolina: Arcadia Publishing, 2005.

Chattanooga Free Press

Chattanooga Times

Douthat, James L., Judy Harris, and Frankie Pope. *The St. Elmo Story.* Chattanooga, Tennessee: The 1986 Heritage Committee of the St. Elmo Improvement League, 1986.

Excerpt From a *History of Tennessee: Hamilton County and the City of Chattanooga Biographies.* Nashville: Goodspeed Publishing Company, 1887. Reprinted by A Plus Printing Company, Tucson, Arizona.

History of Tennessee: Hamilton County and the City of Chattanooga. Nashville: Goodspeed Publishing Company, 1887. Reprinted by A Plus Printing Company, Tucson, Arizona.

Hubbard, Rita Lorraine, *African Americans of Chattanooga.* Charleston, South Carolina: History Press, 2007.

Hughes, Nathaniel C. Jr. and John C. Wilson. *Confederate Soldiers of Hamilton County, Tennessee.* Signal Mountain, Tennessee: Mountain Press, 2001.

Livingood, James, *A History of Hamilton County, Tennessee.* Memphis: Memphis State University Press, 1981.

Poole, Wanda R.N. and Susan Sawyer, *The Baroness Collection Erlanger Medical Center 1891–1991.* Chattanooga: Erlanger Medical Center, 1993.

White, J. Bliss, *1904 Biography and Achievements of the Colored Citizens of Chattanooga.* Signal Mountain, Tennessee: Mountain Press, reprinted 2004.

Wilson, John. *The Dorothy Patten Story.* Chattanooga, Tennessee: Chattanooga News-Free Press, 1986.

Wilson, John and Nathaniel Hughes Jr. *The Confederate Soldiers of Hamilton County, Tennessee.* Signal Mountain, TN: Signal Mountain Press, 2001.